DAVID REMEMBERED

DAVID REMEMBERED

Kingship and National Identity in Ancient Israel

Joseph Blenkinsopp

WILLIAM B. EERDMANS PUBLISHING COMPANY
GRAND RAPIDS, MICHIGAN / CAMBRIDGE, U.K.

Published 2013 by
Wm. B. Eerdmans Publishing Co.
2140 Oak Industrial Drive N.E., Grand Rapids, Michigan 49505 /
P.O. Box 163, Cambridge CB3 9PU U.K.

Library of Congress Cataloging-in-Publication Data

Blenkinsopp, Joseph, 1927-
    David remembered: kingship and national identity in ancient Israel /
    Joseph Blenkinsopp.
       pages   cm
    Includes bibliographical references and index.
    ISBN 978-0-8028-6958-6 (pbk.: alk. paper)
    1. David, King of Israel — Family.
    2. Bible. O.T. — Criticism, interpretation, etc.
    3. Judaism — History — Post-exilic period, 586 B.C.–210 A.D.
    4. Jews — History — 586 B.C.–70 A.D.
    5. Monarchy.   I. Title.

DS121.B59   2013
933'.02 — dc23

                          2012045983

www.eerdmans.com

To Jean with love and gratitude

Contents

Contents

Abbreviations

AB	Anchor Bible
ABD	*Anchor Bible Dictionary,* ed. David Noel Freedman. 6 vols. New York, 1992
AGJU	Arbeiten zur Geschichte des antiken Judentums und des Urchristentums
AGSU	Arbeiten zur Geschichte des Spätjudentums und Urchristentums
AJP	*American Journal of Philology*
AJSL	*American Journal of Semitic Languages and Literature*
ANET	*Ancient Near Eastern Texts Relating to the Old Testament,* ed. James B. Pritchard. 3rd ed. with Supplement. Princeton, 1969
Anton	*Antonianum*
AOAT	Alter Orient und Altes Testament
ArBib	Aramaic Bible
ATD	Alte Testament Deutsch
ATDan	*Acta theologica danica*
BA	*Biblical Archaeologist*
BAR	*Biblical Archaeology Review*
BASOR	*Bulletin of the American Schools of Oriental Research*
BBET	Beiträge zur biblischen Exegese und Theologie
BEATAJ	Beiträge zur Erforschung des Alten Testaments und des antiken Judentum
BETL	Bibliotheca ephemeridum theologicarum lovaniensium
Bijdr	*Bijdragen*
BJS	Brown Judaic Studies
BKAT	Biblischer Kommentar: Altes Testament
BM	*Beth Mikra*
BN	*Biblische Notizen*
BRS	Biblical Resource Series

BWANT	Beiträge zur Wissenschaft vom Alten und Neuen Testament
BZAW	Beihefte zur Zeitschrift für die alttestamentliche Wissenschaft
CAH	*Cambridge Ancient History*
Camb. B.	Cambridge Bible for Schools and Colleges
CAT	Commentaire de l'Ancien Testament
CBQ	*Catholic Biblical Quarterly*
CC	Continental Commentaries
CHJ	*Cambridge History of Judaism,* ed. W. D. Davies and Louis Finkelstein. Cambridge, 1984-
ConBOT	Coniectanea biblica: Old Testament Series
DDD	*Dictionary of Deities and Demons in the Bible,* ed. Karel van der Toorn, Bob Becking, and Pieter W. van der Horst. Leiden and Grand Rapids, 1999
DJD	Discoveries in the Judaean Desert
EBib	Etudes bibliques
EDSS	*Encyclopedia of the Dead Sea Scrolls,* ed. Lawrence H. Schiffman and James C. VanderKam. 2 vols. Oxford, 2000
FAT	Forschungen zum Alten Testament
FRLANT	Forschungen zur Religion und Literatur des Alten und Neuen Testaments
GKC	*Gesenius' Hebrew Grammar,* ed. Emil Kautzsch; trans. A. E. Cowley. 2nd ed., Oxford, 1910
HAT	Handbuch zum Alten Testament
HKAT	Handkommentar zum Alten Testament
HSM	Harvard Semitic Monographs
HTKAT	Herders theologischer Kommentar zum Alten Testament
HTR	*Harvard Theological Review*
ICC	International Critical Commentary
IDB	*Interpreter's Dictionary of the Bible*
IDBS	*Interpreter's Dictionary of the Bible Supplement*
IEJ	*Israel Exploration Journal*
IOS	*Israel Oriental Studies*
JAOS	*Journal of the American Oriental Society*
JB	Jerusalem Bible
JBL	*Journal of Biblical Literature*
JJS	*Journal of Jewish Studies*
JNES	*Journal of Near Eastern Studies*
JSJ	*Journal for the Study of Judaism in the Persian, Hellenistic, and Roman Periods*
JSNT	*Journal for the Study of the New Testament*
JSOT	*Journal for the Study of the Old Testament*
JSOTSup	Journal for the Study of the Old Testament: Supplement Series (Continued as LHB/OTS)
JSS	*Journal of Semitic Studies*
JTS	*Journal of Theological Studies*
Jud	Judaica

Abbreviations

KAT	Kommentar zum Alten Testament
LCL	Loeb Classical Library
LD	Lectio divina
LHB/OTS	Library of Hebrew Bible/Old Testament Studies
MdB	Le Monde de la Bible
NAB	New American Bible
NCBC	New Century Bible Commentary
NechtB	Neue Echter Bibel
NIBCOT	New International Biblical Commentary on the Old Testament
NRSV	New Revised Standard Version
OBO	Orbis biblicus et orientalis
Or	*Orientalia*
OTE	*Old Testament Essays*
OTL	Old Testament Library
OTP	*The Old Testament Pseudepigrapha,* ed. James H. Charlesworth. 2 vols. Garden City, 1983
OtSt	*Oudtestamentische Studiën*
PEQ	*Palestine Exploration Quarterly*
RB	*Revue biblique*
REB	Revised English Bible
SB	Sources bibliques
SBLMS	Society of Biblical Literature Monograph Series
Sem	*Semitica*
SNTSMS	Society for New Testament Studies Monograph Series
SOTSMS	Society for Old Testament Studies Monograph Series
SSN	Studia semitica neerlandica
TA	*Tel Aviv*
TDOT	*Theological Dictionary of the Old Testament,* ed. G. Johannes Botterweck, Helmer Ringgren, and Heinz-Josef Fabry. 17 vols. Grand Rapids, 1974–
TLOT	*Theological Lexicon of the Old Testament,* ed. Ernst Jenni. Peabody, 1997
TLZ	*Theologische Literaturzeitung*
TOTC	Tyndale Old Testament Commentaries
TSAJ	Texte und Studien zum antiken Judentum
TynBul	*Tyndale Bulletin*
VT	*Vetus Testamentum*
VTSup	Supplements to Vetus Testamentum
WBC	Word Biblical Commentary
WMANT	Wissenschaftliche Monographien zum Alten und Neuen Testament
ZAW	*Zeitschrift für die alttestamentliche Wissenschaft*
ZTK	*Zeitschrift für Theologie und Kirche*

Introduction

A historian does not roam about at random through the past, like a ragman in search of bric-a-brac; rather, he sets out with a specific plan in mind, a problem to solve, a working hypothesis to test. . . . To describe what one sees is one thing; but to see that which must be described, that is the hard part.[1]

My aim in this book is to trace one strand in the social and political life of the people of Israel from the sixth century B.C.E. to the early second century of the common era. The narrative begins with the violent dissolution of the Judean state and the suppression of the Davidic dynasty and ends with the revolts against the Roman Empire in Judea and the Diaspora. The theme is monarchy, the Davidic monarchy, and, more specifically, the part played by David and the dynasty founded by him in the collective memory of the Judean and Jewish people, its impact on actual policies pursued, and its role in visions of the end time — all of this after David and the Davidic dynasty had been swept from the scene, an event narrated in Chapter One. I view this investigation as supplementing my *Judaism, the First Phase* published in 2009,[2] with the studies on the period in question, referred to

---

1. Lucien Febvre, *Combats pour l'histoire* (Paris: Colin, 1992) 8, as cited by Carlo Ginzburg, *The Judge and the Historian,* trans. Antony Shugaar (London: Verso, 1999) 35-36.
2. *Judaism, The First Phase: The Place of Ezra and Nehemiah in the Origins of Judaism* (Grand Rapids: Eerdmans, 2009).

1

as the Postexilic period or the Second Temple period, which went into it and which had appeared at intervals in books, journal articles, and contributions to collections of essays over the previous two or three decades. One lacuna in that book, no doubt one of many, was the role of David as a presence in the collective memory, his impact on political life as heroic figure and founder of a dynasty — indirectly also on Nehemiah, as we shall see — and his appearance in end-time scenarios based on the restoration of an idealized past. This deficiency, then, dictated the agenda for the present work.

The sense of loss at the extinction of the dynasty, intensified by subjection to imperial control, is expressed poignantly in Lamentations (4:20):

> The Anointed of the Lord, the breath of our nostrils,
> under whose shadow we thought we might live among the nations,
> was caught in their traps.

Hence the range of attitudes towards empire and strategies for coping with its overwhelming political and military power in the absence of monarchy and the associated state apparatus must be borne in mind throughout.

Coming now to specifics, the questions I ask myself and the reader and attempt to answer include the following: What attempts were made to restore dynastic succession in the postdisaster period? What kind of organization of political and religious life took the place of monarchy, and with what success? What attitudes, strategies, and parties emerged in relation to the overwhelming political and military power of successive empires — Babylonian, Persian, Macedonian and Roman? What forms did aspirations for and predictions of a future restoration of the dynasty assume in prophetic and apocalyptic end-time scenarios? What impact, if any, did these have on social life and politics? Did the more prominent political and military aspects of the traditional profile of David undergo change and development during these centuries and, if so, in what directions?

I realize that this will look like an almost absurdly ambitious project. It involves, in the first place, the risk of punishment for transgressing familiar academic specializations and chronological boundaries (Persian, Hellenistic, Greco-Roman) in search of answers. In recent publications on Second Temple Judaism the departmentalization is especially in evidence in the divide between the Persian (Achaemenid) and Hellenistic periods, each with its own different linguistic demands and range of sources. The source material on which answers have to be based is also unevenly distributed, generally unsatisfactory, and often simply not available. In one instance, in connection with the prophetic books Haggai and Zechariah, we have exact dates which, together with the Bisitun (Behistun) trilingual inscription (Elamite, Babylonian, Old Persian) and a little help from Herodotus, permit, in places, a reconstruction of the early years of the reign of Darius I precise to the month and even to the day (Chapter Five). Elsewhere, however, the sources speak in arcane, symbolic language notoriously difficult to decode, as with the strange fate of the shepherd in Zechariah 9–14 (Chapter Eight). And there are stretches of time, especially in the long period between Nehemiah in the mid-fifth and the Seleucids in the second century, when there are no directly relevant data at all.

I am also aware of the problem of keeping abreast of the overwhelming flood of writing on messianic, apocalyptic, and millennarian movements which continues unabated to this day. While some acquaintance with these larger issues is obviously necessary, my decision was to stay out of this vast hinterland as far as possible, keeping the David theme steadily in view throughout.

In studies of this kind the question of relevance or, in contemporary official British parlance, "impact," is apt sooner or later to raise its ugly little head. Our theme is monarchy or, if we prefer a broader category, monocracy, and who in our enlightened, liberal-democratic and largely secular world is interested in such a thing? As Francis Oakley points out in his excellent study of the subject, of the 191 states around the world recognized as such by the United Nations only a handful have monarchical regimes of any kind, and most of these are largely ceremonial.[3] So the theme of monarchy would not seem to be one to quicken the pulse or stir the blood. We may nevertheless make the point, with all due deference to the contemporary *Weltanschauung,* that an institution which has been dominant in practically every part of the world for most of human history, from at least the Bronze Age down to the recent past, should be of interest to anyone who is serious about understanding the world we live in, how we arrived at where we are, and what our future prospects may be. During these millennia, the institution of monarchy exercised enormous influence on all aspects of social life, religious as well as political, serving among other things as the focus and conduit of sacrality for the community of the governed. This aspect of the institution will be evident to anyone with

---

3. Francis Oakley, *Kingship: The Politics of Enchantment* (Oxford: Blackwell, 2006) 2-3.

even a superficial knowledge of ancient cultures. It is nowhere more clearly in evidence than in those regions which lie in one way or another within our cultural memory — for most of us, the ancient Near East including Palestine, the Greek-speaking world, and the Mediterranean rim in general.

We may even venture a step further and raise the question whether such a study as we contemplate is of purely historical interest, whether assumptions about the taken-for-granted character, superiority, and permanence of our own Western, liberal-democratic institutions are entirely justified. No one will lightly advocate a return to absolutist monocratic government, but history teaches that there is often a price to be paid for attributing absolute validity to our current political institutions. The Roman Republic had been in existence for five centuries, it seemed indestructible, and yet a ruinous civil war led in 27 B.C.E. to the Principate beginning with Octavian. Throughout recent history political systems which seemed to be permanent have been displaced and those which displaced them have proved to be equally impermanent. The French revolutionaries, heir to the enlightened philosophy of the *Encyclopédie,* put an end to the monarchy with the guillotining of Louis XVI in 1793, yet about a decade later Napoleon was crowning himself emperor of the French to public acclaim. The Russian revolution was greeted with immense enthusiasm, yet evolved in a relatively short time into the monarchic, or at any rate monocratic, rule of Stalin. The last century saw constitutional monarchies with more or less liberal constitutions in developed European nations displaced in a short space of time by absolutist rulers during the Fascist era.

The defects of our democratic institutions are, moreover, obvious enough, and the institutions themselves vulnerable enough, to justify us standing back and taking in the broader range of possibilities which a knowledge of the past affords. We might then come to realize, perhaps as a result of financial collapse, unsolvable disputes over control of scarce natural resources, military confrontation, or the gradual subversion of the democratic process, that these defects are systemic as well as contingent. If the source of legitimacy is the will of the majority, what if expressions of that will eventuate in policies which perpetuate racism, rapacious capitalism, and imperial aggrandizement? And, on the urgent, practical level, the failure of Western democracies to reach and implement a consensus on collective action addressing the absolutely basic planetary issues should provoke reflection. The need to take in a broader historical and cultural arc was a lesson we were taught by Max Weber, who, in his ground-breaking writings, refused to take for granted our characteristic Western modes of life and thought and the institutions in which they find expression. Weber insisted on viewing Western political experience from the outside, which is to say from the perspective afforded by world history. And events taking place in the world as he was writing fully justified his approach.

These issues are of general, universal concern, but David, the central figure in our investigation, is, of course, of special interest to Jews and Christians both as a major presence in the Scriptures common to both religions and as messianic figure. The principal biblical presentation of David's life and times, in the historical books of the Bible (1 Samuel 16–1 Kings 2), is a composite image, a combination of different profiles from different sources. Details can be left to the commentaries, but the points at which these sources have been stitched together can often be detected. He is first anointed by Samuel guided by divine inspiration, for which no earthly reason is given other than that he was a very handsome youth (1 Sam 16:1-13). This is a standard topos, often repeated: David's son Absalom (2 Sam 14:25-26) and Absalom's sister and daughter (2 Sam 13:1; 14:27), both called Tamar, were all beautiful people. David first enters Saul's service as a musician capable of soothing his master — though his performances sometimes had the opposite effect — yet after his giant-slaying feat some time later Saul meets him as if for the first time and recruits him again (1 Sam 17:55-58). His role as a musician, as the Hebrew Orpheus,[4] would come to prominence when he was adopted as founder and patron by the Levitical guilds of musicians in the second temple and celebrated as such by the author of Chronicles (Chapter Six). The record also contains variants of several incidents: for example, Saul's attempt to pin David to the wall with his spear (1 Sam 18:10-11; 19:9-10) and David's coming upon Saul unawares and sparing his life (1 Sam 24:1-22; 26:6-25).

These aspects of what we can call "the David legend,"[5] in the first place David as ruler and founder of a dynasty, form one of the liveliest chapters in what biblical scholars are wont to call the Deuteronomistic History (Dtr). It is generally allowed that Dtr went through at least two

---

4. On the depiction of David as Orpheus on mosaics from Jerusalem and Gaza, see *BAR* 20/2 (1994) 58-63, 94; 35/2 (2009) 34-45, 68.

5. I use the term in the etymological sense of *legendum*, something to be read, not necessarily fictional but rather allowing for a basic historical substratum. See the classical treatment of this genre in André Jolles, *Einfache Formen: Legende, Sage, Mythe, Rätsel, Spruch, Kasus, Memorabile, Märchen, Witz* (Darmstadt: Wissenschaftliche Buchgesellschaft, 1958).

and possibly more than two editions before attaining its final form. If so, it makes sense to suppose that the David legend developed more or less along the same trajectory. The royal annals of Judah *(sēper dibrê malkê yĕhûdâ)* cover the reigns of Judean kings from Rehoboam, Solomon's son, to Jehoiakim, Josiah's second son. The summary of Solomon's reign diverges slightly from the pattern (1 Kgs 11:41-43), and there are at least some annalistic traces dealing with David: lists of his sons (2 Sam 3:2-5; 5:13-16), the length of his reign (2 Sam 5:4-5), his officials (2 Sam 8:15-18; 20:23-26), and his death, burial, length of reign (again), and successor (1 Kgs 2:10-12).

Beyond this point speculation is inevitable, but one or two probable stages on the legend's journey to its mature form may nevertheless be mentioned. For the Dtr author Hezekiah ranks as incomparable: "There was none to compare with him among all the kings of Judah after him, nor any among those before him" (2 Kgs 18:5). This statement will call for qualification when we go on to read the same praise of Josiah less than a century later (2 Kgs 23:25). According to the historian of Hezekiah's reign (2 Kgs 18–20), Hezekiah is presented as, in effect, a second David. He followed David's example in all things religious (2 Kgs 18:3). Though humiliated by the Assyrians, he attacked the Philistines as David had done (18:8). Like David, he went to "the house of God" to pray (2 Kgs 19:1; 2 Sam 12:20), and, like him, he heeded prophetic admonitions (2 Kgs 19:2-7) and received a communication from David's God (20:5-6). A rabbinic opinion even accords him quasi-messianic status *(b. Sanh.* 94a). More to the point, tradition assigns the composition of Proverbs 25–29 to "Hezekiah and his men" (Prov 25:1), he is credited with the composition of a psalm (Isa 38:9), and there is archaeological evidence for a significant increase in scribal activity during his reign in the second half of the eighth century when the Judean state was in the process of consolidation. This would therefore have been the right time to expand the traditions about David as a great and good ruler over Judah and Israel, especially with a view to attracting survivors of the Assyrian conquest of Samaria in 722 B.C.E. to move a few miles south and live under a benign descendant of David.[6]

The other great Davidic embodiment was King Josiah. The thesis of a redaction of Dtr during the reign of Josiah, Hezekiah's grandson, first proposed by Frank Moore Cross of Harvard University, has won wide ac-

---

6. The fall of Samaria and subsequent deportations took place either during or shortly before Hezekiah's reign, depending on which dating system is adopted, respectively 727-698 and 715-687.

ceptance.[7] The concluding sentence of this edition is identified as the praise of Josiah with which the Historian recapitulates the reign: "Before him there was no king to compare with him, who turned to Yahweh with all his heart, soul, and strength, in keeping with the entire law of Moses" (2 Kgs 23:25; a scribe in the postdisaster period added the sentence following: "nor did any to compare with him arise after him"). Josiah was put on the throne by a group referred to as the "people of the land" (ʿam hāʾāreṣ). Whatever this designation denotes elsewhere, in these last decades of the kingdom of Judah it refers to a strongly nationalistic group, opposed to foreign influences and fiercely devoted to the native dynasty. These characteristics earned sixty of them, unable to leave Jerusalem during the siege, a place among the first to be rounded up and executed by the conquering Babylonians (2 Kgs 25:19-21; see Chapter One). The reign of Josiah, the last significant representative of the dynasty as David was the first, would have provided a further occasion for expanding the narrative of national and dynastic origins including the res gestae of David, the heroic founder of the nation. This would have been especially so in view of Josiah's ambition — or that of his mentors and supporters — to bring about a reunion of north and south, Israel and Judah — a goal which is fairly explicit in the Chronicler's account of his reign (2 Chronicles 34-35), less so in Dtr (2 Kgs 22:1–23:30), but which the international situation at that time would almost certainly have ruled out (Chapter One). Minor additions would no doubt have been made after the last date in Dtr, that is, 560 B.C.E. (2 Kgs 25:27-30), in fact at practically any time to the Hellenistic period, though it has proved difficult to provide convincing examples.[8]

As for the legend itself, popular traditions about iconic figures like King David often share similar characteristics and follow a similar trajectory, created by the memories and aspirations of different societies often in

7. Frank Moore Cross, Canaanite Myth and Hebrew Epic (Cambridge, MA: Harvard University Press, 1973) 286-89; Richard D. Nelson, The Double Redaction of the Deuteronomistic History (JSOTSup 18; Sheffield: JSOT, 1981); Thomas C. Römer, The So-Called Deuteronomistic History (London: T. & T. Clark, 2005) 27-29.

8. The most ambitious attempt is that of Professor John Van Seters, who identifies in 1 Samuel 16–1 Kings 2 (excluding 2 Samuel 21–24) what he takes to be a version of "the Saga of King David" inserted into Dtr with the purpose of discrediting David and Solomon. He claims that this massive attempt to disparage David, which he regards as pure fiction, originated in "an anti-messianic tendency in certain Jewish circles" some time in the postexilic period, but unfortunately does not provide further details. Van Seters's most recent defense of this hypothesis at this writing is The Biblical Saga of King David (Winona Lake: Eisenbrauns, 2009).

widely diverse cultures. An example which is remarkably close to the David legend in theme, development, and political impact, and may therefore help to contextualize it as a literary work, is the equally complex Arthurian legend. The story of King Arthur, reputed to have lived a millennium and a half after David's time, comes to us in its mature form in Geoffrey of Monmouth's *Historia Regum Britanniae,* written some time between 1135 and 1140. This historical work, which contains a long section on Arthur's exploits, may be taken as the counterpart to the biblical history of the monarchy in Dtr beginning with David.[9] Like David, Geoffrey's Arthur gathered a warrior band around him, was crowned king at an early age, and secured the survival and freedom of his people against Saxon inroads as David did against the Philistines and other neighboring peoples. Arthur was, withal, pious, attentive to the seer Merlin, the counterpart of Samuel, and in regular consultation with the local clergy, Davidic traits which come to the fore in the Chronicler's work. David's killing of Goliath has its counterpart in Arthur's despatching of a giant in Mont Saint-Michel, and Goliath's sword, which became David's trophy (1 Sam 21:8-9), corresponds to Arthur's famous sword Excalibur (originally Caliburn) of supernatural origin. There is also the dark side. The rebellion of Arthur's nephew Mordred and the adultery of his wife Guinevere with Mordred or, in later versions, Lancelot parallel Absalom's rebellion and David's adultery with Bathsheba. Arthur received a mortal wound in battle, was carried to the island of Avalon, later identified with Glastonbury, where, in 1191, the resident monks, anxious to attract tourists, claimed to have discovered his grave. Doubts about whether he really died persisted nevertheless, and from that point on "his legend made him a messiah, answering to an ancient pattern of the imagination."[10]

Doubts about the historical character of the events recorded in the

9. The work was translated with an introduction by Lewis Thorpe in Geoffrey of Monmouth, *The History of the Kings of Britain* (London: Penguin, 1966). The comparison with Dtr was not lost on the translator, who comments that the work "may be said to bear the same relationship to the story of the early British inhabitants of our own island as do the seventeen historical books in the Old Testament . . . to the early history of the Israelites in Palestine" (p. 9). For a recent study of the book, see Karen Jankulak, *Geoffrey of Monmouth* (Cardiff: University of Wales Press, 2010).

10. Geoffrey Ashe, ed., *The Quest for Arthur's Britain* (London: Pall Mall, 1968) 15. Geoffrey of Monmouth reports that Cadwallader, last king of the indigenous Britons (principally the people of Wales and Cornwall), heard an angelic voice telling him that God did not wish the Britons to rule any longer until the moment should come which Merlin had prophesied to Arthur (xii 17).

lives of both David and Arthur, and even about the existence of these two heroic figures, have been around since the beginnings of critical scholarship in biblical studies and the study of the sub-Roman period in the British Isles, respectively. In both cases sources have been evaluated — for Arthur, early historical writings, Welsh genealogical records, religious tracts and bardic compositions — and the relevant archaeological data argued over and analyzed.[11] These discussions and debates will doubtless continue, but experience attests that once an iconic personality or event from the past enters the realm of legend and myth, becomes lodged in the collective memory of a society, and is reinforced by repetitive ritual action, lack of historical credibility becomes irrelevant. Affective communities which cherish the legends do not have the same concern as academic historians to get the past right.

To show what forms this cherishing took with respect to David after the dynasty founded by him came to a violent end will be one of the goals in what follows. After rehearsing the events leading to the dissolution of the Judean state and the eclipse of the dynasty (Chapter One), the next five chapters will deal with attempts under Babylonian and Persian rule either to restore the dynasty (Chapters Two, Three, Five) or, failing that, to find a way of coping with the overwhelming political and military power of empire in the absence of the apparatus of an independent state and native dynasty (Chapters Four and Six). After an examination of the dynastic theme in prophetic projections of the end time (Chapter Seven) and an attempt to penetrate the almost impenetrable parabolic account of the mission and death of the Shepherd leader in Zechariah 9–14 (Chapter Eight), our investigation will conclude with the revival after long silence of the David theme as the focus of resistance, spiritual and physical, to Rome, the new Babylon. This last chapter (Chapter Nine) will therefore seek traces of the

---

11. For a recent and accessible discussion of the principal issues and opinions on the archaeology of early Iron Age Israel with reference to the biblical story of David, see Israel Finkelstein and Neil Asher Silberman, *David and Solomon: In Search of the Bible's Sacred Kings and the Roots of the Western Tradition* (New York: Free Press, 2006); and Israel Finkelstein and Amihai Mazar, edited by Brian B. Schmidt, *The Quest for the Historical Israel* (Atlanta: Society of Biblical Literature, 2007) 99-139. On the archaeology of sites with Arthurian connections in Wales, Cornwall, and other parts of the west of England, especially Cadbury South, once identified as Camelot, see Leslie Alcock, *Arthur's Britain: History and Archaeology* (2nd ed., London: Penguin, 1989); and Peter Salway, *Roman Britain* (New York: Oxford University Press, 1981) 485. Debates about Cadbury would be the Arthurian counterpart to those about Jerusalem of the time of David.

David theme in the relations between the Jewish people and imperial Rome, ending with some observations on Jesus as Son of David, events leading up to the great revolt of A.D. 66–73 C.E., and the Bar Kokhba revolt six decades later.

CHAPTER ONE

The Eclipse of the House of David

Thus, then, did the kings of David's line end their lives; there were twenty-one of them including the last king, and they reigned altogether for five hundred and fourteen years, six months and ten days.

Josephus, *Antiquities* 10:143

The Final Phase (609-586 B.C.E.)

If not the end of the world, the fall of Jerusalem to Nebuchadnezzar and the Babylonian army in the summer of 586 B.C.E. was the disaster which determined for long into the future the course of history for the people of Israel. According to the biblical record, our only source of information on this event since the Babylonian Chronicle breaks off in 593 B.C.E., the Babylonians laid siege to the city in January 587 and the wall was breached in July of the following year (2 Kgs 25:1-3; Jer 39:1-4). Zedekiah attempted to flee the city with a military escort but was captured, was obliged to watch his sons being slaughtered to bring the dynasty to an end, and was then blinded and led shackled into captivity (2 Kgs 25:3-7; Jer 39:3-7; 52:8-11). Supporting evidence for the biblical account includes charred remains from the Jewish quarter of the Old City, including Scythian arrowheads known to have been used by the Babylonians, and ostraca discovered at Lachish which document the approach of the Babylonian army from the southwest.[1] A month later the Babylonian generalissimo Nebuzaradan arrived with the explicit charge of burning the temple, executing the chief priests who had provided the religious legitimation for the revolt, and arranging the logistics for the deportation of those members of the aristocracy and artisan class who had survived the siege and its aftermath (2 Kgs 25:8-21).

The sack of Jerusalem and the ignominious end to the reign of the last of David's line to occupy the throne was the climactic event long remembered in psalm, lament, and liturgical prayer. The eclipse of the dynasty, and with it the collapse of an entire way of life, was the outcome of about a quarter of a century of incompetent rule by the last four rulers, three sons and one grandson of Josiah, the last significant king of Judah who died at the age of thirty-five in 609 B.C.E. The first task is therefore to retell this final chapter of the history of the Judean monarchy in the expectation of finding clues as to how and why the catastrophe happened and what it boded for the future.

During that final quarter of a century these four descendants of Josiah, all in their early twenties or late teens at their accession, contributed by their ineptitude, or by following imprudent advice, to the final extinction of the dynasty at the hands of the great powers of that time, the Egyptians first, then the Babylonians. According to the genealogy of the house of David in 1 Chr 3:15, the order of birth of Josiah's four sons is Johanan, Jehoiakim, Zedekiah, and Shallum. The first of the four to reign, Shallum, renamed Jehoahaz, was anointed and put on the throne ahead of his older brother Jehoiakim by a faction referred to as "the people of the land" (*'am hā'āreṣ*, 2 Kgs 23:30). This term, which can mean different things at different times and in different situations,[2] often has a quite general connotation with reference to the population of Judah outside of Jeru-

---

1. J. C. L. Gibson, *Textbook of Syrian Semitic Inscriptions*. Vol. 1: *Hebrew and Moabite Inscriptions* (Oxford: Clarendon, 1971) 32-49; Nahman Avigad, *Discovering Jerusalem* (Nashville: Nelson, 1980) 49-53. On the revolt and fall of Jerusalem in general, see Oded Lipschits, *The Fall and Rise of Jerusalem* (Winona Lake: Eisenbrauns, 2005) 68-84; J. Maxwell Miller and John H. Hayes, *A History of Ancient Israel and Judah* (2nd ed., Louisville: Westminster/John Knox, 2006) 474-77.

2. Ernst Würthwein, *Der 'am ha'aretz im Alten Testament* (BWANT 17; Stuttgart: Kohlhammer, 1936); Ernest W. Nicholson, "The Meaning of the Expression 'am ha'arez in the Old Testament," *JSS* 10 (1965) 59-66; Antonius H. J. Gunneweg, "'AM HA'ARES — A Semantic Revolution," *ZAW* 95 (1983) 437-40; other references in Joseph P. Healey, "'Am Ha'arez," *ABD* 1 (1992) 168-69; Edouard Lipiński, "The People of the Land of Judah," *TDOT* 11 (2001) 174-75.

salem, in the Judean countryside. But there are occasions, especially towards the end of the Judean state, where the expression refers to a distinct and identifiable political category with its own leaders and representatives, in some respects analogous to the institution of elders. Conservative, traditionalist and nationalistic in their political views, its members were attached to the native dynasty and fiercely opposed to foreign influences. More than two centuries earlier, they had played a leading role in the coup responsible for the dethronement and death of Queen Athaliah and the restoration of the Davidic dynasty in the person of Joash (Jehoash), the seven-year-old son of the former king Ahaziah (2 Kgs 11:14, 18-20; 12:1). More than two centuries later the same group emerged once again, putting the eight-year-old Josiah on the throne after avenging the assassination of Amon, his father (2 Kgs 21:24). After Josiah's death they intervened yet again on behalf of his son Shallum/Jehoahaz in preference to Jehoiakim, an older brother (2 Kgs 23:30). As king-makers, they must have exercised considerable influence on state affairs during this last, fateful period, especially in view of the youth of all four rulers. In these last decades of the Judean monarchy they were at the opposite end of the political spectrum from those whom their enemies would have known as the appeasement party. The principal representatives of the party opposed to these "people of the land" came from the territory of Benjamin north of Jerusalem, among whom the most prominent were members of the family of Shaphan, a prominent statesman during Josiah's reign. The public voice of this powerful faction was that of the Benjaminite prophet Jeremiah. In view of the high political profile and ideology as nationalists and royalists of the *'am hā'āreṣ*, it is not surprising that sixty of them, confined to Jerusalem during the siege of 588-586, were rounded up and executed by the Babylonians after the fall of the city (2 Kgs 25:19-21).

The historian of the monarchy, known in scholarly circles as the Deuteronomistic Historian (hereafter Dtr or simply the Historian), reports that Jehoahaz, first of the four, reigned for three months, but it may be doubted whether he actually reigned at all. Shortly after executing Josiah, Pharaoh Necho II imprisoned Jehoahaz at the Egyptian army headquarters in Riblah on the Orontes in Syria, put his own nominee Eliakim, older brother of Jehoahaz, on the throne, and took Jehoahaz off to Egypt where he presumably died (2 Kgs 23:34; Jer 22:11-12). The twenty-five-year-old Eliakim, second son of Josiah, renamed Jehoiakim by Pharaoh Necho, was left with the task of raising the heavy tribute imposed by this most recent imperial overlord, which could not have endeared him to the population as a whole (2 Kgs 23:34-35). The Historian provides no information on the first period of Jehoiakim's eleven-year reign (609-598/597 B.C.E.) during which Judah was under Egyptian rule. But after the Egyptian defeat by the Babylonian army led by Nebuchadnezzar at Carchemish on the upper Euphrates in 605 (Jer 46:1-12), the Judean kingdom was ruled from Babylon rather than Memphis. Then, following on the failure of Nebuchadnezzar's attempt to invade Egypt in 601, Jehoiakim was persuaded to participate in a revolt in the western provinces of the Babylonian Empire which was no more successful than previous attempts to throw off the imperial yoke and which left Jehoiakim's successor to pick up the pieces.

There are conflicting accounts of Jehoiakim's fate. According to 2 Chr 36:6, repeated in Dan 1:1-2, he was exiled to Babylon, a version which some accept but which may be due to confusion between Jehoiakim and his successor Jehoiachin. The Historian reports that he "slept with his ancestors," in other words, was buried with his royal antecedents in Jerusalem (2 Kgs 24:6) or, following the Lucianic version of the Septuagint, in the garden of Uzzah alongside the remains of Manasseh (2 Kgs 21:18). Jeremiah, however, predicted that his body would be dragged out of the city and buried like a dead donkey, meaning probably no burial at all (Jer 22:18-19; cf. 36:30), a prediction which Josephus says was fulfilled, but only after Jehoiakim was put to death by Nebuchadnezzar (*Ant.* 10:97). Jeremiah's extremely hostile oracle about this young man's sad end is, however, a prediction, not a statement of fact. It may have been intended as incitement to assassination, but there is no evidence that anyone took the hint.[3] But enemies would not have been lacking, and they would have included the (probably Benjaminite) family of the Shaphanids, patrons and protectors of Jeremiah. Their opposition to movements of national independence and rebellion during the quarter century following the death of Josiah, a position opposed by the "people of the land" as noted earlier, would be rewarded by favorable treatment accorded Jeremiah by the Babylonians after the fall of Jerusalem and the appointment of Gedaliah, grandson of Shaphan, to govern the province on behalf of the Babylonian overlord.[4]

Like Jehoahaz, Jehoiachin (also known as Coniah and Jeconiah), the

---

3. Jer 26:24; 29:3; 36:9-19. That he was in fact assassinated is suggested by John Bright, *A History of Israel* (3rd ed., Philadelphia: Westminster, 1981) 327. J. Maxwell Miller and John H. Hayes, *A History of Ancient Israel and Judah* (Philadelphia: Westminster, 1986) 406, however, read Jeremiah's prediction as an invitation to assassination for which, however, there were apparently no takers.

4. 2 Kgs 25:22-26; Jer 39:11-14; 40:1-12.

eighteen-year-old son of Jehoiakim, is said to have reigned for only three months (2 Kgs 24:8).[5] These three months witnessed the final unravelling leading to the last phase of the punitive campaign of Nebuchadnezzar, the siege and capture of Jerusalem, and the surrender of Jehoiachin's person and family to the Babylonian conqueror. At first, Nebuchadnezzar contented himself with inciting the Transjordanian kingdoms to harass Judah (2 Kgs 24:1-2), but in March 597 B.C.E. Jerusalem was taken by the Babylonian army after a brief siege, which once again snuffed out dynastic rule (2 Kgs 24:10-12). The biblical account is supported by the Babylonian Chronicle for that year which reads as follows:

> In the seventh year, in the month of Kislev, the king of Akkad mustered his troops, marched to the Hatti-land (Syria-Palestine), and encamped against the city of Judah, and on the second day of the month of Adar he seized the city and captured the king. He appointed there a king of his own choice, received its heavy tribute, and sent them to Babylon.[6]

Jehoiachin's reign, therefore, equalled that of Jehoahaz in insignificance as well as length. Unlike Zedekiah eleven years later, he surrendered both the city and his own person to the Babylonians with the result that, instead of laying the city waste, Nebuchadnezzar contented himself with looting palace and temple of their precious metals and other treasures before departing. With respect to the administration of the province, the same procedure was followed as with the Egyptian takeover eleven years earlier: deportation and exile of the current ruler, appointment of a substitute, in this instance Mattaniah, son of Josiah and Jehoiachin's uncle, and the conferring of a new throne name on the client king, in this instance Zedekiah (2 Kgs 24:17).[7]

5. According to 2 Chr 36:9-10 Jehoiachin was eight years old and reigned for three months and ten days, but "eight" is probably a scribal error for "eighteen." The same more precise length of reign is reproduced in Josephus, *Ant* 10:98.

6. Donald J. Wiseman, *Chronicles of the Chaldaean Kings (626-556 B.C.) in the British Museum* (London: Trustees of the British Museum, 1961) 72-73. For the history of the period, see Miller and Hayes, *A History of Ancient Israel and Judah*, 406-8.

7. Zedekiah was Jehoiachin's uncle (*dôd*) according to 2 Kgs 24:17, but his brother (*'āḥîw*) according to 2 Chr 36:10, in keeping with the genealogical datum in 1 Chr 3:16. The latter option would make a better fit with the parallelistic structure of 2 Chr 36:1-14: two sons of Josiah followed by two grandsons and alternating reigns of three months and eleven years. According to the LXX, Syriac, and Vulgate of 2 Chr 36:10, however, *'āḥîw* ("his brother") should probably be emended to *'āḥî 'ābîw* ("his uncle").

It turned out, however, that the exiled Jehoiachin rather than Zedekiah continued to be regarded by many, certainly by nationalists and royalists like the ʿam hāʾāreṣ and perhaps especially in the Babylonian Diaspora, as the legitimate ruler *in absentia*. At best, Zedekiah would have been seen by many as regent until Jehoiachin's anticipated return and resumption of his interrupted reign. After Zedekiah's sons had been slaughtered at Riblah, a deliberate act aimed to exclude the possibility of dynastic succession and bring the Davidic line to an end (2 Kgs 25:7),[8] any remaining interest in Zedekiah's Davidic legitimacy would have disappeared, and we know nothing about what happened to him subsequently. One indication that Jehoiachin continued to be seen by some, perhaps many, as the legitimate ruler is the dating system in Ezekiel calculated from the beginning of the exile, therefore from the date of Jehoiachin's accession. These dates run from 593 to 573 B.C.E.[9] Hananiah, Jeremiah's prophetic opponent, perhaps a spokesman for the "people of the land," also foresaw and predicted the return of Jehoiachin to the throne (Jer 28:1-17). The high level of nationalistic-prophetic activity in the Babylonian Diaspora, which was savagely suppressed by Nebuchadnezzar (Jer. 29:1-32), may have been driven by the same aspirations for the restitution of the banished Jehoiachin. At any rate, Jeremiah decisively rejected this nationalistic movement which produced its own martyrs, and predicted its failure (Jer 29:15-23). Even if legitimate — he is described as "the signet ring on Yahweh's right hand" — the exiled Jehoiachin would have no successor (Jer 22:24-30).

Zedekiah was the third of Josiah's four sons named in the Chronicler's genealogical list (1 Chr 3:15). He was the son of Hamutal, also mother of Jehoahaz,[10] and destined to have the dubious distinction of being the last of David's line to occupy the throne of Judah. The Historian has little to say about his eleven-year reign apart from his decision to rebel and the terrible fate that awaited him after the failure of the rebellion. Jeremiah records more than one attempt to dissuade Zedekiah from joining a coalition of western rebels with the anticipated support from Egypt under the

---

8. Nebuchadnezzar evidently did not view Jehoiachin and his sons, confined in Babylon, as a threat (2 Kgs 25:28-29).

9. Ezek 1:2; 8:1; 20:1; 24:1; 29:1; 30:20; 31:1; 32:1; 33:21; 40:1.

10. The three sons (Jehoahaz, Jehoiakim, Zedekiah) and one grandson (Jehoiachin) of Josiah who reigned during this quarter century were the sons of three different mothers: Hamutal (Jehoahaz, Zedekiah), Zebidah (Jehoiakim), and Nehushtah (Jehoiachin). We have no information on Johanan, first-named of Josiah's sons (1 Chr 3:15).

newly crowned Pharaoh Psammeticus II. This was shortly before the Babylonian punitive expedition (Jer 27:1-22), in which Jeremiah was opposed by the nationalist prophet Hananiah who predicted the downfall of the Babylonian Empire in two years' time (28:1-17). After Zedekiah had made his fateful decision, no doubt encouraged by such overly optimistic prophets like Hananiah, he nevertheless continued to consult with Jeremiah even during the siege (Jer 21:1-2; 37:1-10). Jeremiah seems to have regarded him as weak and impressionable rather than evil; he was, after all, only twenty-one years old when he came to the throne. Ezekiel, on the other hand, brands him intemperately as "the vile, wicked prince of Israel" who broke his oath of allegiance to Nebuchadnezzar (Ezek 21:30-32[Eng 25-27]) and therefore deserved the fate awaiting him.

It seems likely that in its original form Dtr concluded on a low note with the bald statement that "Judah went into exile from its land" (2 Kgs 25:21b). If so, two historical appendices must have been added: the first, the reign and assassination of Gedaliah, the subject of Chapter Three (2 Kgs 25:22-26); the second, the rehabilitation of Jehoiachin (25:27-30).[11] This final episode relates how Nebuchadnezzar's successor, Amel-Marduk (written dysphemistically as Evil-Merodach),[12] in his first regnal year granted amnesty to Jehoiachin in the thirty-seventh year of his exile, therefore in the fifty-fifth year of his age. The benevolence demonstrated by Amel-Marduk included a special allowance, the right to dine at the royal table, and a preeminent position vis-à-vis other kings in exile with him (2 Kgs 25:27-30). This information makes a good fit with one of several administrative texts dated to the thirteenth year of the reign of Nebuchadnezzar II, therefore 592 B.C.E., which attests to the presence of Jehoiachin *(Ia-ku-ú-ki-nu)* together with his five sons and eight other Judaeans, unfortunately not named, at the Babylonian court.[13] The presence of Jehoiachin together with

11. On the conclusion to Dtr see Walter Dietrich, *Prophetie und Geschichte: Eine redaktionsgeschichtliche Untersuchung zum deuteronomistischen Geschichtswerk* (FRLANT 108; Göttingen: Vandenhoeck & Ruprecht, 1972) 140-43; Richard Elliott Friedman, *The Exile and Biblical Narrative: The Formation of the Deuteronomistic and Priestly Works* (HSM 22; Chico: Scholars, 1981) 35-36; Christopher T. Begg, "The Interpretation of the Gedaliah Episode (2 Kgs 25:22-26) in Context," *Anton* 62 (1987) 3-11; Mark A. O'Brien, *The Deuteronomistic History Hypothesis: A Reassessment* (OBO 92; Freiburg: Universitätsverlag and Göttingen: Vandenhoeck & Ruprecht, 1989) 271; Thomas Römer, *La première histoire d'Israël, l'Ecole deutéronomiste à l'oeuvre* (Geneva: Labor et Fides, 2007) 152, 170-71, 185.

12. Hebrew *'ĕwîl mĕrōdak;* a contemptuous way of referring to Marduk, imperial deity of Babylon, as stupid *('ĕwîl).*

13. See E. F. Weidner, "Jojachin, König von Juda in Babylonischen Keilschrifttexten,"

other exiled client rulers at the Babylonian court may have been intended as an implicit threat of replacement directed at reigning vassals, and therefore a motivation to obedience and fidelity to their oaths. The release of Jehoiachin by Amel-Marduk also suggests that he was grooming this grandson of Josiah to return to Jerusalem as a client ruler, a move perhaps inspired by anxiety about the expansionist policies of Amosis (Ahmose) II and the consequent need to promote the *pax babylonica* in a not unimportant western province adjacent to Egypt. In fact, the precision of the date at this point — the twenty-seventh of the twelfth month (Adar) in the thirty-seventh year since his accession (2 Kgs 25:27) — may indicate that this was regarded as marking the official resumption of Jehoiachin's interrupted reign. But if this was Amel-Marduk's plan, it came to nothing since he was assassinated a few months later by his brother-in-law Neriglissar, who succeeded him.[14] Jeremiah's prediction that Jehoiachin would die in Babylon was therefore fulfilled after all (Jer 22:26), but the prophetic-messianic enthusiasm which focused on his grandson Zerubbabel two generations later showed that the hopes of the nationalists and royalists would not so easily be extinguished.

Josiah the Incomparable

Looking back on this sad final chapter from the other side of the disaster of 586 B.C.E., the Historian is telling his readers that the Davidic line in effect came to an end with the death of Josiah twenty-three years before the fall of Jerusalem. The reigns of Jehoiakim and Zedekiah could be discounted as illegitimate since these two sons of Josiah were put in place by foreigners. The illegitimacy of Zedekiah is especially in evidence in the final paragraph of the History which intimates that the exiled Jehoiachin continued to be regarded as the rightful heir *in absentia*. The other two, Jehoahaz and Jehoiachin, could hardly be said to have reigned at all since for the three

---

in *Mélanges syriens offerts à Monsieur René Dussaud* II (Paris: Geuthner, 1939) 923-35; translation in *ANET*, 308. On the background to Jehoiachin's imprisonment and rehabilitation, see Rainer Albertz, "In Search of the Deuteronomists: A First Solution to a Historical Riddle," in *The Future of the Deuteronomistic History*, ed. Thomas Römer (BETL 147; Leuven: Leuven University Press and Peeters, 2000) 15-17.

14. Since the author of the second appendix anticipated the restoration of Jehoiachin to the throne but did not record it, 560 B.C.E., the date of the death of Amel-Marduk, may be taken to be the conclusion of Dtr in its present form.

months each occupied the throne they were under the coercive power of foreign rule, that of Egypt and Babylon, respectively. Moreover, three of the four died as captives in a foreign land — all four if we accept the Chronicler's statement that Jehoiakim ended his days in Babylon (2 Chr 36:6). And it was self-evident to the Historian that all four "did what was evil in the sight of Yahweh" (2 Kgs 23:32, 37; 24:9, 19).

The end of the line for the Davidic dynasty is also foreshadowed in the Historian's account of Josiah's reign (2 Kings 22–23). An editor contemporary with Josiah summed up the reign as follows: "Before his time there was no king to compare with him who turned to Yahweh with all his heart, soul and strength in keeping with the law of Moses" (2 Kgs 23:25a), to which has been added some time after the fall of Jerusalem, "Nor did any to compare with him arise after him" (23:25b).[15] This praise of Josiah as incomparable among all the descendants of David is followed by an announcement of imminent disaster on Judah and Jerusalem in which the blame is assigned to the religious infidelity, injustice, and violence of Manasseh, Josiah's grandfather, whose reign ended with his death a year before Josiah's accession (23:26-27). Here, too, the language betrays the hand of a postdisaster Deuteronomist[16] who is anxious to come up with a theological explanation for Josiah's violent, untimely, and apparently senseless death after such notable demonstrations of piety and fidelity to the law. This statement about the incomparability of Josiah conveys a sad sense of finality, of the end of the line, and is rounded out with a brief account of his death at Megiddo (2 Kgs 23:28-30).

The coming disaster is intimated in oracular manner by the prophetess Huldah in a message transmitted to Josiah by a delegation of five notables sent to consult her (2 Kgs 22:14-20). This oracular utterance predicted good news of sorts for the king in the short term (vv. 18-20), but really bad news for everyone else in the longer term (vv. 15-17). It conforms to a familiar pattern of oracles presaging disaster, most recently one delivered by "Yahweh's servants the prophets" to Manasseh (2 Kgs 21:10-15). Close par-

---

15. The existence of a Hezekian edition of Dtr has at time been argued on the basis of the somewhat similar commendation of that king in 2 Kgs 18:5: "After his time there was no king to compare with him among all the kings of Judah, and (those) who were before him." Since there is no textual justification for emendation, this statement presupposes knowledge of several kings subsequent to Hezekiah and therefore cannot serve as proof of a Hezekian edition of the History. The final sentence, *wa'ăšer hāyû lĕpānâw* ("and those who preceded him"), is generally treated as a rather clumsy addition perhaps inspired by 2 Kgs 23:25.

16. Cf. 2 Kgs 21:10-15; 24:3-4; Jer 15:3-4.

allels to Huldah's pronouncement of doom are also to be found in prose additions to Jeremiah which also date from some time after the disaster. Huldah, the Judean Cassandra, speaks, in fact, as if she were the female counterpart to Jeremiah.[17] The combination in a prophetic utterance of good news in the short term and bad news in the long term also follows a familiar pattern. Elijah announces to Ahab that, since he had torn his clothes and humbled himself, Yahweh would not bring about the disaster in his days, but that it would fall on his "house" (i.e., dynasty) in the person of his son Joram, last of the Omrids after his death (1 Kgs 21:27-29; 2 Kgs 9:14-26). An earlier example is the announcement of doom on the house of Eli communicated to Eli by Samuel, again with distinctly Deuteronomistic associations (1 Sam 3:10-14).

The lesser evil predicted for the king by Huldah, that he would be gathered to his ancestors and to his grave in peace before the disaster happened, seems to be contradicted by Josiah's death at the hands of the Egyptian king at Megiddo. This is not necessarily the case, however. The phrase "in peace" *(bĕšālôm)* may be referred to the statement immediately preceding, "you will be gathered to your own burial place." The peace in question would then consist in being buried in one's own ancestral place, thereby aggregated to the greater unity of the dead and living members of the lineage, as Abraham was buried "in peace" (Gen 15:15): Peace in the final and fullest sense, therefore.

The End of the Line

Josiah both reproduces the essential features of the David of the traditions and recapitulates the history of the dynasty. That he is a kind of replica or avatar of David is intimated at the beginning of the account of his reign, where we are told that "he did what was right in the sight of Yahweh, conducting himself in every respect after the manner of David his ancestor, without deviating either to the right or the left" (2 Kgs 22:2). No other ruler of the sixteen preceding him since David received this measure of praise. Solomon conducted himself according to the statutes of David (1 Kgs 3:3a),

17. Cf. Jer 6:9; 11:11; 35:17; 45:5, and esp. 19:3-9 addressed to the kings of Judah and inhabitants of Jerusalem. In his discussion of 2 Kings 22–23 as the foundation myth of the Deuteronomistic School, Thomas Römer observes that Huldah speaks to the delegation as if she were Jeremiah. See *The So-Called Deuteronomistic History: A Sociological, Historical, and Literary Introduction* (London: T. & T. Clark, 2007) 50.

but this statement is immediately followed by serious qualifications. Asa did what was right following the example of David, but not in every respect since he tolerated the existence of the local sanctuaries and their cults, the so-called "high places" (*bāmôt*, 1 Kgs 15:14). Hezekiah even went further than most of the kings preceding him in banning the "high places" and, in general, following David's example (2 Kgs 18:3). He is one of the Historian's heroes, but after his recovery from a life-threatening sickness he foolishly entertained envoys from Babylon and showed little concern for the coming disaster predicted by Isaiah (2 Kgs 20:12-19). A less flattering account of his political activity can also be deduced from certain passages referring to him directly or indirectly in Isaiah.[18] Josiah's fidelity to the law is in evidence throughout. The work of repair and restoration on the temple (2 Kgs 22:3-7, 9), based on the account of the same operation during the reign of Jehoash (2 Kgs 12:10-16),[19] provided the narrative context for the discovery of the law book which has been worked into it (22:8, 10-11). The discovery of this book in the temple and its consequences have been rightly seen as a defining moment in Dtr and the foundation myth of the Deuteronomistic School.[20] Huldah's oracular utterances are also Deuteronomistic in language and theme, and the religious reforms carried out under Josiah's direction correspond either explicitly or by implication to stipulations in the book of Deuteronomy.[21]

---

18. Esp. in chs. 28–31, on which see my "Hezekiah and the Babylonian Delegation," in *Essays on Ancient Israel in Its Near Eastern Context: A Tribute to Nadav Na'aman,* ed. Yairah Amit *et al.* (Winona Lake: Eisenbrauns, 2006) 107-22.

19. Hilkiah, Josiah's priest, corresponds to the priest Jehoiada during the minority of Jehoash, and Shaphan corresponds to the anonymous royal secretary co-responsible for the work of repair. In both episodes the funds are collected (2 Kgs 12:10; 22:4) and handed to the workers who had oversight of the temple (2 Kgs 12:12; 22:5, 9). During both reigns the work was done by carpenters, builders, and masons (12:11-12; 22:6), who used timber and quarried stone (12:12; 22:6) and from whom no accounting was called for since they were honest (12:16; 22:7).

20. Römer, *The So-Called Deuteronomistic History,* 49-56.

21. This is so with the abolition of the "high places" and the resettlement of their priests in Jerusalem (2 Kgs 23:5, 8, 13; cf. Deut 12:3; 18:6-8), in keeping with the centralization of cult in the Jerusalem temple (Deut 12:8-12, 13-15). The same for the rejection of cult images of Baal, Asherah, and other deities (2 Kgs 23:4-6; cf. Deut 4:15-18, 25-26; 5:8-10); the rejection of astral deities, probably of Assyrian origin (2 Kgs 23:4-5, 11; cf. Deut 4:19); the cult of Molek (2 Kgs 23:10; cf. Deut 18:10); destruction of *massēbôt* and *'ăšērîm* (monoliths in honour of male and female fertility deities, 2 Kgs 23:14; cf. Deut 7:5); expulsion of male cult prostitutes from the temple (2 Kgs 23:7; cf. Deut 23:17-18); and the prohibition of necromantic practices and practitioners (2 Kgs 23:24; cf. Deut 18:10b-11).

The account of Josiah's reign in 2 Chronicles 34–35 presents him much more unequivocally and comprehensively as the counterpart at the end of the dynasty to David at its beginning. The author had evidently read his principal source, 2 Kings 22–23, closely, but could not accept the implication that Josiah had tolerated pagan cult practices for eighteen years and had undertaken the repair of the temple when it was still full of idolatrous cult objects and accommodated male cult prostitutes. The Chronicler's solution was to revise the chronology of the reign so as to limit Josiah's infidelity to his minority and attribute his reforms not to the discovery of the law of Moses but to his own religious initiative. At the age of sixteen, ten years before the discovery of the law book in the temple (2 Chr 34:8, 14-18), Josiah had a religious experience and "began to seek the God of his ancestor David" (34:3). This adjustment of the chronology of the reign allowed the author to elevate David to a position comparable to that of Moses, a position which is in evidence throughout 1-2 Chronicles and testifies to the author's relative freedom from tradition. David is presented as founder of the temple cult, guided certainly by the law of Moses, but also by direct prophetic inspiration (1 Chr 25:2; 28:19). Josiah also reestablished the temple clergy after the apostasies of Manasseh on the basis of *written* instructions of David comparable to those of Moses (2 Chr 35:4; cf. 1 Chr 28:19).

The Chronicler's Josiah is superimposed on David in another respect, one which called for a more drastic revision of his principal source: he is now the one who recovered for Judah territories which, according to tradition, had belonged to David's "Greater Israel." The Historian (2 Kings 22–23) states at several points that the king's reforms were limited to Jerusalem and the cities of Judah (23:5-6, 8, 24) and provides little support for reforming activity outside of that region. The notice about the destruction of local shrines in Samaria could imply nothing more than a raid or one-time foray dictated by religious zeal into the province of Samerina, territory belonging to the Assyrian Empire, after which, we are told, he returned to Jerusalem (2 Kgs 23:19-20). In any case, his activity in Bethel and Samaria, which is said to fulfil an ancient prophecy, has for several commentators the appearance of a later insertion (23:15-20; cf. 1 Kgs 13:1-3). For the author of Chronicles, on the other hand, the religious reforms of Josiah extended into Ephraim, Manasseh, Naphtali, and Simeon, all the way, therefore, from the extreme north to the extreme south of the country (2 Chr 34:6-7, 9). In the context of the author's general ideology, the intent was to cleanse all the territory once under David's rule from the same religious "abominations" from which Judah was now, for the time being, free (34:33). This is an important point for the author since it meant that Judah and Ephraim, north and south, were once more united under a descendant of David as at the beginning.

This account of Josiah's reconquest of the irredentist provinces of David's one-time kingdom is often accepted as historically reliable, but it appears that the situation of the great empires at that time left no opening for such a campaign of conquest. Ashurbanipal (668-627 B.C.E.) was active in the west about the time Josiah came to the throne, subduing a revolt in Tyre and campaigning against Arab tribes. During the relatively peaceful last two decades of the same king's reign there was no question of Assyria losing, or giving up, the western provinces, certainly not as a result of pressure from the much-discussed and probably fictitious Scythian invasion of Palestine.[22] The collapse of Assyria came about quite suddenly and could not have been seriously contemplated before the Babylonian revolt and the civil war which followed Ashurbanipal's death. Even during the decade preceding the fall of Nineveh in 612 B.C.E., Assyrian armies were still on the offensive in spite of several defeats, and we are told, for good measure, that the idea of a territorially weakened Assyria is not supported by the evidence from contemporary Assyrian economic documents.[23] The situation appears to have been that, already during Josiah's reign, Egypt was the dominant power in the region west of the Jordan river (*'ēber nāhri*, "Across the River"). It controlled the famous *Via Maris*, the main south-north highway along the Mediterranean coast, and therefore also Megiddo, and as far north as the Phoenician cities. It is therefore highly unlikely that Josiah could have operated freely any further north of Jerusalem than Bethel, about 12 kilometers north of Jerusalem, at the southern edge of the Assyrian province of Samerina.[24]

The other prop for the hypothesis of territorial expansion — as far north as the Esdraelon Valley — is the death of Josiah at Megiddo. The

22. Richard P. Vaggione, "Over All Asia? The Extent of the Scythian Domination in Herodotus," *JBL* 92 (1973) 523-30; Nadav Na'aman, "The Kingdom of Judah under Josiah," *TA* 18 (1991) 3-71 (36-37); Miller and Hayes, *A History of Ancient Israel and Judah,* 445-47.

23. Joan Oates, "The Fall of Assyria (635-609 B.C.)" in *CAH*, 2nd ed., 3/2, ed. John Boardman *et al.* (1991) 178-79.

24. On the situation during Josiah's reign, see Nadav Na'aman, "The Kingdom of Judah under Josiah," 3-71; Oates, "The Fall of Assyria," 162-88; Donald B. Redford, *Egypt, Canaan, and Israel in Ancient Times* (Princeton: Princeton University Press, 1992) 441-42; Miller and Hayes, *A History of Ancient Israel and Judah,* 439-77.

Historian says nothing about his death in battle. All that we are told is that Josiah went to Megiddo to meet Pharaoh Necho (Nekau II) and the Pharaoh killed him (2 Kgs 23:29). Why he did so we do not know. He may have accused him of seditious intentions or actions against Assyria, his imperial overlord and an Egyptian ally, or he may have been summoned to take the oath of allegiance to the new overlord, the pharaoh himself. At any rate the evidence, deficient as it is, supports the conclusion that there was no hiatus in imperial control of Judah during Josiah's reign, in much the same way that control passed without a break from Egypt to Babylonia after the Egyptian defeat at Carchemish on the Upper Euphrates in 605 B.C.E. Already in control of the Phoenician cities, therefore also of the *Via Maris* and the key point Megiddo, Egypt simply took the place of Assyria, perhaps by mutual agreement.[25] By the time assigned in Dtr to Josiah's reforming activities, perhaps even earlier, Egypt was the dominant presence in Syria and Palestine.[26] Certain allusions in roughly contemporary prophetic texts could lead to the same conclusion. Jer 2:16-18, 36 states that the people of Israel will be shamed by the Egyptians as formerly by the Assyrians, possibly with reference to the Egyptian takeover of Syria-Palestine towards the end of the reign; Zeph 2:4-5 predicts that the Philistine cities will be devastated, a possible reference to the campaigns of Psamtek (Psammeticus) I in the Philistine region in the 630s and 620s.

The conviction that Josiah's reign marks the end of the Davidic line comes to expression most clearly in the Chronicler's drastically rewritten version of Josiah's death and obsequies (2 Chr 35:20-25). The Chronicler fills in the gaps in his own way in Dtr's brief notice of the death and burial (2 Kgs 23:29-30). Josiah confronted Pharaoh Necho in battle and, after rejecting the latter's plea to heed a warning from one of his Egyptian gods, disguised himself, went into the thick of the fight, was shot by archers, and taken in a chariot back to Jerusalem where he died. That this account has been modeled on the death of Ahab of Israel in battle as described in 2 Chr 18:28-34 (cf. 1 Kgs 22:29-37) seems to be beyond cavil. Like Ahab, Josiah disguises himself, is shot by an archer, tells his attendants he is mortally

25. Na'aman, "The Kingdom of Judah under Josiah," 38-40; Miller and Hayes, *A History of Ancient Israel and Judah,* 446-48.

26. Redford, *Egypt, Canaan, and Israel in Ancient Times,* 441-51. Marvin A. Sweeney, a proponent of the thesis proposed by Hermann Barth in 1977 of a Josian redaction of Isaiah, argues that Josiah aimed to restore the united kingdom of David and Solomon, but gives too little weight to the actual situation in the Trans-Euphrates region during Josiah's reign. See his *King Josiah of Judah: The Lost Messiah of Israel* (Oxford: Oxford University Press, 2001).

wounded in much the same terms as Ahab, and is conveyed in a chariot to Jerusalem as Ahab is to Samaria. Both ignore a prophetic warning before the battle (1 Kgs 22:28; 2 Chr 18:27), and both are told that they will be spared witnessing the final disaster on their dynasties (1 Kgs 21:29; cf. 2 Chr 34:28). The prophet Elijah's assurance addressed to Ahab prefigures the prophetess Huldah's prediction addressed to Josiah — good news in the near future for the king, bad news in the more distant future for others: "Because he (Ahab) has humbled himself before me, I shall not bring disaster on his house in his lifetime but in that of his son" (1 Kgs 21:29). So however we interpret Huldah's oracle, the message is that the end is near.

Ahab's death in battle marked the end of the dynasty founded by Omri in the same way that Josiah's death under similar circumstances marked the end of the dynasty founded by David. Another striking intertextual link in Chronicles between beginnings and endings can be detected in the author's account of the death of Saul. Saul too was killed by an archer in a battle against greater odds (1 Sam 31:3; 1 Chr 10:3). Like Josiah, he had three sons destined to reign after him (1 Sam 14:49; 31:6). His death nevertheless marked the end of the dynasty since we are told that "Saul died together with his three sons, *and all his house died with him*" (1 Chr 10:6). Saul certainly intended to found a dynasty, and but for David would have done so. Another son, Ishbaal, did succeed to the throne but was assassinated after a brief and insignificant reign.[27]

The Chronicler's account of Josiah's reign ends with a ritual of mourning for the dead king:

> All Judah and Jerusalem were in mourning over Josiah, and Jeremiah intoned a dirge over him. To this day all the male and female rhapsodists commemorate Josiah in their dirges, and they made it a custom in Israel. A written version can be found in the Book of Dirges. (2 Chr 35:24b-25)

This solemn conclusion to Josiah's reign is unique in the author's account of the twenty-one rulers of Judah beginning with David. No other king is said to have been honored in this way. Spices were burned for Asa (2 Chr

---

27. 2 Sam 2:8-10; 3:1, 6; 4:1-8. He is identified as a son of Saul (2 Sam 2:8, 12) but is not one of the three sons — Jonathan, Malchishua, and either Ishvi or Abinadab — listed elsewhere (1 Sam 14:49; 31:2), unless Ishvi is an alternative form of his name. For a summary of events during his brief reign, see Miller and Hayes, *A History of Ancient Israel and Judah,* 145-47.

16:13-14), honor was shown to Hezekiah's corpse (2 Chr 32:33), and his people did *shiva* for Saul (1 Chr 10:12), but the Chronicler mentions no other rituals of mourning for dead kings in any way comparable to those for Josiah. Unique also is the statement about the preservation of the memory of his tragic death down to the time of the composition of Chronicles. In view of the indications noted above about Josiah as the recapitulation and point of termination of the Davidic line, the conclusion suggests itself that the mourning was not just for Josiah but for the passing of the dynasty itself and, with it, the end of everything the dynasty stood for.

Mourning for Josiah as a form of remembering lacks the calendric precision with which the destruction of both the first and second temples continues to be commemorated on Tisha b'Av (the ninth day of the month of Av, the fifth month in the Babylonian calendar, corresponding to a date in the Gregorian calendar in July or August). Mourning the loss of the temple began early, as we learn from Zech 7:5, where it is linked with commemorating the assassination of Gedaliah in the month of Tishri, probably four years after the sack of Jerusalem. Somewhat later, fast days marking the beginning and end of the siege of the city were added (Zech 8:19).[28] This concentration of grief accentuates the depth of the sense of loss of the essential institution which for centuries had made possible a common life and identity.

Following on the account of Josiah's death, the Chronicler's historical narrative down to the fall of Jerusalem (2 Chr 36:1-23) reads like an appendix to the history which began with Saul and David. It is basically a much abbreviated version of the Historian's account, but adds that the disaster was caused by the apostasy of the leading priests and people and the desecration of the temple. No doubt the author had in mind the undoing of the religious reforms of Josiah after his death (2 Chr 36:14). The narrative concludes, however, in a quite different way. To repeat: in its original form, Dtr concluded with exile (2 Kgs 25:21b), since the Gedaliah episode (25:22-26) and the release of Jehoiachin from confinement by Amel-Marduk (25:27-30) are appendices to Dtr bringing the story down to 560 B.C.E., the assassination of Amel-Marduk. The author of Chronicles makes a quite different point by simply omitting events subsequent to the fall of Jerusalem recorded in 2 Kgs 25:22-30, passing at once from the deportations following on the sack of the city to the return made possible by the establishment of the Persian Empire in fulfillment of prophecy (2 Chr 36:20-21). To that

28. For the sources of these dates, see 2 Kgs 25:1, 8-9, 25; Jer 39:1-2; 52:4, 6-7.

conclusion the opening paragraph of Ezra-Nehemiah has been added as an appendix (36:22-23). The outcome is that, whereas Dtr in its final form ends by opening up a future for the Davidic line in the person of the deported Jehoiachin (2 Kgs 25:27-30), for Chronicles the next chapter of the history will feature not a descendant of David but the Persian Cyrus, who will be inspired by the God of Israel not to restore the dynasty but to rebuild the temple in Jerusalem.

CHAPTER TWO

After the Disaster: The Benjamin-Saul Alternative

It is idle to speculate what might have happened if some small circumstance in the past had been other than it was; if, for example, Alexander had not plunged into the icy water at Babylon (if indeed he did), or Julius Caesar had caught a chill and stayed home on the Ides of March. Yet I cannot resist the temptation of reflecting how different the history of Israel would have been if Saul had paused to take aim before trying to pin David to the wall with his spear. We may not have had the Psalms of Saul, or hosannas sung to the Son of Saul, but there would have been no Davidic "empire," no Davidic Messiah, and perhaps no pilgrims singing the songs of Zion on the way to the City of the Great King. But Saul, already possessed by an evil spirit from Yahweh, missed; and from that point on his beraka drained away like blood from an open wound.[1]

Surviving the Disaster

The liquidation of the Judean state and suppression of the native dynasty by the Babylonians in 586 B.C.E. left the survivors with questions to which

---

1. I take the liberty of citing this first paragraph from my contribution to the Festschrift for John L. McKenzie entitled "The Quest of the Historical Saul." See James W. Flanagan and Anita Weisbrod Robinson, eds., *No Famine in the Land: Studies in Honor of John L. McKenzie* (Missoula: Scholars, 1975) 75. I will not argue with anyone who questions the historicity of the spear-throwing incidents.

there were no easy answers. There were the question why it had happened and an urgent need for someone to explain to them how their God who had made so many promises and commitments, a God who neither slumbers nor sleeps in watching over Israel (Ps 121), a God who had set them free from the imperial power of Egypt in the distant past, and who, a little more than a century earlier, had miraculously saved Jerusalem from the Assyrian emperor Sennacherib, could now have abandoned them to their fate. There was the more immediate question whether further resistance, or at least nonacquiescence, was still possible faced with the Babylonian Empire and its overwhelming political and military power. These questions, and the answers elicited in the aftermath of the catastrophic events of 586 B.C.E., will call for discussion in due course. But the first issue demanding attention from the survivors, if life was to continue, was the form of political and social organization to be adopted at the local level now that imperial control had been reaffirmed with overwhelming and annihilating force. Analogous cases of national and societal collapse, in both ancient and modern times, would lead us to expect the survivors of this disaster to fall back on the kind of broad kinship network — household, clan, tribe — which had functioned prior to the formation of the state and, as we know from the prophets of the eighth and seventh centuries, had suffered controls and checks at the hands of the state apparatus under the monarchy. Something like this seems to have happened in Judah after the Babylonian conquest. One aspect of this situation with important implications for the future was the revival of a sense of tribal identity and tribal loyalty. Nowhere was this more in evidence than in territory formerly assigned to Benjamin, the tribe of King Saul dispossessed and replaced by David but not forgotten.

Judah and Benjamin: Different Approaches to Imperial Babylon

The tribe of Benjamin was originally associated with its northern neighbors Ephraim and Manasseh, the Joseph tribes. But since it was the only one of the ten tribes to survive the Assyrian conquest of the kingdom of Samaria in 722 B.C.E., it was inevitably thrown into contact with Judah lying immediately to the south. Both tribes cherished their respective traditions of origins, of which the rivalry between Saul the Benjaminite and David the Judean, preserved only in the Judean version with a very overt Judean bias, formed a major component. And so it happened that in the last decades of the existence of Judah old animosities were revived, and the Benjaminite region came to be the focus of opposition to policies pursued at the court in Jerusalem, especially its fateful decision to rebel against the imperial power of Babylon as described in the previous chapter. After the rebellion was crushed, the administrative center of the province was moved from Jerusalem to Mizpah in Benjamin (now on the site of the village of Tell en-Naṣbeh, 12 km north of Jerusalem), and the government of the province was confided to Gedaliah, grandson of Shaphan, head of a distinguished family opposed to rebellion, almost certainly of Benjaminite origin, of which we shall hear more in due course. A study of destruction sites and settlement patterns from the late Iron Age, the decades following the fall of Jerusalem, has shown that major sites in Benjaminite territory — Mizpah (Tell en-Naṣbeh), Gibeah (perhaps Tell el-Fûl), Gibeon (el-Jib) — were spared destruction during the suppression of the revolt.[2] Jeremiah, from Anathoth in Benjamin (Jer 1:1), now a northern suburb of Jerusalem, shared the same opposition to revolt as the Shaphanids and was protected by members of the family. After the Babylonian conquest, he was treated with consideration by the Babylonian authorities, given gifts, and confided to the care of Gedaliah by the Babylonian commander Nebuzaradan (Jer 40:1-6). Benjaminite-Judean hostility was therefore a prominent feature of the history of the half-century or so between the fall of Jerusalem and the fall of Babylon in 539 B.C.E. and probably on into the early Persian period.

Benjamin has always been the most mysterious of the twelve tribes. In the first place, it is the only one of the twelve whose patronymic ancestor was not born in Mesopotamia. It is therefore, in origin, the only Palestinian tribe.[3] The paradigmatic character of the ancestor narratives in Genesis might even encourage us to ask whether this unique feature reflects an awareness that Benjaminites were not deported by the Babylonians.[4] Other possibilities exist, but this hypothesis would be consistent with Benjaminite politics in the last decades of the kingdom of Judah and

2. Oded Lipschits, "The History of the Benjamin Region under Babylonian Rule," *TA* 26 (1999) 155-90; *The Fall and Rise of Jerusalem* (Winona Lake: Eisenbrauns, 2005) 237-49.

3. The birth of Manasseh and Ephraim, sons of Joseph, in Egypt (Gen 46:20), represents a secondary development in the traditions of tribal origins.

4. Ezra 1:5 and 4:1-4 have the families of Judah and Benjamin coming from Babylonia to rebuild the temple, but the wording reflects the later use in Chronicles and Ezra-Nehemiah of the expression "Judah and Benjamin" for the surviving representatives of the ideal Israel in the postdisaster period. See below, 35-36.

the period immediately following, especially their rejection of the policy of revolt against the Babylonian overlord pursued at the Judean court.

Other aspects of the story of ethnic origins in Genesis reveal striking parallels with the situation in Judah in the aftermath of the Babylonian conquest. One of the most striking of these is the account of the death of Rachel in giving birth to Benjamin on the last leg of Jacob's return from Mesopotamia after a twenty-year exile (Gen 35:16-20):

> They set out from Bethel, and when they were still some distance from Ephrath, Rachel was in childbirth and her labor pains were severe. While her pains continued, the midwife said to her, "Don't be afraid, for this is yet another son for you." With her dying breath — for she did die — she called him Ben-Oni but his father called him Benjamin. So Rachel died and was buried on the way to Ephrath (that is, Bethlehem). Over her grave Jacob set up a sacred pillar, and to this day it is called The Pillar of Rachel's Grave.

This is the last stage of Jacob's (Israel's) return from exile in Babylon. Although his journey takes him finally to Hebron/Mamre to visit Isaac who then dies (Gen 35:27-29), he is told to *settle* at Bethel (Gen 35:1), site of the sanctuary famous in the preexilic period and adjacent to Mizpah in Benjamin after the fall of Jerusalem and destruction of its temple. Rachel's death and Benjamin's birth take place near Ephrath-Bethlehem in Judah. But it is explicitly attested that Rachel's tomb was originally in Benjaminite territory (1 Sam 10:2), and the same location is hinted at in that strange passage in Jeremiah, a kind of ghost story, in which the weeping of the long-dead Rachel for her children can be heard in Ramah (Jer 31:15). Ramah is certainly in Benjamin (Josh 18:25), but the Judean tradition locates Rachel's grave in Judah, where it remains to this day (Gen 35:16-20) and from which no amount of weeping and sobbing could have carried as far as Ramah. An alternative explanation of this Jeremian tradition may be proposed. After the Babylonian conquest, Benjaminite Ramah was no doubt long remembered as the assembly point for the deportees preparatory to departure for Babylon (Jer 40:1). In retrospect, it may be this sad circumstance which occasioned Rachel's weeping.[5]

---

5. On the Judean appropriation of Rachel's grave site, see my "Benjamin Traditions Read in the Early Persian Period," in *Judah and the Judeans in the Persian Period*, ed. Oded Lipschits and Manfred Oeming (Winona Lake: Eisenbrauns, 2006) 630-33.

Another case reflecting the tension between Judah and Benjamin and its eventual resolution in the postdisaster period is the Judean takeover of the town of Kiriath-jearim, originally a member of the Gibeonite tetrapolis (Gibeon, Chephirah, Beeroth, Kiriath-jearim) and therefore in Benjamin (Josh 9:17; 18:28). The transfer to Judah of this one city only of the four (Josh 18:14; 1 Chr 13:6) was no doubt occasioned by the sojourn of the holy ark at Kiriath-jearim, from which it was taken, in not so solemn procession and not without fatalities, to Jerusalem (1 Sam 7:1-2; 2 Sam 6:12-19), an event commemorated in the temple liturgy:

> We heard of the ark in Ephrathah,
> we found it in the region of Jaar.
> Let us enter his dwelling;
> let us bow down at his footstool.

(Ps 132:6-7)

Bethel, a border town between Benjamin and Judah (Josh 18:13) and originally in Benjamin (Josh 18:22), also played a part in these intertribal hostilities in the interim period between the destruction and rebuilding of the Jerusalem temple. On his return from exile, Jacob received a divine command to settle in Bethel, site of an ancient and prestigious sanctuary, and build an altar there (Gen 35:1). It was there that he had a vision in which he received the new name Israel and the assurance that he would found a nation and that kings would be among his descendants (Gen 35:1-15).[6] The sanctuary of Bethel, which survived both the fury of the Assyrians in 722 B.C.E. (2 Kgs 17:24-28) and the reforming zeal of Josiah a century later (2 Kgs 23:15-20), was situated in Benjaminite territory, in close proximity to the administrative center at Mizpah set up by the Babylonian overlord. If, as I have argued, Bethel served as the imperially authorized cult center for the province in place of the now destroyed Jerusalem temple, its close proximity to the administrative center of the province would help to explain the choice.[7] It would also reinforce the suspicion that the account of

6. Jacob's vision at Bethel after his return from Mesopotamia is generally taken to be the Priestly (P) version corresponding to the vision at Bethel before his departure twenty years earlier, attributed to a different source, generally J or JE (Gen 28:10-22). In the narrative context, however, it is presented as a second and more significant visit and vision. It is perhaps surprising that in the patriarchal stories the prediction about a future monarchy occurs only in revelations attributed to a Priestly hand (Gen 17:6; 35:11).

7. See my "The Judaean Priesthood during the Neo-Babylonian and Achaemenid Pe-

the vicissitudes of Jacob after his return from exile mirrors the experience of Judeans and Benjaminites during the exilic and early postexilic periods.

The situation during the period immediately preceding and following the fall of Jerusalem also appears to be reflected at the beginning and end of the book of Judges. The first of two introductions to the book (Judg 1:1–2:5) presents an account of the conquest and occupation of Canaan under the divinely sanctioned guidance of Judah (Judg 1:1-2), therefore in direct contradiction to the account immediately preceding in the book of Joshua. While highlighting the role of Judah, it also goes out of its way to disparage Benjamin. In the course of the conquest, Judah and its associated tribe of Simeon take Jerusalem, slaughter its inhabitants, and burn the city (1:8). Benjamin, on the other hand, failed to dislodge its original inhabitants (1:21); indeed, according to later sources, their descendants were still living there at the time of writing (Neh 11:7-9; 1 Chr 8:32; 9:3, 7-9). In sum, "Yahweh was with Judah" (Judg 1:19). In this Judean version, therefore, Judah and not Ephraim, Joshua's tribe, with which Benjamin was at first associated, was favored by Yahweh throughout the conquest and occupation of Canaan.

The episode at the end of Judges (chs. 19–21) embodies even more clearly this pro-Judean and anti-Benjaminite ideology. It describes a war of extermination against the tribe of Benjamin waged by the other tribes under divinely sanctioned Judean leadership (20:18). The occasion was the gang rape of the female companion of a man from the tribe of Levi and the homosexual aggression against the Levite himself, planned but not carried out by the male inhabitants of the Benjaminite town of Gibeah, which also happened to be Saul's town. These Benjaminites are described as "a depraved lot" (*'anšê běnê-běliya'al,* Judg 19:22). The dismemberment of the body of the murdered woman and the dispatch of the parts to the other tribes provoked a plenary tribal assembly at Mizpah and a consultation with the deity at Bethel, where the decision was taken that Judah should be the leader. The account of successive campaigns waged by the confederates, punctuated by visits to sanctuaries, prayer, and penitential exercises is, quite patently, a product of fantasy. As George Foot Moore, still one of the best commentators on the book of Judges, put it more than a century ago: "It is not history, it is not legend, but the theocratic ideal of a scribe

riods," *CBQ* 60 (1998) 25-27; "Bethel in the Neo-Babylonian Period," in *Judah and the Judeans in the Neo-Babylonian Period,* ed. Oded Lipschits and Joseph Blenkinsopp (Winona Lake: Eisenbrauns, 2003) 93-107.

who had never handled a more dangerous weapon than an imaginative pen."[8] On the third attempt, after the loss of forty thousand men, the confederates succeeded in defeating the Benjaminites. Since the eventual success of the tribal league with the near-extermination of Benjamin resulted in a deficit in the canonical number of tribes, an outcome the confederates appear not to have foreseen, two solutions were proposed. The first was another war of extermination, this time against the inhabitants of Jabesh-gilead who had absented themselves from the plenary gathering and who, as it happened, belonged to Saul's short-lived kingdom.[9] In the course of this operation the surviving Benjaminites were to capture four hundred virgins with the purpose of repopulating their tribe (21:8-14). The second solution, which may be an alternative version of the first and will inevitably bring to mind the rape of the Sabine women, involved instructing these same Benjaminite survivors to frequent the annual festival at Shiloh, lie in ambush during the dancing of the young women in the vineyards, and carry them off to serve the same purpose (21:15-24).

This disedifying narrative has been assigned different dates in the commentaries, but the opinion that in its final form, possibly as a retelling of an earlier internecine tribal war story, it cannot be earlier than the late Babylonian or early Achaemenid period, is well represented.[10] In keeping with the common practice of biblical narrators to build on existing narratives and narrative patterns, the homosexual aggression of the men of

8. George Foot Moore, *A Critical and Exegetical Commentary on Judges* (ICC; New York: Scribner's, 1895) 411.

9. Gilead is listed as a region of Ishba'al's extensive kingdom on both sides of the Jordan (2 Sam 2:9). The Jabesh-gileadites repaid Saul's avenging their honor (1 Sam 11:1-11) by a like act of rescuing his body and those of his sons from Beth-shan, cremating them, burying the ashes, and mourning and doing *shiva* (1 Sam 31:11-13).

10. See Moore, *Judges,* xiii, 421-22: no earlier than the fourth century B.C.E., but perhaps based on an earlier narrative; G. A. Cooke, *The Book of Judges* (Camb. B.; Cambridge: Cambridge University Press, 1913) 171-72: an ancient story line reworked in the manner of the P source and Chronicles; John Gray, *Joshua, Judges and Ruth* (NCBC; (Grand Rapids: Eerdmans, 1967) 239-43: an ancient core with postexilic redaction; Robert G. Boling, *Judges* (AB 6A; Garden City: Doubleday, 1975) 278-79: an old story tacked onto the history by an exilic redactor; J. Alberto Soggin, *Judges,* trans. John Bowden (OTL; Philadelphia: Westminster, 1981) 278-83: elements of two Deuteronomistic redactions. See further Yairah Amit, "Literature in the Service of Politics: Studies in Judges 19–21," in *Politics and Theopolitics in the Bible and Post-Biblical Literature,* ed. Henning Graf Reventlow, Yair Hoffman, and Benjamin Uffenheimer (JSOTSup 171; Sheffield: Sheffield Academic, 1994) 28-40; "The Saul Polemic in the Persian Period," in Lipschits and Oeming, *Judah and the Judeans in the Persian Period,* 647-61.

Gibeah imitates the similar threat directed at Lot's guests in Sodom (Gen 19:1-11), and the war of extermination against Benjamin seems to reflect similar action taken by Moses against Midian (Numbers 31). Mizpah as the place of assembly for the pan-Israelite "congregation" (Judg 20:1, 3; 21:1-12) and Bethel as the place for encounter with the deity and the performance of sacrifice and other cultic acts (Judg 20:18, 23, 26-28) fit the administrative situation which obtained in the aftermath of the Babylonian conquest: Mizpah was certainly the administrative hub of the province and Bethel was probably the state-sponsored sanctuary associated with it. A further point: the exogamy-endogamy issue, represented in the war narrative by the confederates' oath not to intermarry with Benjaminites (Judg 21:1, 18), began to be acute in the late Neo-Babylonian–early Persian period at the level not only of relations with outsiders but also within Jewish communities.

The conflicts of that period of confusion and crisis, and their eventual resolution, were read back into the record not only of tribal and national origins, as we have seen, but throughout the later historical record, most clearly in the Chronicler's version. After the secession of the northern and central tribes from Solomon's kingdom, Rehoboam prepared to attack the separatists at the head of a Judean-Benjaminite army but was prevented from doing so by the intervention of Shemaiah, a man of God (2 Chr 11:1-5). Rehoboam therefore had to content himself with securing the defenses of Judah-Benjamin against its northern neighbor and appointing his sons as governors of districts in Judah and Benjamin, clearly considered to be one territorial entity (2 Chr 11:5-12, 23). This situation persisted under later Judean rulers.[11] As the end approached, all Judah and Benjamin pledged themselves to observe the stipulations of Josiah's covenant (2 Chr 34:32), and members of the same two tribes are said to have been involved in the rebuilding of the temple and the resolution of the intermarriage crisis (Ezra 1:5; 4:1-4; 10:9).

The eventual settlement of this intertribal conflict is apparent from the frequent allusion in Chronicles and Ezra-Nehemiah to "Judah and Benjamin" as a single entity.[12] We also hear of Judeans and Benjaminites settling together in Jerusalem after returning from Babylonia,[13] and there were Judeans who took Benjamin as a personal name.[14] Depending on the

---

11. 2 Chr 14:8; 25:5-10; 31:1; 34:8-9, 32.
12. 2 Chr 11:1-23; 14:8; 25:5; 31:1; 34:9, 32; Ezra 1:5; 4:1; 10:9; Neh 11:4, 7-9.
13. 1 Chr 8:32-40; 9:7-9; Neh 11:4, 7-9.
14. Ezra 10:32; Neh 3:23; 12:34.

date one assigns to the Joseph novella, a Judean-Benjaminite reconciliation or settlement may also be reflected in Judah's offer to stand surety for Benjamin, whose life was thought to be in danger (Gen 43:1-10; 44:32-34). In sum: while the twelve-tribal Israel was never lost from sight, its sole surviving representatives were the conjoined tribes of Judah and Benjamin.

Saul

The revival of a sense of tribal identity in Benjamin, together with Benjaminite hostility towards Judah, would inevitably have rekindled interest in Saul, his progress towards the kingship, and the traditions about his conflict with, and eventual replacement by David. The question to be asked is therefore the following: Do the few sources at our disposal provide any grounds for concluding that the revival of Saul's dynasty, long extinguished, was an option at that time? In other words, was there support for replacing a descendant of David with one of Saul's family after the Davidic dynasty had come to a violent end?

Those Benjaminites who still cherished the memory of the first Israelite king, a member of their tribe, would not have been deceived by the pro-Davidic propaganda transmitted by means of the Judean version of David's rise to power in Dtr. If an alternative Benjaminite narrative had survived, it would have insisted that Saul was the first king to reign in Israel and that his kingship was fully legitimated by prophetic anointing (1 Sam 9:1–10:16) and the demonstration that he possessed the requisite charisma after winning a great victory (1 Sam 11:1-15).[15] Dtr's account of how David entered his service and excited Saul's jealousy is patently biased in David's favor. Anti-Saul animus is also apparent in the account of David's marrying into Saul's family. Saul offered him his elder daughter

---

15. In addition to the commentaries, see Volkmar Fritz, "Die Deutungen des Königtums Sauls in den Überlieferungen von seiner Entstehung, 1 Sam 9–11," *ZAW* 88 (1976) 246-62; Nadav Na'aman, "The Pre-Deuteronomistic Story of King Saul and Its Historical Significance," *CBQ* 54 (1992) 638-58. Philip Davies has argued that a *written* Benjaminite version of the story of David and Saul did exist, that Dtr was written to counter it or, better, to expunge it from the record, and that this version would have been put together at Mizpah sometime after it became the administrative center of the province. If this hypothesis could be established it would have significant consequences for the date, place of origin, and purpose of Dtr, but unfortunately evidence is lacking. See Philip R. Davies, *The Origins of Biblical Israel* (LHB/OTS 485; New York: T. & T. Clark, 2007) 105-15.

Merab in exchange for his services in the Philistine war and in the hope that he would be killed in battle, but at the last moment withdrew the offer (1 Sam 18:17-19). It was then the turn of the younger daughter Michal to play the same role in Saul's nefarious plans, this time accompanied by the absurd demand for a marriage price of a hundred Philistine foreskins (18:20-29). David, however, like the legendary hero that he was, returned unscathed and delivered the marriage price in full, thus legally obliging Saul to give him his daughter in marriage. Marriage to Michal was a turning point in David's relations with Saul, but a Benjaminite reading of this incident would have interpreted it somewhat differently from Dtr, in which Saul's motive in encouraging the marriage is a particularly flagrant example of anti-Saul bias in the Judean historiographical tradition. For David, however, marriage to Michal was a key move in attempting to legitimate his ambition to succeed or supplant Saul in the kingship. After the relations between the two men soured even further, Saul may have come to suspect David's motives, since he took Michal back and gave her to another husband (1 Sam 25:44). This seems definitive enough, but even after Saul's death David insists with his (Saul's) successor Ishbaal that she be returned to him. Here, too, the insistence is dictated by ambition as much as by affection for his absent wife (2 Sam 3:13-16).

This overt bias in the account of the marriage issue is confirmed by the sequel. After securing his hold on the throne, David eliminated all those who might challenge the legitimacy of his claim. This is what usurpers have always done, as history attests. By showing a pretense of good will to Mephibaal, Saul's grandson, he rendered him innocuous by maintaining him as a guest at his court. Mephibaal is told repeatedly that he is to eat at David's table, which is neither more nor less than a standard form of surveillance (2 Sam 9:1-13); compare Saul's anger at seeing David's place at table empty (1 Sam 20:18, 24-34). Worse still, the rest of Saul's descendants — two sons and five grandsons — were handed over to the Gibeonites to be victims of a ritual killing, ostensibly to atone for Saul's attack on Gibeon and its associated cities (2 Sam 21:1-9) but in reality to exclude the possibility of succession. Here, too, an action of Saul, praiseworthy in the Israelite context of that time, is buried under another example of a calculated act of David aimed to eliminate any further obstacle to his accession to Saul's throne.[16] After Saul's death, David succeeded with the help of Abner, one

16. On the ethnic identity of the Gibeonite tetrapolis, see my *Gibeon and Israel: The Role of Gibeon and the Gibeonites in the Political and Religious History of Early Israel*

of several odious characters with whom David surrounded himself, in taking over the territory ruled by the hapless Ishbaal (2 Sam 1:1–5:3).

For those Benjaminites who continued to cherish the memory of Saul and his tragic death, their reading of the tradition would probably have looked something like this. But in fact any attentive reader of the account in 1 Samuel will detect, at several points in the story of Saul's fall and David's rise, hints of a contrapuntal account favorable to Saul which, however, cannot be put together to form a coherent narrative. Saul is made king by acclamation at Gilgal (1 Sam 11:15), and it was he and not Samuel (as in 1 Sam 7:5-16) who was the first to take on the Philistines. The point need not be labored. Early traditions of Benjaminite origin, favorable to Saul, have been submerged in Dtr by extensive editing in the official Judean version,[17] and the juxtaposition of these two conflicting perspectives in the historical record constitutes the literary counterpart to Judean-Benjaminite relations in the years following the fall of Jerusalem.

The shadowy figure of a defeated and discredited Saul is also discernible in the background of the war of extermination against Benjamin waged under the leadership of Judah in which, as we have seen, the crime which precipitated the conflict was committed by the male inhabitants of

---

(SOTSMS 2; Cambridge: Cambridge University Press, 1972) 14-27. G. Hentschel, "Die Hinrichtung der Nachkommen Sauls (2 Sam 21,1-14)," in *Nachdenken über Israel, Bibel und Theologie: FS. für Klaus-Dietrich Schunck zu seinem 65. Geburtstag*, ed. H. Michael Niemann, Matthias Augustin, and Werner H. Schmidt (BEATAJ 37; Frankfurt am Main: Lang, 1994) 93-116, perhaps overelaborates in assigning pro-Saulide and pro-Davidic parts of this brief narrative to distinct redactions.

17. One of the clearest and most persuasive expositions of this hypothesis is still that of Nadav Na'aman, "The Pre-Deuteronomistic Story of King Saul and Its Historical Significance," *CBQ* 54 (1992) 638-58. I mention only a few other studies from a large body of writing on the subject over the last few decades: Niels P. Lemche, "David's Rise," *JSOT* 10 (1978) 2-25; P. Kyle McCarter Jr., "The Apology of David," *JBL* 99 (1980) 489-504; W. Lee Humphreys, "The Rise and Fall of King Saul: A Study of an Ancient Narrative Stratum in 1 Samuel," *JSOT* 18 (1980) 74-90; "From Tragic Hero to Villain: A Study of the Figure of Saul and the Development of 1 Samuel," *JSOT* 22 (1982) 95-117; Karel van der Toorn and Cees Houtman, "David and the Ark," *JBL* 113 (1994) 209-31; Meir Malul, "Was David Involved in the Death of Saul on the Gilboa Mountain?" *RB* 103 (1996) 517-45; Jacques Vermeylen, "La maison de Saül et la maison de David: Un écrit de propagande théologico-politique de 1 Sm 11 à 2 Sm 7," in *Figures de David à travers la Bible*, ed. Louis Dorousseaux and Vermeylen (LD 177; Paris: Cerf, 1999) 35-74; John Van Seters, *The Biblical Saga of King David* (Winona Lake: Eisenbrauns, 2009); Steven L. McKenzie, "Saul in the Deuteronomistic History," in *Saul in Story and Tradition*, ed. Carl S. Ehrlich in cooperation with Marsha C. White (FAT 47; Tübingen: Mohr Siebeck, 2006) 59-70.

Gibeah, Saul's town. In the first place, Jabesh-gilead, which refused to send representatives to the assembly at Mizpah and was on that account the object of a second war of extermination (Judg 21:8-12), lay within the kingdom of Saul and his son Ishbaal (1 Sam 11:1-11; 2 Sam 2:9). But the clearest allusion in Judges 19–21 to the story of Saul is the grotesque manner in which the Levite summoned the tribes to avenge the crime of Gibeah. The Levite's action in dismembering the dead and abused body of his female companion and sending the parts round the tribes to call them to battle quite transparently reflects, perhaps in satirical mode — and if so in execrable taste — Saul's call to warfare in defense of Jabesh-gilead by carving up his oxen and sending the parts around the tribes (Judg 19:29; 1 Sam 11:7). These undertones and hints below the surface of the narrative show that Saul was still alive, whether in favor or disfavor, in the collective memory at the time of the final redaction of Judges 19–21, certainly in the postdisaster period.

Support for the revival of the Saulite claim to replace the extinguished Davidic dynasty in the postdisaster period has also been sought in the genealogical material relevant to Saul preserved in Chronicles. The first of two practically identical genealogical lists begins with the sequence Ner, Kish, and Saul and ends with Ulam and his sons and grandsons in the twelfth generation from Saul (1 Chr 8:33-40). The second, also embedded in a Gibeonite (therefore Benjaminite) genealogy, ends with the six sons of a certain Azel, also it seems in the twelfth generation (9:39-44). Calculating thirty years for a generation, about the maximum in antiquity,[18] the lists would extend no further than the reign of Manasseh (698 or 687-642 B.C.E.), perhaps not even so far. The much longer Davidic genealogical list

---

18. Some examples: Herodotus learned from his priestly interlocutors in Egypt that, in calculating the genealogies of their pharaohs, they reckoned three generations to a century, therefore a little more than thirty years for a generation (*Hist.* 2:142). Sixty generations of the high priests of the god Ptah at Memphis, covering 1,350 years, works out at 22.5 years a generation; see John Harold Plumb, *The Death of the Past* (Boston: Houghton Mifflin, 1970) 29. Generations in Anglo-Saxon genealogies do not exceed thirty years, and the Welsh-Brythonic dynasty of Dyfed comes out closer to twenty-five years; see Leslie Alcock, *Arthur's Britain* (2nd ed., London: Penguin, 1989) 10-11. The same calculations do not hold for the genealogies of Jesus in Matthew 1 and Luke 3, which are strictly schematized and in which the only name in common with the Chronicler's Davidic genealogy is Zerubbabel. On the biblical genealogies in general, see Robert R. Wilson, *Genealogy and History in the Biblical World* (Yale Near Eastern Researches 7; New Haven: Yale University Press, 1977); "Genealogy, Genealogies," *ABD,* 2:929-32; Marshall D. Johnson, *The Purpose of the Biblical Genealogies* (SNTSMS 8; 2nd ed., Cambridge: Cambridge University Press, 1988).

in 1 Chr 3:1-24, which differs from the Saul genealogies in that its first part deals with reigns, averages out at or near twenty-nine years a generation. At any rate, the Saul genealogies raise a serious question as to whether a suitable candidate would have been available anytime after the fall of Jerusalem, even if the restoration of the Saul line at that time had been a realistic option.[19]

Saul no doubt intended to found a dynasty. He was succeeded by his son Ishbaal who, we are told, reigned two years (2 Sam 2:8-10) before being assassinated (4:5-8). Jonathan's son and Saul's grandson Mephibaal (2 Sam 4:4; 9:1-3) was tempted to profit by Absalom's rebellion against David to regain the throne for the Saul line, though the report to that effect by his servant Ziba may well have been self-interested and mendacious (2 Sam 16:3-4). After the defeat and death of Absalom, Mephibaal made his submission to David, his life was spared (2 Sam 19:24-30), he and his son Mica[20] remained, probably not entirely on a voluntary basis, at David's court, and we hear no more about a Saul dynasty. The author of Chronicles goes further in his account of Saul's defeat and death at the hands of the Philistines: "Thus Saul and his three sons died, and all his house perished together" (1 Chr 10:6). The parallelism with Josiah and the three sons who followed him on the throne and brought the Davidic line to an end would probably not have been lost on the author.

The bias against Saul is not confined to Dtr. It is a feature of the historiographical tradition in general. Ben Sira avoids mentioning his name, simply observing that "Samuel . . . anointed rulers over his people" and "made known to the king his death" (Sir 46:13, 20). In his long account of Saul's vicissitudes, Josephus praises his heroism, but notes that he was subject to a demoniacal disorder and adds that his fall was due to disobedience to the divine will (*Ant.* 6:45-350). The *Liber antiquitatum biblicarum* (sections 58 and 54) adds its own purely fictional embellishments. Saul spared Agag in the expectation that he would reveal the whereabouts of hidden treasure, and he expelled the mediums out of vainglory, not piety.

19. On the genealogies as evidence for dynastic rivalry, see Diana V. Edelman, "Did Saulide-Davidic Rivalry Resurface in Early Persian Yehud?" in *The Land That I Will Show You: Essays on the History and Archaeology of the Ancient Near East in Honour of J. Maxwell Miller*, ed. J. Andrew Dearman and M. Patrick Graham (JSOTSup 343; Sheffield: Sheffield Academic, 2001) 77-80. The relevance of the genealogies is questioned by Yairah Amit, "The Saul Polemic in the Persian Period," in Lipschits and Oeming, *Judah and the Judeans in the Persian Period*, 655-56.

20. Mica *(mîcā')* in 2 Sam 9:12, Micah *(mîcâ)* in 1 Chr 8:34; 9:40.

The portrait in rabbinic texts is mixed. Saul is praised for disposing of the Gibeonites. He was also zealous for Torah study, but is taken to task for not sharing the results of his study with others — definitely an original touch (*b. 'Erub.* 53b). His failure to kill Agag was especially reprehensible since Agag was the ancestor of Haman, who features as "the enemy of the Jews" in the book of Esther (*b. Meg.* 13a).

To sum up: We cannot rule out the possibility that some Benjaminites of that time entertained hope for the restoration after many centuries of the short-lived dynasty of Saul under the aegis of the Babylonian or Persian imperial power. But the bottom line is that evidence is lacking, and what little we do know would seem to render such hopes illusory. In the first place, as we have seen, the genealogical record of Saul's descendants does not extend to that time. If, moreover, Gedaliah — a Benjaminite in all probability, but at any rate not a descendant of Saul — was appointed to govern the province as a client king, a hypothesis which will be defended in the following chapter, his appointment would confirm the likelihood that no candidate with more acceptable credentials was available.

CHAPTER THREE

Under the Yoke of Babylon: The Gedaliah Episode

Settle down in the land, serve the king of Babylon, and all will be well with you.

2 Kings 25:24

The Shaphan Family and Jeremiah

Though unknown to Nebuchadnezzar and his officials, at the fall of Jerusalem the Babylonian Empire had less than half a century to run its course (586-539 B.C.E.). Some time after the sack of the city, the burning of the temple, and the executions, Nebuchadnezzar appointed Gedaliah over the conquered province of Judah, now seriously reduced in both size and population. Gedaliah was the grandson of Shaphan, a high-ranking official during the reign of Josiah. The office held by Shaphan was that of *sōpēr*, usually translated "scribe," but the duties attached to the office went well beyond the familiar secretarial routine.[1] His descendants went on to play

---

1. 2 Kgs 22:3-20; 2 Chr 34:8-28. The office has also been translated "adjutant-general," "secretary," and "head of the royal chancellory," none of which covers all of the activities attributed to *sōpĕrîm* in Hebrew Bible texts. See Joachim Begrich, "Sōpher und Mazkīr: Ein Beitrag zur inneren Geschichte der davidisch-salomonischen Grossreiches und des Königreiches Juda," *ZAW* 58 (1940-41) 1-29; Roland de Vaux, *Ancient Israel: Its Life and Institutions* (1961; repr. BRS. Grand Rapids: Eerdmans and Livonia: Dove, 1997) 131-32; T. N. D. Mettinger, *Solomonic State Officials: A Study of the Civil Government Officials of the Israelite Monarchy* (ConBOT 5; Lund: Gleerup, 1971) 52-60; Edouard Lipiński, "Royal and State

an important role in affairs of state during the quarter century or so following the reign of Josiah. A clay bulla (seal impression) stamped with the words *lgdlyhw [']šr 'l hbyt*, "belonging to Gedalyahu who is in charge of the house (i.e., palace)," dated palaeographically to Iron IIC/III (ca. 600-550 B.C.E.), came to light during James Leslie Starkey's excavation of Lachish. It may refer to Gedaliah and his office during Zedekiah's reign, and being "over the house," i.e., majordomo of the palace, was probably included in or identical with the position of *sōpēr* held by Shaphan during Josiah's reign.[2] If so, Gedaliah's administrative experience would help to explain his appointment by the Babylonians. What we know of the Shaphanite family tree can be represented as follows, with the names of sons and grandsons not necessarily in order of birth:

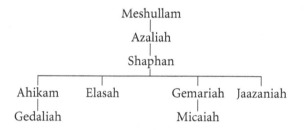

Gedaliah is the son of Ahikam, according to 2 Kgs 25:22 and Jeremiah 40–41. To judge by his role in the mission to Huldah the prophetess during Josiah's reign, where he is listed before his father and second after the chief priest (2 Kgs 22:12-14), Ahikam was probably the oldest of the four sons of Shaphan. But the most important piece of information about him is that he used his influence on behalf of Jeremiah, in the aftermath of the prophet's trial, to prevent him falling into the hands of those who planned to put

---

Scribes in Ancient Israel," in *Congress Volume, Jerusalem, 1986*, ed. J. A. Emerton (VTSup 40; Leiden: Brill, 1988) 157-64; Herbert Niehr, *"sōpēr," TDOT* 10 (1999) 318-19; Yitzhak Avishur and Michael Helzer, *Studies on the Royal Administration in Ancient Israel in the Light of Epigraphic Sources* (Tel Aviv-Jaffa: Archaeological Center Publications, 2000) 54-62.

2. See S. H. Hooke, "A Scarab and Sealing from Tell Duweir," *PEQ* 67 (1935) 195-96; J. L. Starkey, "Excavations at Tell el-Duweir 1934-1935," *PEQ* 67 (1935) 198-208; Olga Tufnell, *Lachish III: The Iron Age* (Oxford: Oxford University Press, 1953) 348. Nahman Avigad, *Hebrew Bullae from the Time of Jeremiah: Remnants of a Burnt Archive* (Jerusalem: Israel Exploration Society, 1986) 24-25, maintains that a bulla bearing the inscription *lgdlyhw 'bd hmlk*, "belonging to Gedalyahu servant (i.e., officer) of the king," may refer to the same Gedaliah since the script is identical with the Lachish bulla. Since, however, the bulla was purchased from an antiquities dealer and is therefore unprovenanced, caution is in order.

him to death (Jer 26:24). The role of "the people" in proceedings before, during, and after Jeremiah's trial for treason,[3] together with that of temple personnel (priests and prophets), chief officers of Judah, and elders, was obviously important but it is not entirely clear who these "people" were. Together with priests and prophets they bring Jeremiah to trial, but only the priests and prophets charge him before the officials acting as judges. "All the people" are persuaded by his speech to declare him innocent, but after the trial he is in danger of death at the hands of "the people." The term is too ambivalent to allow for sure identification, but the allusion may well be to the ʿam hāʾāreṣ encountered earlier whose political convictions were diametrically opposed to those of Jeremiah. At any rate, Ahikam's intervention after the trial provides a first insight into the role of the Shaphanids at this fateful juncture of Judean history. In the person of Gedaliah, the family would intervene once again on Jeremiah's behalf after the Babylonian occupation of Jerusalem (Jer 39:14; 40:5-6).

Further confirmation of the Shaphanid-Jeremiah connection is at hand with the role of another son, Elasah, who served as emissary to the Babylonian Diaspora on behalf of the prophet (Jer 29:3; 1 Chr 8:37). His principal task was to convey a letter from Jeremiah to the leaders of the Judean expatriate community in Babylon urging them to settle down and resist incitement to rebellion from prophets active among them, three of whom — Ahab ben Kolaiah, Zedekiah ben Maaseiah, and Shemaiah of Nehelam — are named in the letter (Jer 29:21-23, 24-32). These would be counterparts in the Diaspora to the nationalist prophet Hananiah, Jeremiah's opponent, in Judah (Jer 28:1-17). Their execution for refusal to acquiesce in the overwhelming power of the imperial overlord would have qualified them as martyrs by the nationalist and dynastic party, but as agitators and disturbers of the peace by Jeremiah who, for good measure, adds the accusation of adultery, a depressingly familiar form of denigration (Jer 29:23). The third son, Gemariah, together with his son, Micaiah, were active in Judean politics during the reign of Jehoiakim. The father had quarters in the temple precincts, and the son served as a kind of liaison officer on behalf of Elishama the "scribe," probably the successor in that office to Shaphan, Micaiah's grandfather. They too were involved with Jeremiah at a crucial moment in Judah's history, the transition from Egyptian to Babylonian vassalage after the decisive victory of Nebuchad-

---

3. kol-hāʿām (Jer 26:7-9, 11-12, 16); kol-qĕhal hāʿām (26:17); kol-ʿam yĕhûdâ (26:18); or simply hāʿām (26:24).

nezzar at Carchemish on the upper Euphrates in 605 B.C.E. referred to in Jer 36:9-13.[4]

The last of the four sons, Jaazaniah, is mentioned only once, in Ezekiel's visionary tour of the temple in Jerusalem where he sees Jaazaniah ben Shaphan serving as leader and hierophant with seventy Judean elders, offering incense before wall paintings of animals (Ezek 8:7-13). So it seems that this son, engaging in pagan rituals, was the black sheep of Shaphan's family. The theriomorphic nature of this cult, suggesting an Egyptian origin, would be consonant with the need for alignment with Egypt five or six years after the first Babylonian conquest of Jerusalem (i.e., 592 B.C.E.), the date assigned to this vision (Ezek 8:1). For the many who would have echoed the lament of these worshippers — "Yahweh does not see us, Yahweh has abandoned the land" (8:12) — Egypt and its gods might well have seemed the only remaining recourse.[5]

The Appointment and Assassination of Gedaliah

The appointment of Gedaliah soon after the suppression of the revolt, followed by an equally succinct account of events leading to his assassination, is reported briefly in what is probably an appendix to Dtr (2 Kgs 25:22-26). It was added after the stark notice that "Judah went into exile from its land," which strikes a note of finality and was probably the original conclusion to the History (2 Kgs 25:21b). The same events are recorded at greater length in Jeremiah (Jer 39:11-14; 40:1–41:18), and it is probably from this narrative that 2 Kgs 25:22-26 has been excerpted. The Gedaliah episode is absent from Chronicles, where the interest focuses more on the restoration of the temple than of the dynasty and which therefore passed directly from the fall of Jerusalem and the deportations to the first year of the reign of Cyrus, leaving the period of Babylonian control a blank (2 Chr 36:20-23). 2 Kgs 25:22-26 reads as follows:

4. For the seal impression from the City of David inscribed *lqmryhw bn špn* ("belonging to Gemaryahu son of Shaphan") see Oded Lipschits, *The Fall and Rise of Jerusalem* (Winona Lake: Eisenbrauns, 2005) 85.

5. The Egyptian character and origin of the cult is accepted by most commentators including Walther Eichrodt, *Ezekiel,* trans. Crosslett Quin (OTL; Philadelphia: Westminster, 1970) 124-25; Hans F. Fuhs, *Ezechiel 1-24* (NechtB; Würzburg: Echter, 1986) 50-51; Andrew Mein, *Ezekiel and the Ethics of Exile* (Oxford: Oxford University Press, 2001) 124-27.

As for the people left in the land of Judah, those whom Nebuchadnezzar king of Babylon had left behind, he appointed Gedaliah ben Ahikam ben Shaphan over them. When all the army commanders — Ishmael ben Nethaniah, Johanan ben Kareah, Seraiah ben Tanhumeth from Netophah, and Jaazaniah son of the Maacathite — together with their men heard that the king of Babylon had appointed Gedaliah they came to him at Mizpah. Gedaliah gave them and their men his solemn assurance in the following terms: "Have no fear of the Babylonian officials. Settle down in the land, serve the king of Babylon, and all will be well with you." But in the seventh month Ishmael ben Nethaniah ben Elishama of the royal line came with ten men and assassinated Gedaliah. He also killed the Judeans and Babylonians who were with Gedaliah at Mizpah. Thereupon, all the people of high and low estate and the army commanders fled to Egypt for fear of the Babylonians.

The more detailed narrative in Jeremiah, in which understandably the principal focus is on the role of the prophet himself, begins by noting Nebuchadnezzar's personal concern to protect Jeremiah through the agency of his supreme commander Nebuzaradan, who set him free and entrusted him to Gedaliah. Jeremiah was then permitted to return home, which is to say to Benjaminite territory, and to reside among his own people, which is to say among his fellow Benjaminites (Jer 39:11-14; cf. 1:1). In what appears to be an alternative account, he was set free in Ramah, a Benjaminite settlement (Josh 18:25), in which, as we learn from this version, the Babylonians had established the assembly point for the deportations (Jer 40:1-6). After playing back to the prophet his own theological explanation of the disaster, the Babylonian official referred to as the *rab-ṭabbāḥîm*[6] offered Jeremiah the choice between residence in Babylon under the patronage of the king or at Mizpah with Gedaliah. Jeremiah chose Mizpah, upon which Nebuzaradan gave him provisions and a present to show his appreciation for Jeremiah's support of the Babylonians and sent him on his way.

The Jeremian narrative has a list of Judean commanders of Zedekiah's destroyed or disbanded army only slightly different from that of the Historian (Jer 40:8; cf. 2 Kgs 25:23), but adds the information that Judeans

6. "Captain of the guard" (REB) or something of the sort, but surely not "chief cook," as Mordechai Cogan and Hayim Tadmor, *II Kings* (AB 11; Garden City: Doubleday, 1988) 318-19, translate. The verb *ṭbḥ* is used in a military (e.g., Jer 25:34; Ezek 21:15; Lam 2:21) as well as a culinary context. While court officials were often sent on special missions, Nebuchadnezzar would not have put his head chef in charge of a subjugated province.

who had fled to the Transjordanian kingdoms and further afield at the approach of the Babylonian army also answered Gedaliah's summons to return and settle down (Jer 40:7-12). This version thus fills in the gaps in the bare account of the assassination in 2 Kgs 25:25-26. The army commanders led by Johanan ben Kareah warn Gedaliah that one of their number, Ishmael, was planning with the connivance of the Transjordanian Ammonite king Baalis to assassinate Gedaliah. The motive for Ishmael's plan supplied by the text is that he was, or claimed to be, a member of the Judean royal family (*mizzera῾ hammĕlûkâ*, lit., "of the seed of the kingdom") and might therefore be expected to harbor resentment against a successor to Zedekiah who was not of Davidic descent.[7] He had probably taken refuge with Baalis to escape the fate of other relatives of Zedekiah. In 595 B.C.E., on the occasion of the accession of Psammeticus II to the pharaonic throne, Baalis had taken part with other Transjordanian rulers in a local summit meeting to plan revolt and coordinate action (Jer 27:1-7), but seems to have escaped sharing the fate of Judah. Ezekiel (Ezek 21:25[Eng 20]) imagines Nebuchadnezzar attempting by means of divination to decide whether to attack Ammon or Judah. Judah drew the short straw, but according to Josephus (*Ant.* 10:181-82) the turn of the Ammonites came five years later.[8] At any rate, Gedaliah rejected the warning and

7. The name Ishmael does not appear in the Chronicler's list of David's descendants, but the name of his grandfather, Nethaniah, is a variant of Nathan, one of David's many sons (1 Chr 3:5). In addition, Elishama, his father's name, occurs twice in the list (1 Chr 3:6, 8). An unprovenanced bulla with the inscription *lyšm῾l bn hmlk* ("belonging to Ishmael the king's son") was published by Gabriel Barkay, "A Bulla of Ishmael, the King's Son," *BASOR* 290/291 (1993) 112-13, who identified this Ishmael wth the assassin of Gedaliah. This is certainly possible, but there are many biblical and nonbiblical individuals with that name, the interpretation of *bn hmlk* is disputed, and the bulla was purchased on the notoriously suspect antiquities market.

8. Baalis, or Baalisha, appears on a seal impression discovered at Tell el-Umeiri in what was Ammonite territory (*mlkm῾r ῾bd b῾lyš῾*) and on another unprovenanced bulla (*b῾lyš῾ mlk bny ῾mn*). On the Umeiri seal impression, see Larry G. Herr, "The Servant of Baalis," *BA* 48 (1985) 169-72; Ulrich Hübner, *Die Ammoniter: Untersuchungen zur Geschichte, Kultur und Religion eines transjordanischen Volkes im 1. Jahrtausend v. Chr.* (Wiesbaden: Harrassowitz, 1992) 86-87; Bob Becking, "Baalis King of the Ammonites: An Epigraphical Note on Jeremiah 40:14," *JSS* 38 (1993) 15-24; "Inscribed Seals as Evidence for Biblical Israel? Jeremiah 40.7–41.15 *par exemple,*" in *Can a 'History of Israel' Be Written?* ed. Lester L. Grabbe (JSOTSup 245; Sheffield: Sheffield Academic, 1997) 80-82; "The Seal of Baalisha King of the Ammonites: Some Remarks," *BN* 97 (1999) 13-17; *From Babylon to Eternity: The Exile Remembered and Constructed in Text and Tradition,* with Alex Cannegieter, Wilfred van de Poll, and Anne-Mareike Wetter (London: Equinox, 2009) 9-12.

paid the price; he was murdered in the course of a meal, bringing his brief tenure of office to an end.[9]

The flight to Egypt recorded in Dtr (2 Kgs 25:26) is preceded in the Jeremian account by Ishmael's murder, while still in Mizpah, of eighty pilgrims from the north who were coming with offerings for "the house of Yahweh."[10] This took place before knowledge of the assassination of Gedaliah was common knowledge; hence the reason for this further act of violence was to prevent it becoming known and thus allow time to escape, and so it happened (41:4-9). There follows the encounter between Johanan and Ishmael at Gibeon resulting in the release of the prisoners Ishmael was taking with him to Ammon, Ishmael's escape to that kingdom, and the continuation of the flight into Egypt inspired by fear of Babylonian reprisals for the assassination of their appointee (41:10-18).

The two narratives read together present a credible account of what was happening in the region in the aftermath of the collapse of the rebellion, but they leave several questions unanswered. Among the most pressing are: In what capacity was Gedaliah appointed? Why Gedaliah, and why at Mizpah? When did the assassination take place, and what were its consequences for Judah? We will deal with these briefly in turn.

As to the first question: both accounts — Dtr and Jeremiah — simply state that the Babylonian monarch appointed *(hipqîd)* Gedaliah over the people who remained in the land, without specifying in what capacity. Several modern versions (NRSV, REB, JB, NAB) assume that he was appointed governor and translate accordingly. The issue continues to be discussed,[11] but it seems to me more consistent with a close reading of the

9. Josephus elaborates in his accustomed manner. The heinousness of the crime was, he tells us, intensified by having been perpetrated during a splendid banquet which Gedaliah put on for Ishmael, in the course of which Gedaliah had sunk into a drunken slumber, thus facilitating the dastardly act *(Ant.* 10:168-69).

10. It is emphasized that the pilgrims arrived the day after the murder, before anyone knew of it (41:4). I argued that their destination was Mizpah or, more probably, Bethel rather than Jerusalem in "The Judaean Priesthood during the Neo-Babylonian and Achaemenid Periods," *CBQ* 60 (1998) 25-27; and "Bethel in the Neo-Babylonian Period," in *Judah and the Judeans in the Neo-Babylonian Period,* ed. Oded Lipschits and Joseph Blenkinsopp (Winona Lake: Eisenbrauns, 2003) 97-99.

11. In recent decades by Cogan and Tadmor, *II Kings,* 326-27; Peter Machinist, "Palestine, Administration of," *ABD* 5 (1992), 69-81; David Stephen Vanderhooft, *The Neo-Babylonian Empire and Babylon in the Latter Prophets* (HSM 59; Atlanta: Scholars, 1999) 104-10; "Babylonian Strategies of Imperial Control in the West: Royal Practice and Rhetoric," in Lipschits and Blenkinsopp, *Judah and the Judeans in the Neo-Babylonian Period,*

text, as well as the little we know of Babylonian practice, that he was appointed as a client king. Confirmation may be at hand in a scaraboid seal impression with the emblem of a fighting cock from Mizpah (Tell en-Naṣbeh) which identifies a certain Jaazaniah, the name borne by a member of Gedaliah's entourage at Mizpah (2 Kgs 25:23; Jer 40:8), as an officer of the king.[12] More directly to the point, the frequency with which the verb *hipqîd* occurs — twice in the History (2 Kgs 25:22, 23) and five times in Jeremiah (Jer 40:5, 7, 11; 41:2, 18) — arouses suspicion. At some point we would expect to hear in what capacity he was appointed — as governor *(peḥâ)*, as is the case with Sheshbazzar (Ezra 1:8) and Zerubbabel (Hag 1:1, etc.), and as several modern translations assume (NRSV, REB). What is perhaps suppressed is the knowledge that one who was not of Davidic descent now occupied the throne from which Zedekiah had been thrust. We would therefore not expect either of our accounts to use the term *himlîk*, as with the accession of Zedekiah (2 Kgs 24:17), rather than the less precise *hipqîd*.[13] In addition, there is no indication, and little probability, that Judah was made into a province with its own governor so soon after the devastating punitive expedition of Nebuchadnezzar II.[14] While there is scant documentation for Babylonian imperial administration in general, the Babylonian Chronicle for the first year of Nebuchadnezzar reports that he

---

235-62. J. Maxwell Miller and John H. Hayes, *A History of Ancient Israel and Judah* (2nd ed., Louisville: Westminster/John Knox, 2006) 482-85, argue that Gedaliah was appointed as a client king, a conclusion with which I agree, though not because of the reference to "the king's daughters" at Mizpah (Jer 41:10) alleged by Miller and Hayes. If, ex hypothesi, the writer wished to conceal the appointment of Gedaliah as a client king, he would not have referred to Gedaliah's own daughters as "the daughters of the king." These would more naturally be understood to be Zedekiah's daughters since we hear only of his sons being put to death (2 Kgs 25:7).

12. *ly'znyhw 'bd hmlk*, on which see W. F. Badè, "The Seal of Jaazaniah," *ZAW* 51 (1933) 150-56. The discovery of the bulla at Tell en-Naṣbeh (Mizpah) creates a presumption in favor of the Jaazaniah mentioned here. The name is borne by only three other individuals: a son of Shaphan mentioned earlier (Ezek. 8:11), a Judean official (Ezek. 11:1), and a Rechabite (Jer. 35:3). It therefore seems quite plausible that the king whom this Jaazaniah served, however briefly, was Gedaliah.

13. Pace Machinist, "Palestine, Administration of," 79. His related point, that the Babylonians would have refrained from appointing one not of Davidic descent to avoid provocation, is inconsistent with the brutality of the Babylonians, their determination to punish and at all costs to avoid another dynastic rebellion after the surrender of Jerusalem.

14. In basic agreement on this point with Vanderhooft, *The Neo-Babylonian Empire and Babylon in the Latter Prophets*, 104-10 and disagreement with Machinist, "Palestine, Administration of," *ABD* 5 (1992), 77; and Lipschits, *The Fall and Rise of Jerusalem*, 84-92.

received tribute from "all the kings of Hatti land" *(šarrani ša (māt) hattú kališunu)*,[15] and the Istanbul Prism of Nebuchadnezzar ends with a damaged and obviously incomplete list of client kings from the western reaches of the empire (Tyre, Sidon, Gaza, Ashdod).[16] The appointment of natives as client kings in subject provinces was therefore a recognized feature of Neo-Babylonian provincial administration in keeping with Assyrian policy which the Babylonians followed in its main lines.[17]

It may seem surprising that Nebuchadnezzar would repeat the procedure which he adopted followed the first siege of Jerusalem, namely, exile of the rebellious king and his replacement by a more pliant candidate.[18] There is, however, in this instance one essential difference. Eleven years previously the nominee was a member of the royal Judean dynasty, and from the Babylonian point of view his appointment led to disaster. Gedaliah, on the contrary, was a member of the family which pursued a policy if not exactly pro-Babylonian, then certainly favoring nonresistance. This circumstance prompts us to turn to our second query: Why Gedaliah, and why at Mizpah? The two narratives provide no information on the background of the Shaphanid family, but their patronage of Jeremiah would suggest Benjaminite origins since Jeremiah was certainly Benjaminite (Jer 1:1).[19] After purchasing real estate in Benjaminite territory, Jeremiah was arrested and charged with treason while attempting to leave the besieged city to take possession of his property (Jer 32:6-15; 37:11-16). Shortly thereafter, while still confined in Jerusalem after its capture, he was committed to the care of Gedaliah and escorted to his own place among his fellow Benjaminites. Mizpah, about 12 kilometers north of Jerusalem, was the new administrative center in which Gedaliah was established by the Babylonians. It too lay

---

15. Donald J. Wiseman, *Chronicles of the Chaldaean Kings (626-556 B.C.) in the British Museum* (London: Trustees of the British Museum, 1961) 68-69.

16. Amélie Kuhrt, *The Ancient Near East c. 3000–330 B.C.* (London: Routledge, 1995) 2:605-7; *ANET*, 307-8.

17. On this theme of continuity, see Ronald H. Sack, "Nebuchadnezzar II and the Old Testament: History versus Ideology," in Lipschits and Blenkinsopp, *Judah and the Judeans in the Neo-Babylonian Period*, 221-33.

18. 2 Kgs 24:15-17. The Babylonian Chronicle reports that, in his seventh year (i.e., 598/597 B.C.E.), Nebuchadnezzar seized Jerusalem, captured the king, and "appointed there a king of his own choice *(šarra ša libbi-šú)*." Wiseman, *Chronicles of the Chaldaean Kings*, 72-73.

19. Two Shaphanid names, Meshullam and Elasah, belong to the Benjaminite onomastic repertoire (1 Chr 8:17, 37; 9:7), but Meshullam has too wide a distribution and Elasah is too isolated to be considered characteristically Benjaminite.

in Benjaminite territory, and the point has been made that the nearby venerable shrine of Bethel probably served as the imperially sanctioned religious center after the deliberate and systematic destruction of the Jerusalem temple under the direction of Nebuzaradan. Originally the most important sanctuary of the kingdom of Samaria, established deliberately as a rival to Jerusalem with its own priesthood and liturgical calendar,[20] Bethel survived the Assyrian conquest in 722 B.C.E. (2 Kgs 17:26-28) to rival Jerusalem once again in greatly changed circumstances.[21]

The distinctive character of Benjamin vis-à-vis Judah during this period is indicated by the list of settlements to which, according to the census list in Ezra 2:20-35 = Neh 7:25-38, the Judean expatriates in Babylon returned in the early Achaemenid period. A remarkably high number of these place names — fourteen or fifteen out of twenty-two — are in Benjaminite territory, and this datum has been confirmed by the archaeology of that region. In marked contrast to Judah, a notable number of sites — principally Tell en-Naṣbeh (Mispah), Tell el-Fûl (Gibeah?), Beitîn (Bethel), el-Jib (Gibeon) — escaped destruction.[22] It is now generally accepted that, whatever Gedaliah's status may have been, the Benjaminite region was the center of opposition to the decision of Zedekiah to rebel. If Mizpah was a Babylonian strong point during the siege, it probably would have been the destination of those Judeans who took advantage of the temporary retirement of the Babylonian forces after the arrival in the vicinity of Jerusalem of an Egyptian army (Jer 37:5; 38:19). It was during this interruption of the siege that Jeremiah also attempted to leave the city to take possession of his property in Benjamin, which in turn led to his arrest and a charge of desertion and treason (Jer 37:11-16; cf. 32:6-15).

Coming now to our third and last point: Our two sources are not forthcoming on the length of Gedaliah's tenure. According to Dtr, the

20. 1 Kgs 12:27-29, 31-33. According to Amos 7:13 Bethel was "a royal sanctuary, a national temple" *(miqdaš-melek, bêt mamlākâ)*.

21. See my "Bethel in the Neo-Babylonian Period," 93-107. For a review of recent studies on the Bethel sanctuary, see Philip R. Davies, *The Origins of Biblical Israel* (LHB/OTS 485; New York: T. & T. Clark, 2007) 159-71.

22. Charles E. Carter, "Ideology and Archaeology in the Neo-Babylonian Period: Excavating Text and Tell," in Lipschits and Blenkinsopp, *Judah and the Judeans in the Neo-Babylonian Period*, 301-22. The identifications indicated are accepted by most archaeologists and historians, but it should be borne in mind that archaeological conclusions arrived at for this period are notoriously subject to revision.

Babylonian army entered Jerusalem in the fourth month of the eleventh year of Zedekiah's reign (2 Kgs 25:3), the temple was burned by Nebuzaradan in the fifth month of the same year (25:8), and Gedaliah was assassinated in the seventh month, but unfortunately without indication of the year (25:25). The fact that these three disasters were marked by fasts (Zech 8:18-19) might suggest that the assassination of Gedaliah took place in the same year as the fall of the city. On the other hand, this leaves us with the problem of fitting in between the fall of the city and the assassination the assembly of some thousands of deportees in Ramah, collecting the loot from the temple and palace, and bringing the royal family and other prisoners to Riblah, the principal Babylonian headquarters in the far north of Syria. We would also have to allow time for the return to Judah of Judeans dispersed in the Transjordanian kingdoms and further afield (Jer 40:7-8, 11-12), the conspiracy in Ammon which led to the assassination (Jer 40:13-16), and possibly also the gathering in of the late summer harvest (Jer 40:12). It therefore seems better to assume that the year of Ishmael's deed has fallen out or been omitted. One attractive proposal identifies the mass departure for Egypt which followed (2 Kgs 25:26) with Jeremiah's third deportation in the twenty-third year of Nebuchadnezzar, therefore 582 B.C.E. (Jer 52:30). If this is so, Gedaliah's reign would have lasted about four years.

We can obtain some idea of the changing fortunes of devastated Judah from a close reading of the final chapter of the history as recorded in Dtr and, more remotely, in Chronicles. The original conclusion of Dtr — "Judah went into exile out of its land" soon after the fall of Jerusalem (2 Kgs 25:21) — gives the impression of sad finality in keeping with the predictions and threats of exile in the prophetic writings and the History itself (2 Kgs 17:19-20; 24:13). A first appendix records the appointment and assassination of Gedaliah, ending with a further exile, this time in Egypt (2 Kgs 25:22-26). We might surmise that this new conclusion was seen as the counterpart at the end of the nation's history to the descent into Egypt at the beginning. But, then, a second appendix was added dealing with the release of the exiled Jehoiachin from confinement in Babylon and the special favor granted him by the Babylonian king Amel-Marduk (2 Kgs 25:27-30). This event carries a precise date, the thirty-seventh year of Jehoiachin's exile, therefore 560 B.C.E., not quite in agreement with that monarch's accession year, 562. It strikes a note of hope for the future return of the long-absent grandson of Josiah and the restoration of the Davidic dynasty, a hope which, however, was quickly extinguished by the assassination of

Amel-Marduk in the second year of his reign.[23] As was noted earlier, the fact that this event put an end to any hope of Jehoiachin's return, and therefore the resumption of the Davidic line, suggests that this final coda, holding out a sliver of hope for the future, was added to the history some time between 562 and 560 B.C.E.

The conclusion to the Chronicler's History is quite different. The author looks beyond the exile to the new epoch inaugurated by the fall of Babylon and the advent of Cyrus. The original ending (2 Chr 36:17-21) refers to the exile only as the fulfillment of Jeremiah's seventy-years oracle (Jer 25:11-12; 29:10) understood as the sabbatical rest of the land during the absence of its population. The one appendix, taken from the opening verses of Ezra (2 Chr 36:22-23; cf. Ezra 1:1-3), passes at once to the new epoch, one in which the emphasis will be on temple rather than royal palace and on temple personnel rather than royal courtiers, in keeping with the situation obtaining almost three centuries after the fall of Jerusalem and the destruction of its temple.

This is as far as our sources take us. For the rest, we can only imagine what the condition and mood of the country was like in the aftermath of the disaster, and we have no information, either from the biblical record or external sources, on how Judah was governed during the remaining four decades of Babylonian rule. The latest of several challenges to their hegemony, by Ishmael, his party and his backers, including Baalis ruler of Ammon, would probably have led the imperial overlord to appoint Babylonian governors, abandoning any attempt at proxy rule through local officials. In spite of this gap in the record, questions remain to be asked. In the absence of extrabiblical information, do the biblical texts provide any clues to parties, politics, and positions vis-à-vis the imperial power of the day? Do they provide any clues with respect to the fundamental issue how a subject people can parlay whatever assets it has to best effect faced with overwhelming military power, whether by accommodation or opposition, overt or covert. One answer to this question will claim our attention in the following chapter.

23. The conclusion therefore seems reasonable, if not inevitable, that this second appendix could not have been added after 560 B.C.E., which raises a question about the date of at least one draft of Dtr.

CHAPTER FOUR

The Theological Politics of Deutero-Isaiah

I myself have spoken and have summoned him.
I have brought him thus far; his mission will succeed.

Isaiah 48:15

Coping with Catastrophe

Those of us who have never had to live through a catastrophic situation will find it hard to imagine what life was like for the survivors in Judah in the autumn and winter of 586 B.C.E. The murder and mayhem, destruction of property, loss of the public institutions which sustained communal living, the monarchy in the first place, created a situation of extreme deprivation, disorientation, numbness, and anomie. People had to fall back for survival on whatever resources were still available in the household and kinship network to which they belonged. Sooner or later questions about why it happened and who was responsible would be raised, and sooner or later such questions would be directed at their ancestral deity who had pledged to protect his people, his city Jerusalem, and the house of David and had signally failed to do so. Something like this happens in all comparable situations, but in this instance the questioning would have been rendered more insistent by the religious reforms carried out a few years earlier during Josiah's reign with their heavy concentration on political and religious centralization. Such questioning is implicit in practically all the biblical texts from the exilic period. Our concern is with the fate of the dynasty, on which the whole apparatus of public life depended, and what options were available after it had been extinguished. But before addressing that issue directly, it will be useful to take in the larger picture by presenting a rough sketch of the range of response to the disaster reflected in texts from that time.

One option was simply to reject the official "Yahweh alone" orthodoxy. Following on the assassination of Gedaliah about four years after the fall of Jerusalem, some of the surviving military leaders and many of the ordinary people sought refuge in Egypt from the anticipated Babylonian reprisals, taking a protesting Jeremiah with them (2 Kgs 25:25-26; Jer 41:1–43:7). After settling in the garrison town of Tahpanhes (Daphne, today Tell Defneh), they were once again reminded by Jeremiah that the disaster recently visited on them had come about on account of their addiction to cults other than that of Yahweh (Jer 44:1-14). This time, however, the prophet's listeners, both men and women, rejected Jeremiah's explanation of the disaster in the most peremptory manner. On the contrary, they insisted, responsibility lay with those, including Jeremiah himself, who had tried to persuade them to abandon the cult of "the Queen of Heaven." The veneration of this goddess, they claimed, had been an essential element in public and private religious practice in Judah at all times and with all categories of the population since the beginning.[1] The abandonment of her cult is the real reason, they told him, why we find ourselves in this miserable situation. The women concluded by stating their determination to continue making offerings and libations to the Queen of Heaven and venerating her image.[2] What we have here, then, is an alternative explanation for the disaster of 586 B.C.E.

So much for the religious reforms of Josiah and his supporters! But what happened in Egypt was not an isolated incident. Even before the final catastrophe, the image of the goddess, ejected from the temple precincts by Josiah's reform party (2 Kgs 23:4, 6-7), found its way back there about three decades later, as we read in Ezekiel's visionary tour of the temple (Ezek 8:5-6). A postdisaster literary stratum of Isaiah also testifies to the impact of disaster on the revival in Judah of chthonic cults together with the veneration of the goddess (Isa 1:29; 57:3-13; 66:17). Isaiah even includes a denunci-

---

1. The identity of this *malkat haššāmayim* (the original vocalisation; cf. LXX *hē basilissa tou ouranou*) is uncertain. Similar titles are borne by the Assyrian Ishtar *(malkat šamāmi)* and the West Semitic Anat *(b'lt šmm)*, but the goddess Asherah, so prominent throughout Israelite and Judaean history, cannot be excluded. See Cornelis Houtman, "Queen of Heaven," *DDD*, 678-80.

2. This is one of the very rare occasions in the Hebrew Bible where women are heard speaking on the subject of religion.

ation of the cult of deities presiding over fate, fortune, or chance (Isa 65:11), an anticipation of the Greek *moira*. This is a by no means unfamiliar reaction to disaster and the loss of a sense of control and meaning which major disasters tend to induce.[3]

Those who chose not to follow the example of their fellow Judeans in Egypt, and who in their grief and perplexity remained faithful to Yahweh and the ancestral traditions, would sooner or later have felt obliged to justify their choice to themselves as well as to those, within and outside of their own community, who were asking "Where now is your god?" (Ps 42:4[Eng 3]; 115:2). Much of the writing which has survived from the postdisaster period addresses this question in one way or another. It is especially in evidence in the rereading and reediting of the sayings of prophets, especially those who passed judgment on the religious infidelity of their contemporaries. An example from the Assyrian period may be mentioned. Among the diverse kinds of material in the book named for Amos, active in the middle decades of the eighth century B.C.E., is a brief gnomic poem about the necessity and ineluctability of prophecy:

> Do two walk together unless they have made an appointment?
> Does a lion roar in the forest when it has no prey?
> Does a young lion cry out from its den when it has caught nothing?
> Does a bird fall into a snare on the earth when there is no trap
> for it?
> Does a snare spring up from the ground when it has taken nothing?
> Is a trumpet blown in a city and the people are not afraid?
> Does disaster befall a city unless Yahweh has brought it about?
> [Surely Yahweh God does nothing without revealing his secret
> to his servants the prophets.]
> The lion has roared, who will not fear?
> Yahweh God has spoken, who will not prophesy?
>
> (Amos 3:3-8)

---

3. The deities Gad and Měnî are rendered in LXX by *daimōn* and *tychē*, respectively; Vulg. has only one name, *Fortuna*. On these deities, see S. David Sperling, "Meni," *DDD*, 566-68; Joseph Blenkinsopp, *Isaiah 56–66* (AB 19B; New York: Doubleday, 2003) 278-79. A parallel instance is the "deal with death" contracted by the Judean leadership faced with terminal danger from Assyria towards the end of the eighth century B.C.E. and denounced in Isa 28:14-22. Recourse to necromancy and the occult is a well-attested phenomenon at times of catastrophe. See my "Judah's Covenant with Death (Isaiah xxviii 14-22)," *VT* 50 (2000) 472-83.

The seventh in the list of rhetorical questions which make up the poem has provoked an interpretative scribal comment in the following verse (in parentheses) which, while assuming the required affirmative answer, goes on to observe that, if that is so, Yahweh God always warns of impending and avoidable disaster, and therefore is free of blame. Since "his servants the prophets" is the standard postdisaster Deuteronomistic term for the prophetic succession,[4] the stricken city is Jerusalem, and the fact that the disaster awaiting it was announced in advance by Yahweh's prophetic servants places the blame where it belongs, with the people and their rulers. It therefore at the same time absolves Yahweh from the charge of injustice and caprice.[5]

The same conclusion is reached by a more direct route in the concluding paragraph of Hosea addressed to the reader of the book (Hos 14:10[9]). The language and idiom have persuaded practically all commentators that it was appended to the book during the time of the second temple:[6]

> Let the wise understand these matters, and let the judicious acknowledge them. The ways of Yahweh are straight, and the righteous walk in them, while sinners stumble in them.

The message is addressed especially to those troubled by Hosea's repeated affirmation about the responsibility of Yahweh for putting an end to the kingdom of Samaria. Rather than setting out to prove that this decision of Yahweh was morally justified, the scribe who added the injunction simply asserts that while the justice and wisdom of divine action will be self-evident to the wise and upright, the acceptance of this self-evident truth is obscured and hindered by an immoral way of life. Ezekiel appears to

4. 2 Kgs 9:7; 17:13, 23; 21:10; 24:2; also in passages in Jeremiah attributable to a Deuteronomistic editor: Jer 7:25; 25:4; 26:5; 29:19; 35:15; 44:4.

5. This solution to the problem of theodicy arising from the disaster of 586 B.C.E. is already apparent in Dtr's comment on the extinction of the kingdom of Samaria in 722: "Yahweh warned Israel and Judah by every prophet and every seer . . . but they would not listen; they acted stubbornly like their ancestors . . . therefore Yahweh was angry with Israel and removed them out of his sight" (2 Kgs 17:13-20).

6. On the language of Hos 14:10[9] — "the ways of Yahweh" *(darkê YHWH)*, the stumbling of the wicked and rebellious (verbal stem *kšl*), and the frequent contrast between the righteous *(ṣaddiqîm* and the wicked *(rěšāʿîm)* — cf. Prov 10:30; 24:16. A. A. Macintosh, *A Critical and Exegetical Commentary on Hosea* (ICC; Edinburgh: T. & T. Clark, 1997) 583, draws the conclusion that by the time of its composition in the postexilic period the book of Hosea had become to all intents and purposes Scripture.

make a similar point in replying to the complaint that "the way [i.e., conduct] of Yahweh is not right and just" (Ezek 18:25).[7] Ezekiel rejects this charge only after refuting the idea of intergenerational moral responsibility implicit in the complaint that his contemporaries were being punished for the sins of their forebears. He does this by means of the case history of a three-generational family: a righteous grandfather, a violent and immoral son, a grandson who does not follow his father's example — concluding with a statement of individual moral accountability: whether you are righteous or wicked depends on you alone, not on your parents and antecedents. Only the one who sins dies; moral accountability is not intergenerational (Ezek 18:1-24). More directly relevant to the debate about the morality of divine action, however, is Ezekiel's case history of a land — Judah, for example — devastated by the disasters of famine, wild animals, the sword, and pestilence (Ezek 14:12-23). He concludes that even if Noah, Daniel, and Job, those three models of wisdom and righteousness from ancient times, were living in that land, they would save no one but themselves, not even their immediate family members, by virtue of their righteousness (Ezek 14:12-23).[8]

As to what extent these debates among the literati reflected discussion and self-questioning among the Judean public we can only guess. At any rate, life had to go on even in the aftermath of tragedy and disaster. The survivors would have put their lives back together as best they could, as their forebears did after the ravages of the Assyrian army under

7. "Not right and just" is an attempt to translate *lo' yittākēn*. "The way of the Lord is unfair" (NRSV) seems to be too weak, as if the Lord is not playing according to the rules; "The Lord acts without principle" (REB) is stronger but perhaps not strong enough; "unprincipled" is not the same as "unjust."

8. In this respect Ezekiel appears to differ from the author of the dialogue between Abraham and Yahweh about Yahweh's decision to destroy Sodom in Gen 18:22-33. That this dialogue is a late addition to the narrative from a time after the fall of Jerusalem has often been argued since Julius Wellhausen, *Die Composition des Hexateuchs und der historischen Bücher des Alten Testaments* (4th ed., Berlin: de Gruyter, 1963) 25-36. See, e.g., Claus Westermann, *Genesis* (BKAT 1; Neukirchen: Neukirchener, 1979) 347-48, 352, who attributes it to a postexilic theologian. This kind of dialogue is without parallel in Genesis but is reminiscent of disputations in Ezekiel and Malachi. There are two issues here: the first, the fate of the righteous caught up in divine judgment on an immoral city; the second, whether the righteous can influence the fate of the unrighteous and, if so, under what conditions and at what critical mass. See my articles "Abraham and the Righteous of Sodom," *JJS* 33 (1982) 119-32; and "The Judge of All the Earth: Theodicy in the Midrash on Genesis 18:22-33," *JJS* 41 (1990) 1-12.

Sennacherib a little more than a century earlier. We have no information on how Judah was governed during the remaining forty-three years of Babylonian rule. Mindful of the recent history of rebellion, the imperial overlord would probably have given up any further attempt at proxy rule through local officials and appointed a Babylonian governor instead. During that short half-century, however, fundamental changes were taking place on the international scene. In 550 B.C.E. the Median Empire was overrun by the Iranian Cyrus II, and in the next two years it was the turn of Elam, Parthia, Hyrcania, and Armenia. By the end of the decade Cyrus was the master of the Lydian Empire under the fabled Croesus, together with the rest of Asia Minor, Eastern Iran, and much of Central Asia. By the beginning of 539 Cyrus was ready to advance against Babylon, and in October of that year he entered the city in triumph. Since Judah was a province in the empire ruled from Babylon, these shape-changing events were calculated to have a direct impact on Jewish communities in Judah and elsewhere. The question then arises: did the change from Babylonian to Persian rule elicit a corresponding change in attitude to life under imperial control and the loss of native institutions, including the native dynasty? About that time, the mid-sixth century, we begin to hear a prophetic voice with a new and controversial answer to that question.

Tokens of Faithful Love to David (Isaiah 55:1-5)

The only mention of David in Deutero-Isaiah (chs. 40–55), or for that matter Deutero- and Trito-Isaiah (chs. 40–66), occurs towards the conclusion of Deutero-Isaiah (hereafter DI), at the beginning of the last chapter (55:1-5) in which many of the themes which recur throughout the section are recapitulated. This one reference to the Davidic dynasty provides a point of departure for a discussion of the author's proposed solution to the loss of the dynasty and his theological politics in general.

After the invitation to accept the free gift of food that nourishes (vv. 1-2), the address continues as follows (vv. 3-5):

> Come to me and listen carefully,
> Hear me, and your spirit will revive.
> I shall make a perpetual covenant with you,
> the tokens of faithful love I showed to David.
> As I appointed him a witness to peoples,

so you will summon a nation you do not know,
and a nation that does not know you will come in haste to you,
for the sake of your God,
for the Holy One of Israel who has made you glorious.

The most natural interpretation of this appeal is that God will show you, the prophet's fellow Judeans, the same favor he showed David in the past.[9] These "tokens of faithful love" imply a guarantee of perpetuity for the Davidic dynasty, as stated in Nathan's oracular pronouncement (2 Sam 7:8-17) and elsewhere (2 Sam 23:1-7; Ps 89:27-37), in effect a perpetual covenant *(bĕrît ʿôlām)*, as is explicit in 2 Sam 23:5 and implicit in our text. But the point is being made that the commitment concerning the dynasty has now been reinterpreted, reformulated, and transferred to the people as a whole, those addressed by the author who had survived the disaster which swept the dynasty away.

The passage continues by applying this insight to international relations, always of decisive significance for small nations, then as now, whose fate was to live in the shadow of great empires. David's relations with foreign nations as overlord and source of the blessings of justice and peace are now reformulated in terms of a new relationship of the people as a whole to the outside world which will bring the author's fellow Judeans recognition and honor. Use of the singular, *gôy* ("nation"), in v. 5 (twice) would, in the circumstances, hint at Persia under the rule of Cyrus, a figure overwhelmingly present throughout the first section of DI (chs. 40–48). Moreover, the statement "you will summon a nation you do not know, and a nation that does not know you will come in haste to you" echoes the frequent summons addressed to Cyrus in DI (Isa 41:25; 42:6; 45:3, 4), even though he does not know Israel's God (45:4-5). In 55:3-5, read in the light of

---

9. *hasdê dāwid,* only here and 2 Chr 6:42, is parsed as objective genitive in keeping with the context, as in Hugh G. M. Williamson, "'The Sure Mercies of David': Subjective or Objective Genitive?" *JSS* 23 (1978) 31-49, rather than subjective genitive, referring to deeds performed by David, as in André Caquot, "Les 'grâces de David': À propos d'Isaïe 55,3b," *Sem* 15 (1965) 45-59; W. A. M. Beuken, "Isa. 55.3-5: The Restoration of David," *Bijdr* 35 (1974) 49-64; Pierre Bordreuil, "Les 'grâces de David' et I Maccabee ii 57," *VT* 31 (1981) 73-76. That David is the recipient rather than the origin of the tokens of faithful love is the view of most recent commentators; among English-language commentators, see Norman Whybray, *Isaiah 40–66* (NCBC; Grand Rapids: Eerdmans, 1975) 191; Brevard S. Childs, *Isaiah* (OTL; Louisville: Westminster/John Knox, 2001) 434-45; Joseph Blenkinsopp, *Isaiah 40–55* (AB 19A; New York: Doubleday, 2002) 370-71; John Goldingay and David Payne, *A Critical and Erxegetical Commentary on Isaiah 40–55* (ICC; London: T. & T. Clark, 2006) 2:371-75.

Deutero-Isaiah as a whole, the summons would refer to Cyrus as representative of the nation summoned to act as agent of the God of Israel in the conquest of Babylon anticipated for the near future.

The need to rethink the established dogma of the perpetuity of the Davidic dynasty arose from the intractable data of historical experience. The eclipse of the Davidic dynasty, signaled by the public slaughter of the sons of Zedekiah, last of the line, and the dragging of the blinded king into exile (2 Kgs 25:7), had happened within the lifetime of many of the prophet's audience, and perhaps also that of the prophet himself writing during the last years of Babylonian rule in the mid-sixth century B.C.E. Ps 89 contains one of the most poignant expressions of bewilderment and anguish at the apparently definitive annulment of the covenant by which the permanence of the national dynasty was thought to have been guaranteed. This lament has enough in common with the theme and even the language of Isa 55:3-5 to suggest that the author of our text, and of Isaiah 40–55 as a whole, was familiar with it and had it in mind. Covenant language occurs in both Isa 55:3-5 and Ps 89, where the key term *běrît* appears four times and *ḥesed* seven times.[10] It is clear nevertheless that the Isaian author goes well beyond the psalmist, who can still plead with Yahweh to bear in mind his promises and can still utter the age-old complaint *'ad-mātay?* ("how long? v. 47, emended text). For the Isaian author, on the contrary, the dynastic promise has undergone a fundamental reinterpretation. Hence the complete absence of allusion to David and the Davidic dynasty in DI either as a historical reality, or the object of hope for the future, or a feature of es-

10. Childs, *Isaiah*, 434-37; Goldingay and Payne, *Isaiah 40–55*, 2:372. Otto Eissfeldt, "The Promises of Grace to David in Isaiah 55:1-5," in *Israel's Prophetic Heritage*, ed. Bernhard W. Anderson and Walter Harrelson (New York: Harper & Row, 1962) 196-207, points out the parallels in detail but also a fundamental difference in the psalm vis-à-vis Isa 55:3-5, in that the psalmist is addressing more directly the disconfirmation of the promise to David. Nahum M. Sarna, "Psalm 89: A Study in Inner Biblical Exegesis," in *Biblical and Other Studies*, ed. Alexander Altmann (Cambridge, MA: Harvard University Press, 1963) 29-46, dates the psalm, a composite of hymn, oracle, and lament, to the reign of Ahaz during the Syro-Ephraimite attack on Judah in the eighth century B.C.E. The psalm does not seem to match this situation: the attack of Syria and Samaria on Jerusalem did not succeed (see v. 41) and Ahaz was not dethroned (see vv. 40, 45). Scott R. A. Starbuck, "Theological Anthropology at a Fulcrum: Isaiah 55:1-5, Psalm 89, and Second Stage Traditio in the Royal Psalms," in *David and Zion: Biblical Studies in Honor of J. J. M. Roberts*, ed. Bernard F. Batto and Kathryn L. Roberts (Winona Lake: Eisenbrauns, 2004) 247-65, suggests a date for the psalm in its final form after the death of Josiah and deposition of Jehoahaz, therefore when the dynasty was in terminal crisis.

chatological scenarios, a situation unparalleled in prophetic texts dated to the exilic period.[11] But this situation, remarkable in itself, leaves unaddressed the issue of an acceptable alternative form of governance once the break with the native dynasty is accepted as inevitable. We must now ask whether the author of Isaiah 40–55 had his own answer to that question.

The Historical Context: Prospects and Options

Any attempt to address this issue must take account of the historical context in which the author of DI[12] was active, a context which takes in the period from the extinction of the dynasty to the time of writing, by broad agreement the last decade of Babylonian rule (ca. 550-539 B.C.E.). To recapitulate: The final eclipse of the Davidic dynasty occupied the quarter century following the death of Josiah during which four of his descendants hastened the end by their ineptitude. The public execution of the male children of Zedekiah, last of the four (2 Kgs 25:6-7), was a deliberate act

11. Cf. Jer 17:24-25; 22:1-4; 23:5-6; 30:8-9; 33:14-26; Ezek 34:23-24; 37:24-28; Amos 9:11-12; Mic 5:1-4(Eng 2-5), and frequently in Isaiah 1–39 (9:1-6; 11:1-9; 16:5). Taking in this broader view of DI makes it difficult to accept the more benign alternative that the promise to David is now to be shared with all the people rather than transferred to them, as Walter C. Kaiser, "The Unfailing Kindnesses Promised to David: Isaiah 55:3," *JSOT* 45 (1989) 91-98, has it.

12. Use of the term "author" calls for explanation. Without attempting to argue the case in detail, I am assuming a basic thematic unity throughout chs. 40–55 and must confess to some hesitation with regard to recent attempts to section the work into layers, assigning dates to each. This seems to me to be especially the case with passages which ostensibly, in the context, refer to Cyrus II and have been generally so understood, but are redated to the reign of Darius I. I have in mind the dividing up of Isa 45:1-7, the primary Cyrus text, in the redactional *tour de force* of Reinhard Kratz, *Kyros im Deuterojesaja-Buch: Redaktionsgeschichtliche Untersuchungen zu Entstehung und Theologie von Jes 40–55* (FAT 1; Tübingen: Mohr [Siebeck], 1991), but also the older study of J. M. Vincent, *Studien zur literarische Eigenart und zur geistigen Heimat von Jesaja, Kap. 40–55* (BBET 5; Frankfurt am Main: Lang, 1977); and, more recently, Odil Hannes Steck, "Israel und Zion: Zum Problem konzeptioneller Einheit und literarischer Schichtung in Deuterojesaja," in his collected essays, *Gottesknecht und Zion: Gesammelte Aufsätze zu Deuterojesaja* (FAT 4; Tübingen: Mohr [Siebeck], 1992) 173-207; also Ulrich Berges, *Das Buch Jesaja: Komposition und Endgestalt* (Freiburg: Herder, 1998) 322-413. On the need for a less drastic approach to *Redaktionsgeschichte*, see the remarks of Hans-Jürgen Hermisson, "Einheit und Komplexität Deuterojesajas: Probleme der Redaktionsgeschichte von Jes 40–55," in *The Book of Isaiah/Le Livre d'Isaïe*, ed. Jacques Vermeylen (BETL 81; Leuven: University Press and Peeters, 1989) 286-312.

aimed at finally extinguishing the dynasty and, with it, any hope of independence for "the rebellious city harmful to kings and provinces" (Ezra 4:15). But there remained one surviving representative of the dynasty, the exiled Jehoiachin. An appendix to Dtr records that in the first year of his reign, therefore 562/561, Amel-Marduk granted amnesty to Jehoiachin, giving him a preeminent position among other exiled rulers at the Babylonian court (2 Kgs 25:27-30). If this implies that Jehoiachin was being groomed to return to Jerusalem as a client ruler, as suggested earlier, the plan came to nothing since Amel-Marduk was assassinated a few months later by his brother Neriglissar. Jehoiachin therefore died in Babylon after all, as predicted by Jeremiah (Jer 22:26).

At the time of the composition of DI this was very recent history. In retrospect, it must have seemed to many of this prophetic author's contemporaries who had survived the terrible half-century since the death of Josiah as if that tragic event marked, in effect, the end of the line for the dynasty. This would have made it easier to accept the transfer of the promises to David from the dynasty to the people as a whole. The same view is expressed in a more subtle way in the Chronicler's rewritten version of Josiah's death and obsequies (2 Chr 35:20-27). The latter concludes, uniquely, with a memorial lament which reads like a lament for the Davidic house as a whole and all that it stood for.

In surveying this half-century of turmoil we noted the emergence of different points of view on what kind of future was possible and tolerable in the absence of the native dynasty and faced with the overwhelming imperial power represented by the Babylonians and, in prospect, the Persians. To these points of view corresponded parties with conflicting opinions on the fundamental issue of acquiescence in or active opposition to imperial rule in its different forms. The appointment of Gedaliah over the province sharpened the issue and raised the stakes on the conflicts about a future without the dynasty (2 Kgs 25:22-26; Jer 40:1–41:18); and this would be especially the case if Gedaliah was appointed as client king, since he was certainly not of Davidic descent. It would also render more contextually intelligible the assassination of Gedaliah by Ishmael who was, or claimed to be, of Davidic descent (Jer 41:1).

The biblical account of the situation is obviously incomplete, but the texts have much to say about Jeremiah and the Shaphanids in opposition to policies pursued by those advising Zedekiah and their allies. Party conflict in the last phase of the kingdom of Judah may be reflected in the final chapter of Dtr. It seems likely that its original conclusion was the definitive statement that "Judah went into exile out of its land" (2 Kgs 25:21) rather than the inconsequential bit of information with which it concludes in its present form (25:30).[13] If this is so, two appendices must have been added. The first is the account of the appointment of Gedaliah, his assassination, and an exodus en masse to Egypt to avoid the anticipated Babylonian reprisal (2 Kgs 25:22-26). The second, which holds out a sliver of hope for a future restoration, records the rehabilitation of Jehoiachin by Amel-Marduk and therefore must have been added before the assassination of the latter in 560 B.C.E.[14] All of this is in sharp contrast to the conclusion of Chronicles, where the focus is no longer on the national dynasty but on Cyrus as the divinely inspired agent of Yahweh (2 Chr 36:22-23). And with Cyrus we return to DI and its author's response to the issues of his own day.

Cyrus, Divinely Inspired and Divinely Appointed Successor to the Davidic Line

According to Isaiah 40–48 Cyrus is destined to be the principal agent of national rehabilitation and restoration for Judean communities in Judah and the Diaspora. Karl Budde stated this very clearly many years ago: "Cyrus stands at the very center of the prophet's worldview."[15] He is the one who will defeat Judah's enemies — Babylon in the first place,[16] impose an inter-

---

13. Recent discussion in Thomas Römer, *La première histoire d'Israël: L'Ecole deutéronomiste à l'oeuvre* (MdB 56; Fribourg: Labor et Fides, 2007) 152 (2 Kgs 25:21 or maybe 25:26).

14. The situation is more complex for those who argue for a Josian edition of the History concluding with the statement about the incomparability of Josiah in 2 Kgs 23:25: "Before him there was no king like him who turned to Yahweh with all his heart and soul and strength, according to all the law of Moses." After experiencing the four, or maybe five, rulers who followed him, a later scribe has added: "nor did any like him arise after him," followed by a statement in which Yahweh rejects Judah, Jerusalem, and its temple (23:25b-27). The general sense seems to be that the dynasty ended, in effect, with Josiah. For a summary account of the double redaction theory, together with competing views of the "Cross school" and the "Göttingen school," see Albert de Pury, Thomas Römer, and Jean-Daniel Macchi, *Israël construit son histoire: L'historiographie deutéronomiste à la lumière des recherches récentes* (MdB 34; Geneva: Labor et Fides, 1996) 46-58; Römer, *The So-Called Deuteronomistic History* (London: T. & T. Clark, 2005) 27-35.

15. Cited in Max Haller, "Die Kyros-Lieder Deuterojesajas," in *EUQARISTHRION: Studien zur Religion und Literatur des Alten und Neuen Testaments,* ed. Hans Schmidt (Göttingen: Vandenhoeck & Ruprecht, 1923) 261.

16. Isa 41:1-5, 25-29; 43:14; 45:1-7, 13; 46:11; 48:14-16.

national order based on justice and peace (42:1-4),[17] allow, even facilitate, the repatriation of those forcibly deported (42:7; 45:13), and make possible the rebuilding of Jerusalem and its temple (44:28; 45:13). These tasks are to be discharged under the direct inspiration and aegis of Yahweh, Israel's king.[18] Such expectations would not have seemed unreasonable in view of propaganda of the kind disseminated in the Cyrus Cylinder text published within a year of the fall of Babylon. In the second half of this manifesto Cyrus, speaking in his own name, claimed to have restored the gods of subject peoples to their original sanctuaries and permitted their devotees to return to their native lands.[19] Most commentators conclude that Deutero-Isaiah, or the greater part of it, was composed before the promulgation of this text, some time between 550 and 538. Pro-Persian propaganda would, however, have been in circulation during the last years of the reign of Nabonidus, probably disseminated by Marduk priests offended by Nabonidus's neglect of the *akitu* festival and his alleged other impieties, and the prophet could have become acquainted with it at that time.

On the assumption that the author of Isaiah 40–55 had a particular form of governance in mind for the immediate future, we must go on to ask in what capacity Cyrus was to fulfil this commission assigned to him by Yahweh. I will argue that Deutero-Isaiah is attempting to persuade his public that Yahweh is now bringing about a new dispensation in which Cyrus,

17. The nature of the commission mandated in 42:1-4, that of imposing an international order based on justice (*mišpāt* occurring three times in this short passage), is the function of a ruler not of a prophet or priest. It has several of the features of a royal installation ritual; cf. Pss 2; 72; 110. The identification of the *'ebed* in 42:1-4 with Cyrus has often been argued or assumed, e.g., Haller, "Die Kyros-Lieder des Deuterojesajas," 262-63; Sydney Smith, *Isaiah, Chapters XL–LV* (Oxford: Oxford University Press, 1944) 54-57; Sigmund Mowinckel, *He That Cometh*, trans. G. W. Anderson (1959; repr. BRS; Grand Rapids: Eerdmans and Livonia: Dove, 2005) 189-91. It should be added that since the book of Isaiah has been the object of a continuous and cumulative process of reinterpretation, this first of Duhm's servant passages could have been reapplied to other figures at a later time. See my *Isaiah 40–55*, 209-12.

18. Isa 41:21; 43:15; 44:6. With the verb *hēʿîr*, "stir up," "inspire" in Isa 41:2, 25; 45:13; cf. 2 Chr 36:22; Ezra 1:1.

19. The relevant statements correspond to lines 32-33 of the Cylinder; see the translation in *ANET*, 315-16. It is acknowledged, however, that this is propaganda probably emanating from Babylonian priests hostile to Nabonidus and that Persian policy vis-à-vis subject peoples was not significantly different from that of their imperial predecessors. See, inter alios, R. J. Van der Spek, "Did Cyrus the Great introduce a new policy towards subdued nations?," *Persica* 10 (1982) 278-83; Amélie Kuhrt, "The Cyrus Cylinder and Achaemenid Imperial Policy," *JSOT* 25 (1983) 83-97.

as Yahweh's agent, will take over the succession to the now defunct Davidic dynasty, warranted by an authority which transcends by far descent through the male line, namely, direct divine inspiration not only of the prophetic author but of Cyrus himself.[20] Since this solution called for abandoning beliefs long cherished together with aspirations for political autonomy, we can appreciate that many of the hearers would be predisposed to reject the message. An earlier commentator put this is even stronger terms: "If Cyrus was the anointed of Yahweh, he had taken the place of the line of David, and had become the true king of Judah. . . . The consequence, equally inevitable, of this proclamation of Cyrus must have been that the prophet would seem to some of his own people a traitor, worthy of death."[21] Hence the weight attached to prophetic authority in these chapters, validated by the Deuteronomistic verification-falsification theory (Deut 18:21-22), in other words, the fulfillment of earlier predictions.[22] Hence also the repeated emphasis on the cosmic power of the deity who sponsors and guarantees the truth of the prophet's message.[23] These recurring themes testify to the earnestness of the prophet's claim to a hearing while at the same time betraying an implicit acknowledgment of the likelihood of rejection. One indication of the latter may be detected in the gradually increasing exasperation at the failure of those addressed to accept the message.[24]

That this is the author's political solution to the current crisis is supported by the complete silence of Deutero-Isaiah on David, the Davidic dynasty, and its destiny, with the exception of the passage cited at the head of this essay. It can also be deduced more directly from the titles assigned to Cyrus. These include such familiar designations as "servant" (*'ebed*) and "shepherd" (*rō'eh*) which encapsulate the millennial Mesopotamian ideal of the just ruler and are likewise part of the Davidic titulature.[25] If the first

---

20. The verb *(hē'îr > 'ûr)* can have a meaning analogous to prophetic inspiration, with reference to the Servant of the Lord (Isa 50:4), Zerubbabel and Joshua (Hag 1:14), and Diaspora Jews (Ezra 1:5). I take it that this is the sense in which Cyrus is said to be inspired (Isa 41:2, 25; 45:13; also 2 Chr 36:22; Ezra 1:1).

21. Smith, *Isaiah, Chapters XL–LV,* 74.

22. Isa 41:22-23, 25-29; 44:7-8, 26-28; 48:3-5, 16b.

23. Isa 40:12-14, 21, 26, 28; 42:5; 45:7, 12, 18; 48:13. See Joseph Blenkinsopp, "The Cosmological and Protological Language of Deutero-Isaiah," *CBQ* 73 (2011) 493-510.

24. Isa 42:18-25; 43:22-28; 45:9-13; 46:8-13; 48:1-11.

25. David as the servant of YHWH in 2 Sam 3:18; 1 Kgs 8:24-26; 2 Kgs 19:34; Jer 33:21-22, 26. In Ezek 34:23; 37:24 David is both servant and shepherd. David, who is presented as literally a shepherd, is reminded by the Israelite tribal elders that he was designed by YHWH as shepherd and ruler (*nāgîd,* 2 Sam 5:2 = 1 Chr 11:2; also Ps 78:71-72).

of the four Duhmian *Ebedlieder* (42:1-4), with the following comment (42:5-9), was *at that time* referred to Cyrus, as proposed earlier, it would imply a commissioning of the Persian ruler as Yahweh's royal servant and a presentation of him in that capacity to the people. Isa 42:1-4 reads, in fact, like a solemn verbatim report of a ceremony of installation in office. The idea behind the ruler as servant is not, or at least not primarily, that he is to serve his people, but that he is to function in the service of the deity who commissioned him and whose will he is to implement. Whereas according to the Cylinder text Cyrus is commissioned by and acts in the name of Marduk, in Isaiah he is the servant of Yahweh. An inscription from the Abu-Habba collection in the British Museum, from the reign of Nabonidus, refers to Marduk who "aroused Cyrus, king of Anshan, his young servant," who then went on to defeat the Medes.[26] The metaphor of shepherding, on the other hand, tempers the image of absolute royal power with a concern for justice and care for society's losers and outcasts (Isa 40:10-11). As a metaphor for just and equitable rule, it features in royal annals throughout Mesopotamian history, for example, with reference to Hammurapi and Ashurbanipal.[27] As shepherd, therefore, Cyrus will see to the well-being of the prophet's defeated and dispirited fellow Judaeans, the rebuilding of Jerusalem, and the restoration of the ruined cities of Judah (Isa 44:28).

The most striking of these titles attached to the native dynast in several texts,[28] and to Cyrus in DI, is *mašîaḥ*, "anointed one":

This is what Yahweh says about his anointed one, about Cyrus:
"I have grasped him by his right hand
to beat down nations before him,
depriving kings of their strength;
to open doors before him,
with no gates closed to him."

(45:1)

---

26. Text in Paul-Alain Beaulieu, *The Reign of Nabonidus, King of Babylon, 556-539 B.C.* (New Haven: Yale University Press, 1989) 108. Several scholars have noted parallels between this text and DI.

27. See Gerhard Wallis, *"rā'â; rō'eh," TDOT* 13 (2004) 544-53.

28. E.g., 1 Sam 2:10, 35; 2 Sam 19:21; 22:51; 23:1, and often in Psalms; Lam 4:20 is particularly poignant and relevant to the situation addressed by DI: "Yahweh's anointed, the breath of our life, was taken in their traps, although we had thought to live among the nations, secure under his shadow."

Commentators have experienced problems with the text and syntax of this verse, quite apart from the question whether *lĕkôreš* ("about Cyrus") should be elided as an interpolation.[29] There is certainly more than one way of translating the verse, but the translation offered above is defensible. Anointing is an important element in ceremonies of installation in the office of kingship, in Judah as elsewhere in the Near East, and such a ceremony may be alluded to in the passage which the statement cited above introduces (Isa 45:1-7). In this ceremony the deity addresses the king-designate directly, as here and in Ps 2:7-9, and presents him to the assembly, as in Isa 42:1-4. Other features — holding him by the hand (45:1; also 42:6), calling him by name (45:3 and 4), giving him a title or throne name (v. 4), ending, perhaps, with an allusion to investiture (v. 5: verb *'āzar*, "bind," "gird") — are familiar features of the practice and ideology of royalty in the ancient Near East. Several of them appear on the Cyrus Cylinder with reference to Cyrus as appointee of the imperial Babylonian deity Marduk, and all are familiar from the language of the Babylonian court.[30]

The International Context of Deutero-Isaiah's Endorsement of Cyrus

This prophetic endorsement of Cyrus is rendered more intelligible by what happened in the aftermath of the fall of Babylon in 539 B.C.E. The Cylinder text states the claim of Cyrus to be king of Babylon as legitimate successor

29. On these issues, see Karl Elliger, *Deuterojesaja 40,1–45,7* (BKAT 11/1; Neukirchen-Vluyn: Neukirchener, 1978) 481-503; Klaus Westermann, *Isaiah 40–66* (OTL; Philadelphia: Westminster, 1969) 152-55, 162; Blenkinsopp, *Isaiah 40–55*, 243-45; Goldingay and Payne, *Isaiah 40–55*, 2:17-22. Few have followed Charles C. Torrey, *The Second Isaiah: A New Interpretation* (New York: Scribner's, 1928) 42, 357; and James D. Smart, *History and Theology in Second Isaiah* (Philadelphia: Westminster, 1965) 115-34, who, for quite different reasons, deleted *lĕkôreš* as an interpolation. Klaus Baltzer, *Deutero-Isaiah* (Hermeneia; Minneapolis: Fortress, 2001) 223, agrees that it is interpolated but adds rather mysteriously that DI was the interpolator.

30. Discussion of parallels in Isaiah 40–55 with Babylonian *Hofstil* go back all the way to the much-cited article of Rudolph Kittel, "Cyrus und Deuterojesaja," *ZAW* 18 (1898) 149-62. Kittel argued that the close parallels, even in wording, between Marduk's relation to Cyrus in the Cylinder and YHWH's relation to the same monarch in DI cannot be explained by direct dependence either way but only by familiarity on the part of DI with the traditional and stereotypical language of the Babylonian court. In the almost equally cited article, "II Isaiah and the Persians," *JAOS* 83 (1963) 415-21, Morton Smith, while not questioning the parallels, proposed that the DI author could have drawn on pro-Persian propaganda disseminated among Jewish expatriates in Babylon before the fall of the city.

of Nabonidus, a claim justified by sponsorship on the part of Marduk, imperial god of Babylon. This text records how Marduk was angry with Nabonidus, looked for a replacement, chose Cyrus, and commanded him to take the city and restore the traditional cult.[31] Cyrus was therefore given religious legitimation as successor to the last Babylonian king. Towards the end of the Cylinder text, Cyrus reports the discovery of an inscription of Ashurbanipal whom he describes as "a king who preceded me," that is, as king of Babylon.[32] One of the titles of Cyrus which appears on contemporary inscriptions is therefore "king of Babylon, king of the lands" *(šar babili šar mātāti).*[33] His succession to the discredited Nabonidus, and therefore also to the illustrious Nebuchadnezzar II, was thus accepted as legitimate, at least by the Marduk priesthood, on the theological grounds of their god's sponsorship. After the conquest, Cyrus restored the *akitu* spring festival in Marduk's *esagila* sanctuary, neglected by Nabonidus, and confirmed the legitimacy of his claim to the throne by presiding over the festival, a circumstance which could lead to reflection on the Persian attitude to the Jerusalem temple as emblematic of and instrumental in imperial control of Judah. (One indication of the new function of the Jerusalem temple, viewed from the Persian perspective, is the requirement that prayers for the royal family in Susa be incorporated into the temple liturgy, Ezra 6:9-10). It was the rejection of this *religious* legitimation of Persian succession to the Babylonian throne which led to the dynastic revolt of Nidintu-Bēl, who claimed, perhaps truthfully, to be the son of Nabonidus and heir to the great Nebuchadnezzar II. A second Babylonian revolt followed shortly afterwards led by a certain Arkha, referred to as an Armenian but of obscure antecedents, who was crowned in Babylon as Nebuchadnezzar IV and whose revolt was suppressed towards the end of 521 B.C.E.[34] Both were essentially dynastic revolts.

---

31. *ANET,* 315.

32. Kuhrt, "The Cyrus Cylinder and Achaemenid Imperial Policy," 88; *The Persian Empire: A Corpus of Sources from the Achaemenid Period* (London: Routledge, 2007) 1:72.

33. M. A. Dandamaev, *Persien unter den ersten Achämeniden (6. Jh. v. Chr.)* (Wiesbaden: Reichert, 1976) 96-100; *A Political History of the Achaemenid Empire,* trans. W. J. Vogelsang (Leiden: Brill, 1989) 54-56.

34. The primary source is the Bisitun inscription (cols. I 77–II 5; IV 28-29). Cuneiform texts dated to the autumn of 521, during the brief reign of Arkha-Nebuchadnezzar IV, have come to light in southern Mesopotamia; see Amélie Kuhrt in *CAH,* 2nd ed., 4, ed. John Boardman *et al.* (1988) 129-30. See also Herodotus, *Hist.* 3:150-60, who, however, is not well informed on the reign of Darius I.

A similar pattern emerged after the conquest of Egypt by Cambyses in 525 B.C.E. Cambyses assumed the throne as legitimate successor to the last of the Saitic pharaohs, Psammeticus III, or, since the latter's reign was short and insignificant, that of his predecessor Amasis II (570-526). As such, he was accepted as the founder of the twenty-seventh dynasty and is addressed in these terms in the autobiographical inscription of the Egyptian notable Udjahorresnet.[35]

Jerusalem, however, was not Babylon, one of the nodal points in the Achaemenid Empire, nor was it Memphis. DI's argument for legitimation was along the same lines, but it was evident that Cyrus would rule over Judah neither in his own person nor through a native appointed as a client king, but through a provincial governor who would answer to the satrap of Babylon-Transeuphrates. Perhaps the memory of the convulsive events following on the death of Josiah excluded the more accommodating option of relative autonomy under a native ruling as client king, even if a suitable candidate had been available.

A final note. Deutero-Isaiah's acceptance of the legitimacy of empire was not unconditional. It was contingent in the first place on leaving Jewish communities under Persian rule free to worship their own deity in their own place of worship and to conduct undisturbed their own religious practices. Fortunately, tolerance and even support of local cults was a characteristic of Persian imperial policy. In this respect the Deutero-Isaian solution anticipates the situation described in the opening chapters of the book of Daniel in which Daniel and his companions profit by the educational opportunities available in the Babylonian Empire, serve at the imperial court, and can even rise to high office. They do so, however, while observing strictly the dietary laws and the customary prayers and refusing to worship other deities. Deutero-Isaiah's theological position must have been experienced as radical when it was first enunciated. It is even more so in its implications, since it opened up the possibility of severing religious ties with nationality and territory and contemplating, perhaps for the first time, the possibility of a future without the apparatus of an independent state system.

---

35. Dandamaev, *A Political History of the Achaemenid Empire*, 76-78; Joseph Blenkinsopp, "The Mission of Udjahorresnet and Those of Ezra and Nehemiah," *JBL* 106 (1987) 409-21.

CHAPTER FIVE

Zerubbabel

Here is the man whose name is Branch; he will branch out from where he is and rebuild the temple of the Lord. It is he who will rebuild the temple, he who will assume royal dignity, who will sit on the throne as ruler.

Zechariah 6:12-13

Who Was Zerubbabel?

About the administration of Judah in the last decades of Babylonian rule we know practically nothing. After the failed coup of Ishmael and the extinction of the last hope for the return of Jehoiachin to the throne, we hear no more about attempts to restore the native dynasty. In the absence of information, we may assume that the province was administered by a governor, in view of recent history probably a Babylonian governor. After the conquest of Babylon by the Persians in October 539 B.C.E. the situation promised to be different. It is hardly surprising that Cyrus II, whose advent was proclaimed in advance by Deutero-Isaiah and who was supported and welcomed by many in Judah and the Diaspora, should appoint a native Judean as governor. The nominee was Sheshbazzar, in Ezra-Nehemiah described as ruler of Judah (*nāśî' lîhûdâ*, Ezra 1:8) and governor (*peḥâ*, Ezra 5:14). According to the same source, he was charged with the task of rebuilding the temple in Jerusalem and bringing back the temple vessels looted by the Babylonians (Ezra 1:8-11; 5:13-16). There is no indication that he was of royal Davidic descent, in which respect he differed from Zerubbabel, who would occupy the same office a few years later under Darius I. As is evident from his name, which in Akkadian *(zēr bābili)* means "seed of Babylon," less literally "of Babylonian origin," Zerubbabel belonged to the Judean Diaspora in southern Mesopotamia before his return to Judah to take over the office of governor. According to both Haggai and Ezra-Nehemiah he was the son of Shealtiel, oldest son of the exiled Jehoiachin,[1] but in the Chronicler's list of David's line he is the son of Pedaiah, Shealtiel's brother (1 Chr 3:19). In either case, he was the grandson of the exiled Jehoiachin and great-grandson of Josiah. Since therefore he was certainly of Davidic descent, we may dispense with the often laborious attempts to harmonize these divergent accounts of his parentage.

We can also dismiss the identification of Zerubbabel with Sheshbazzar, an opinion which apparently goes back to Josephus.[2] The mistake arose from the extremely confusing presentation in Ezra 1–6 of events and personalities in Judah in the early Achaemenid period, probably the latest section of the book to be put in place.[3] In the Hebrew section of Ezra (Ezra 1:1–4:7), Zerubbabel was the leader of the pioneer contingent of expatriates which returned to Judah in the first year of the reign of Cyrus, which would be 538 B.C.E. (Ezra 2:2 = Neh 7:7). Together with the priest Jeshua (or Joshua) he built the first altar, celebrated Sukkoth, made preparations for the rebuilding of the temple, and in the second year laid the foundations of the temple and began construction (Ezra 2:2; 3:1-13). In the Aramaic section of the book (Ezra 4:8–6:18), he and Jeshua resume the building project in the second year of Darius, therefore eighteen years later (4:24), with the support of the prophets Haggai and Zechariah (5:1-2). In the three-way correspondence which follows involving Tattenai, satrap of the Transeuphratene province of the Persian Empire (Akkadian: *eber*

---

1. Haggai 1:1, 12, 14; 2:2, 23; Ezra 3:2, 8; 5:2; Neh 12:1.

2. In Josephus's account of the return to Judah under Cyrus, the temple vessels are confided to Abassaros, one of several variants of the name Sheshbazzar (cf. Sanabassaros in LXX[A] and 1 Esdras), but in his version of the edict of Cyrus permitting or mandating work on the temple the vessels are confided to Zorobabēlos (*Ant.* 11:13-14). The identification is still occasionally encountered, e.g., in Aryeh Bartal, "Again, who was Sheshbazzar?," *BM* 24 (1979) 357-69 (Hebrew), opposed by Menahem Ben-Yashar, "On the Problem of Sheshbazzar and Zerubbabel," *BM* 27 (1981) 46-56 (Hebrew). On the individuals and their names, see also Sara Japhet, "Sheshbazzar and Zerubbabel — Against the Background of the History and Religious Tendencies of Ezra-Nehemiah," *ZAW* 94 (1982) 66-98.

3. See my *Ezra-Nehemiah* (OTL; Philadelphia: Westminster, 1988) 47-54.

nāri), Darius I, and the Judean leadership (5:3–6:12), only an unnamed governor and Jewish elders are involved in the building. It is these elders who, with the permission and encouragement of Darius, resume work on the temple and complete it by that monarch's sixth year (516 B.C.E.). According to this source, then, it seems that Zerubbabel disappeared from the scene at some point between 520 and 516. According to this somewhat confused Ezra-Nehemiah version of events, therefore, both Sheshbazzar and Zerubbabel were in a position of authority at the beginning of Persian rule under Cyrus II and both laid the foundations of the new temple, but it would be mistaken to conclude from this that they were one and the same person. They are clearly distinguished in the Aramaic section of Ezra (Ezra 4:8–6:18), and in referring back to the situation under Cyrus in their letter to Darius the elders mention only Sheshbazzar (Ezra 5:13-16). Identifying Zerubbabel with Sheshbazzar would also leave us wondering why a Diaspora Jew would have two Babylonian names.[4] The alternative is to accept that the list of the first immigrants under Cyrus led by Zerubbabel and Jeshua (Ezra 2:1-67 = Neh 7:6-69), together with the account of their activities after their arrival (Ezra 2:68–4:4), reflects the perspective of a considerably later date together with the practice of telescoping events and privileging origins in evidence elsewhere in Ezra-Nehemiah.[5]

4. We should also resist the temptation to equate Sheshbazzar with Shenazzar, Zerubbabel's uncle according to the Chronicler's list (1 Chr 3:18). On linguistic grounds the names are quite different; see P.-R. Berger, "Zu den Namen *ššbssr* und *šn'sr*," *ZAW* 83 (1971) 98-100; Sara Japhet, "Sheshbazzar and Zerubbabel against the Background of the History and Religious Tendencies of Ezra-Nehemiah," *ZAW* 94 (1982) 66-98; Paul E. Dion, "ששבצר and סנור," *ZAW* 95 (1983) 111-12. The linguistic arguments of Berger *et al.* are ignored by Carol L. Meyers and Eric M. Meyers, who identify Sheshbassar with Shenassar; see *Haggai, Zechariah 1–8* (AB 25B; Garden City: Doubleday, 1987), xxxiv; and "The Future Fortunes of the House of David," in *Fortunate the Eyes That See: Essays in Honor of David Noel Freedman in Celebration of His Seventieth Birthday*, ed. Astrid B. Beck *et al.* (Grand Rapids: Eerdmans, 1995) 208.

5. Nehemiah is also included in the list of the first immigrants (Ezra 2:2), and Ezra is presented as son of the priest Seraiah executed by the Babylonians after the fall of Jerusalem (Ezra 7:1; 2 Kgs 25:18). On the list itself, see Loren W. Batten, *A Critical and Exegetical Commentary on the Books of Ezra and Nehemiah* (ICC; Edinburgh: T. & T. Clark, 1913) 71-74 (later Persian period); William Foxwell Albright, *The Biblical Period from Abraham to Ezra* (New York: Harper & Row, 1949) 87, 110 n. 180 (either 538-522 or late fifth century B.C.E.); Wilhelm Rudolph, *Esra und Nehemia samt 3. Esra* (HAT 20; Tübingen: Mohr, 1949) 7-17 (some time between 539 and 515); Kurt Galling, "Die Liste der aus dem Exil Heimgekehrten," in *Studien zur Geschichte Israels im Persischen Zeitalter* (Tübingen: Mohr, 1964) 108 (518 following on a return in 521/520); Hugh G. M. Williamson, "The Composition of Ezra i-vi," *JTS*

The task of reconstructing events and personalities on the basis of sources as disparate and confusing as Ezra-Nehemiah and the prophecies of Haggai and Zechariah (chs. 1–8) is not easy, but we can sum up the results as follows: Zerubbabel, a descendant of King David, was appointed governor of Judah by Darius I and was active in Judah only once, for a relatively brief period in the early years of that reign, a critical time for the emerging Persian Empire as we shall see. He is presented in that role in both the narrative framework of the discourses of Haggai (1:1, 14) and the sayings themselves (2:2, 21), and his name occurs in no nonbiblical text presently available.[6] "Governor" is to be understood in the normal sense of a provincial administrator rather than discharging an ad hoc appointment, for example, as a kind of Commissioner for Provincial Affairs, comparable to Histiaeus in Lydia or Udjahorresnet in Egypt.[7]

Zerubbabel and the New Temple

Like Zerubbabel, the prophet Haggai was active during the critical period of the early years of Darius I when the future of the Persian Empire, and therefore also the fate of Jewish communities under Persian rule, hung in the balance. There are occasions during this period when we are in a position, practically unique in biblical history, of following events to the

---

33 (1983) 1-30; *Ezra, Nehemiah* (WBC 16; Waco: Word, 1985) 30-32 (in its final form not before the reign of Darius I); Blenkinsopp, *Ezra-Nehemiah*, 42, 83-84 (mid-fifth century, close to the time of Nehemiah).

6. Contrary to the claim of Meyers and Meyers, "The Future Fortunes of the House of David," 208, Zerubbabel is not mentioned in a list of governors of Judah uncovered in Jerusalem, nor has such a list been discovered in Jerusalem or anywhere else. Their reference is to Nahman Avigad, *Bullae and Seals from a Post-Exilic Judean Archive* (Qedem 4; Jerusalem: Hebrew University Institute of Archaeology, 1976), but this publication contains neither the name Zerubbabel nor a list of governors. The authors are relying on the entirely speculative identification of a certain Shelomit, whose name appears on an unprovenanced scaraboid seal (Avigad's #14), with the Shelomit, daughter of Zerubbabel, of 1 Chr 3:19. The authors, moreover, elevate the Shelomit of the seal, maidservant or concubine of Elnathan (*'āmāh 'elnātān*), to the position of coregent with this Elnathan, successor to Zerubbabel as governor of Judah.

7. Rudolph, *Esra und Nehemia samt 3. Esra*, 52, refers to him as "Hochkommissar für Juda." Histiaeus from Miletus obtained permission from Darius I to attempt the pacification of Ionia (Herodotus, *Hist.* 5:106-8; 6:1-5). Udjahorresnet was sent back to Egypt to reform the cult in the third year of Darius; see my *Judaism, The First Phase* (Grand Rapids: Eerdmans, 2009) 94-97.

month and even to the day, though at the center of these events the significance of Zerubbabel is often concealed under the arcane, symbolic language proper to prophecy at that time. In the prophecies of Haggai,
Zerubbabel is linked with the high priest Jeshua, and both together are
charged with the essential task of rebuilding the temple and restoring its
worship. In all epochs throughout the history of the ancient Near East
temple-building or temple-rebuilding was a royal prerogative and task.
The temple was the property of the dynastic ruler who was responsible for
its upkeep and proper functioning, its personnel were employees of the
ruler and answerable to him, and the king played an indispensable role in
the most important liturgies, for example, the Babylonian New Year *akitu*
ritual.[8] The intense concentration in Haggai and Zechariah 1–8 on the
temple, its symbolism and significance, raises the further possibility that
both prophets stood in the tradition of cultic or temple prophecy well attested in ancient Mesopotamia and certainly a feature of the religious life
in both kingdoms during the time of the monarchy.

It may be helpful to set out Haggai's five brief discourses with their
original dates and the approximate equivalent in the Gregorian calendar.
For all five the year is 520 B.C.E., the second regnal year of Darius I.

1.	1:1-11	1st Elul	29th August
2.	1:15a + 2:15-19	24th Elul	21st September
3.	1:15b–2:9	21st Tishri	17th October
4.	2:10-14	24th Chislev	18th December
5.	2:20-23	24th Chislev	18th December

These prophetic discourses are dated with unusual chronological precision,
beginning on the first day of the month of Elul in the second regnal year of
Darius I, therefore, according to one calculation, 29th August 520 B.C.E.
(Hag 1:1), and ending on the 24th day of Chislev, the ninth month, therefore,
according to the same computation, December 18th of that year (2:20).[9] This

---

8. Arvid Kapelrud, "Temple Building, A Task for Gods and Kings," *Or* 32 (1963) 56-62;
Richard S. Ellis, *Foundation Deposits in Ancient Mesopotamia* (New Haven: Yale University
Press, 1968) 20-26; David L. Petersen, "Zerubbabel and Jerusalem Temple Reconstruction,"
CBQ 36 (1974) 366-72; Antti Laato, "Zechariah 4,6b-10a and the Akkadian royal building in-
scriptions," *ZAW* 106 (1994) 53-69.

9. It will be seen that there is some dislocation in the sequence of discourses. Computation of dates follows Richard A. Parker and Waldo H. Dubberstein, *Babylonian Chronology
626 B.C. to A.D. 45* (Brown University Studies 19; Providence: Brown University, 1956) 15-17,

last was the date on which the prophet, addressing Zerubbabel, predicted a convulsive event of cosmic dimensions to take place in the near future which would result in the overthrow of the current world order, meaning in the first place the Persian Empire, and would lead to Zerubbabel entering into his inheritance and ascending the throne as scion of the Davidic line (Hag 2:20-23). Zerubbabel therefore held office in Judah at least through the autumn and early winter of 520, a conclusion consistent with information given in the Aramaic section of Ezra-Nehemiah (Ezra 5:1-2) and the oracular utterances of Zechariah (Zech 4:6-10). In all these texts he is associated with the high priest Jeshua/Joshua ben Jehozadak in the task of rebuilding the temple with the support of Haggai, Zechariah, and no doubt other prophets.

A brief summary of these five discourses will be helpful. In the first (1:1-11), delivered August 29th 520 B.C.E., the prophet rejects the popular view that the time was not ripe for rebuilding the temple (1:2). This opinion may simply imply that circumstances were not seen to be propitious either in view of the drought and the consequently bad economic situation to which Haggai alludes in his response, or as a matter of political expediency, coming so soon after the brutal suppression by Darius of numerous revolts throughout the empire. Some may also have been indifferent or hostile to the project on account of their attachment to alternative cults or cult centers.[10] Some, again, may have opposed the rebuilding on theological grounds, either because the time of divine anger announced by prophetic revelation had not yet run its course,[11] or on account of the convic-

---

but allowance should be made for a margin of error of a few days in converting to the Gregorian calendar. For a critique of Elias Bickerman's argument for the year 521 rather than 520 in "La seconde année de Darius," *RB* 88 (1981) 23-28, see Hans Walter Wolff, *Haggai*, trans. Margaret Kohl (Minneapolis: Augsburg, 1988) 74-76.

10. For the practice of such cults in the postexilic period, see Isa 57:3-13; 65:1-7, 11-12; 66:17. For the hypothesis of the revival of the ancient Bethel sanctuary after the destruction of the Jerusalem temple, see my "Bethel in the Neo-Babylonian Period," in *Judah and the Judeans in the Neo-Babylonian Period,* ed. Oded Lipschits and Joseph Blenkinsopp (Winona Lake: Eisenbrauns, 2003) 93-107.

11. Hag 1:2; cf. Zech 1:12 ("these seventy years") with reference to Jer 25:11-12 or 29:10. If the seventy-year period was thought to begin with the destruction of the temple in 586 B.C.E., the right time, taking account of the date of Haggai's activity, would be only four years in the future, in which case the seventy years of the divine anger would end with the completion of the rebuilding of the temple in 516, which is the date assigned to that event in Ezra 6:15. On the "seventy years" topos, see Charles Whitley, "The Term Seventy Years Captivity," *VT* 4 (1954) 60-72; Avigdor Orr, "The Seventy Years of Babylon," *VT* 6 (1956) 304-6; Peter R. Ackroyd, "Two Old Testament Historical Problems of the Early Persian Period," *JNES* 17 (1958) 23-27; *Exile and Restoration* (London: SCM, 1968) 239-42.

tion that the right time could only be the messianic age which lay in an unknown future. Haggai's answer to this objection is that the present unsatisfactory situation — drought, bad harvests, inflation, low wages and high prices for the many contrasted with luxurious living for the few — will change dramatically once the temple is rebuilt and its worship restored (Hag 1:4-11). The editor of this first address concludes by recording how Zerubbabel, Joshua and "the remnant of the people" responded to the prophet's admonition by beginning work on the temple site (1:12-14).

The chronology of the second discourse (1:15a + 2:15-19),[12] is somewhat confusing. The initial date in Hag 1:15a, the 24th of Elul, the sixth month, corresponding to September 21 520 B.C.E., places it three weeks after the first admonition and suggests that the work of rebuilding, or at least clearing the site, had made some progress. It is nonetheless apparent that the decisive moment, the passage from misery to well-being, from curse to blessing, is the laying of the foundation stone of the rebuilt temple, always an event of deep symbolic significance (Hag 2:15a, 18b-19). The precise date of this turning point — the twenty-fourth day of the ninth month (Chislev), corresponding to December 18, 520 B.C.E. in the Gregorian calendar — is added shortly afterwards in what is almost certainly an interpolation (2:18).[13] The event itself is anticipated in the third discourse (1:15b–2:9) delivered on the 21st of Tishri, October 17, and therefore coincident with the festival of Sukkoth.[14] Addressing Zerubbabel the governor, Jeshua the high priest-designate, and "the remnant of the people,"[15] the

---

12. On the arguments for attaching 2:15-19 to 1:15a and the textual problems of this confusing discourse, see Wolff, *Haggai*, 57-68.

13. On *yussad hêkal YHWH*, Hag 2:18, as referring to the laying of the foundation stone of the rebuilt temple, see Rudolf Mosis, "*yāsad*," *TDOT* 6 (1990) 109-21. Anthony Gelston, "The Foundations of the Second Temple," *VT* 16 (1966) 232-35, rightly points out that the verbal stem *yāsad* has a broader semantic range than laying the foundations of a building and that the temple would not have had to be rebuilt from the foundations up, but he neglects the ritual aspect of the work, the recovery of the foundation stone or foundation deposit of the previous temple, and the ceremonial laying of the first stone or brick. This will come up again for discussion at a later point.

14. For detailed discussion of this passage, see Wim A. M. Beuken, *Haggai — Sacharja 1–8: Studien zur Überlieferungsgeschichte der frühnachexilischen Prophetie* (SSN 10; Assen: Van Gorcum, 1967) 49-64; Wilhelm Rudolph, *Haggai — Sacharja 1–8 — Sacharja 9–14 — Maleachi* (KAT 13/4; Gütersloh: Mohn, 1976) 40-44; David L. Petersen, *Haggai and Zechariah 1–8* (OTL; Philadelphia: Westminster, 1984) 60-70; Wolff, *Haggai*, 69-86.

15. This term, *šĕʾērît hāʿām*, also at Hag 1:12, 14; Zech 8:6, 11, 12; Neh 7:71, carries a strong prophetic resonance as referring to Diaspora Jews associated with Zerubbabel and Joshua, both of diasporic origin.

prophet invites those old enough to have seen Solomon's temple, destroyed sixty-six years earlier, to compare that splendid structure with the miserable heap of ruins now before them. The scene is re-created in Ezra 3:12-13, set however in the reign of Cyrus, with many of the leading priests, Levites and laity unable to hold back their tears. Haggai promises that, appearances to the contrary notwithstanding, the second temple will be more splendid than the first. There is shortly to take place an event of catastrophic cosmic dimensions which will transform not only the natural world but the political scene. The outcome will be tribute from the nations of the world, a temple more glorious than its predecessor and, as a direct consequence, well-being for the land and its people, a vision of the future inspired by traditional prophetic ideas about "the Day of Yahweh" and a glorious future for Jerusalem, the latter especially prominent in Isaiah.

The date of the fourth discourse, the 24th of the ninth month (Chislev), therefore approximately 18 December 520, is identical with that of the climactic proclamation made to Zerubbabel alone about the coming event and the part he was destined to play in it. In this fourth discourse (2:10-14), Haggai is told to request a ruling on the laws of ritual purity from the priests, one of whose duties was to establish, maintain, and explain distinctions between the holy or consecrated and profane and between the ritually clean and unclean (Lev 10:10-11). The request is couched in the form of two case histories. The first makes the point that indirect contact between consecrated food and ordinary foodstuffs does not affect the ritual status of the latter. The second, more relevant to the situation, purports to demonstrate that any contact of such foodstuffs with a corpse-contaminated person infects the food and renders it unclean and therefore unsuitable as sacrificial material. The main problem for the reader arises from the recondite way in which Haggai applies these *responsa* to the situation at hand: "So it is with this people and so it is with this nation in my presence, and so it is with everything they do; what they offer there is unclean." The issue, therefore, is the ritual status of the religious activities ("everything they do") of "this people, this nation," and of the sacrifices that they offer *there*, in an unnamed place other than the location of the prophet. That the people and nation in question refer to the settler population in and around Samaria has often been argued, or at least restated, since it was proposed by J. W. Rothstein more than a century ago.[16] This hypothesis seemed to be

---

16. Johann W. Rothstein, *Juden und Samaritaner: Die grundlegende Scheidung von Judentum und Heidentum* (BWANT 3; Leipzig: Hinrich, 1908); adopted by Beuken, *Haggai*

supported by the account in Ezra 4:1-5 of the offer of assistance in rebuilding the Jerusalem temple extended by settlers in the former kingdom of Samaria and rejected by Zerubbabel, Joshua, and the tribal chiefs. But this account was composed long after the time of Haggai and is set during the reign of Cyrus rather than Darius. The wording "this people, this nation" rather than "that people, that nation" would also more naturally refer to the indigenous Judean population castigated in 1:1-11 and referred to as "this people" in the opening discourse (Hag 1:2). Here and elsewhere — for example, where Isaiah denounces the obtuseness of "this people," meaning his contemporaries (Isa 6:9) — the expression has an unmistakably dismissive sound. In the present context "this people" stands in contrast to "the remnant of the people," those who had survived the trial of exile and returned from the Babylonian Diaspora with the goal of rebuilding the temple and renewing its interrupted cult.

A Cosmic Upheaval and the Reign of Zerubbabel Foretold

Haggai's climactic fifth discourse (Hag 2:20-23) reads as follows:

> On the twenty-fourth day of the month the word of Yahweh came to Haggai a second time: "Give the following message to Zerubbabel, governor of Judah: 'I am about to shake the heavens and the earth. I shall overthrow the throne of kingdoms and destroy the power of the kingdoms of the nations. I shall overthrow chariots and their riders, and horses and their riders will fall by the sword of their comrades. On that day [Word of Yahweh of the hosts] I will take you, Zerubbabel, son of Shealtiel, my servant [word of Yahweh] and wear you as my signet ring, for it is you that I have chosen [Word of Yahweh of the hosts].'"

It consists in two distinct but connected statements (vv. 20-22 and 23), the second introduced with the familiar prophetic formula "on that day." It bears the same date as the fourth (Hag 2:10), that is, December 18th of the year 520 B.C.E. The month is missing, but the addition of "a second time" removes any ambiguity. It is addressed to Zerubbabel alone, which sug-

---

— *Sacharja 1-8*, 64-77; Rudolph, *Haggai — Sacharja 1-8 — Sacharja 9-14 — Maleachi*, 44-50, and many others more recently.

gests that the revelation was passed on in secret, no doubt for reasons of political expediency, since the "overthrow of the throne of kingdoms" could refer only to the collapse of the Persian Empire under Darius. The first of the two statements (2:21-22) repeats the prediction in the third discourse of an imminent event of cosmic proportions which will have an immediate and drastic effect at the level of international affairs. The main difference is that in Hag 2:6-9 the restored temple is to be the beneficiary of the predicted cosmic and political upheaval, whereas in 2:20-23 the upheaval will lead to the restoration of the national dynasty in the person of Zerubbabel.

This depiction of the cataclysm to come is cast in traditional theophanic language, including images suggestive of devastating meteorological and tectonic events, the most notable biblical paradigm being the destruction of Sodom and Gomorrah. The overturning of chariots, horses, and their riders brings to mind the Song of Miriam at the Papyrus Sea (Exod 15:21), and the self-destruction of the panicked enemy is a familiar "holy war" topos (e.g., Judg 7:22; Ezek 38:21; Zech 14:13). The overturning the throne of kingdoms and destroying the power of the realms of the nations describes fairly succinctly what Darius had been doing during the previous two years in suppressing insurrections over a vast area, including two in Babylon.

The oracle addressed directly to Zerubbabel, Yahweh's servant, consists in three statements: I shall take you; I shall wear you as a signet ring; and I have chosen you for a special task. The language is deliberately reminiscent of the initial election of David, taken from the pasture to serve Yahweh as ruler of Israel:

> Now this is what you must say to my servant David: Thus says Yahweh of the hosts: I took you from the pastureland, from tending the sheep, to be leader over my people, over Israel. (2 Sam 7:8)

> He chose his servant David, and took him from the sheepfolds.
> (Ps 78:70)

> I have exalted one chosen from the people,
> I have found my servant David,
> With my holy oil I have anointed him.
> (Ps 89:20b-21[Eng 19b-20])

The title "servant" *('ebed)* is conferred on David and his descendants in Nathan's dynastic oracle (2 Sam 7:1-29) and Solomon's prayer at the dedication of the temple (1 Kgs 8:24-26, 66).[17] When set over against Deutero-Isaiah's identification of Cyrus as Yahweh's servant (Isa 42:1) and anointed one (45:1), this designation of Zerubbabel as servant highlights a fundamental difference in theologically based attitudes to imperial power.

Yahweh will also wear Zerubbabel like a signet ring *(ḥôtām)*, perhaps on a finger of his right hand (Jer 22:24). The signet ring was an essential royal accessory worn either on a finger or hanging round the neck. It contained a precious stone carved by a gem cutter with the owner's name or insignia. It could then serve as a seal stamped on wet clay and as a symbol of authority used for authorizing decrees, letters, and documents in general. We may recall how Jezebel made use of Ahab's signet ring to authorize the murder of Naboth and secure his property (1 Kgs 21:8). The immediate reference in Haggai's fifth and last discourse is to Jeremiah's disavowal of Jehoiachin, grandson of Josiah (Jer 22:24-27):[18]

> By my life, Yahweh says, even though you, Conyahu son of Jehoiakim king of Judah, are the signet ring on the finger of my right hand, I shall pull it off from there and hand you over to those who are seeking to kill you, to those you fear, Nebuchadnezzar king of Babylon and the Chaldeans. Together with the mother who gave you birth, I shall thrust you into another country, one in which neither of you was born, and there both of you will die. You will never come back to the land to which you long to return.

Haggai's designation of Zerubbabel, Jehoiachin's grandson, as the signet ring worn by Yahweh, turns the prophetic curse on Jehoiachin and the queen mother into a blessing on their descendant. At the same time, it implicitly repudiates the theological politics of Jeremiah and his patrons, influential members of the prominent Shaphanid family including Gedaliah, a predecessor of Zerubbabel as overseer of the province, who died at the hands of an assassin.

---

17. Also in many other places including 1 Kgs 11:29-39 (the prophet Ahijah to Jeroboam); Jer 33:21-22, 26; Ezek 34:23; 37:24-25; Ps 78:70; 89:4(Eng 3); 132:10.

18. The Hebrew text begins and ends in the third person inconsistently with the rest of the passage. This version follows REB in using second person throughout.

Zerubbabel and the Crisis of the Persian Empire

After the death of Cyrus II in the autumn of 530 B.C.E., Cambyses II, his son and successor, greatly expanded the extent of the empire with the conquest of Egypt and the lands dependent on it, including Cyrene (Libya) and Cyprus. After Cambyses' death en route to Persia in 520, the struggle for succession between his brother Bardiya and Darius, the latter belonging to the cadet branch of the royal family, resulted in the seizure of the throne by Darius. The obscure course of events leading to his usurpation, narrated in the overtly propagandistic Bisitun (Behistun) Inscription of Darius and in novelistic fashion in Herodotus 3:61-88, was followed almost immediately by revolts throughout the empire which Darius succeeded in suppressing only after almost two years (autumn 522 to spring 520) of incessant warfare. Judging by the relatively lengthy account in the trilingual Bisitun rock inscription (Old Persian version) and the fact that in this instance Darius himself took the lead against the rebels, the most serious of the numerous insurrections following on his usurpation of the throne was the Babylonian revolt under Nidintu-Bēl who claimed to be son of Nabonidus and legitimate heir to Nebuchadnezzar II.[19] After the revolt was suppressed and Nidintu-Bēl put to death in December 522, Darius remained in Babylon until early in the following summer, thus emphasizing the serious threat which the city still presented. Babylon would, in fact, continue to be a thorn in the side of successive Achaemenid rulers including a major revolt under Xerxes. In the autumn of 521, barely two months after Darius had left the city, another insurgent named Arkha (Old Persian Arxa), reputed to be of Armenian extraction (Bisitun IV 28-29), raised the standard of revolt in southern Mesopotamia.[20] The revolt spread to the north, where Arkha was crowned in Babylon as, in effect, Nebuchadnezzar IV. It would not be surprising if *ebernāri*, the Transeuphrates region including Judah, was affected by this serious challenge to Darius's authority. In his *History of the Persian Empire*, Albert Olmstead argued that Judah would have been seriously compromised by the Babylonian revolt in the eyes of Darius simply on account of its being in the same Babylon-Trans-Euphrates satrapy; Darius therefore appointed Zerub-

---

19. Bisitun I 77–II 5; Herodotus (*Hist.* 3:150-60), whose account of a nineteen-month-long siege of Babylon and the remarkable way in which it was concluded strains credibility. He may, in addition, have conflated the two Babylonian rebellions.

20. Cuneiform texts dated to his reign, from late August and early September 521, have come to light in southern Mesopotamia. See Amélie Kuhrt in *CAH*, 2nd ed., 4, ed. John Boardman *et al.* (1988) 129-30.

babel, resident at the imperial court, as governor to minimize the risk of insurrection. Not in itself implausible, the hypothesis however lacks evidence.[21] At any rate, the revolt was suppressed by the Persian commander Intaphernes towards the end of 521, and Arkha was captured and executed.

It is against this bare outline of the critical early years of the reign of Darius that we have to reconstruct the course of events in Judah and the role of Zerubbabel. In doing so, our only recourse is the information extracted from contemporary or near-contemporary material in Haggai and Zechariah 1–8 (Proto-Zechariah). Zechariah's prophetic activity dates from some time in late October or early November 520 B.C.E. (Zech 1:1) at least until the last date in the collection, which corresponds to 7 December in the fourth year of Darius I, therefore 518 (7:1). Haggai had therefore been active for two or three months before Zechariah's earliest dated discourse. The first in the series of visions in Zechariah 1–8 carries a date corresponding in the Gregorian calendar to 15 February 519 (1:7). Since none of the other visions is dated, this is most likely meant to apply to the entire series. The visions came therefore rather less than two months after Haggai's prediction of the great upheaval and the designation of Zerubbabel as dynastic ruler of Judah (Hag 2:20-23). We shall bear in mind the possibility of a connection between this prediction and the visions of Zechariah.

The incidence of the introductory formula ("I looked up and saw" or some variation), together with the bracketing of the series between Zech 1:7-17 at the beginning and 6:1-8 at the end, both of which deal with patrols, suggests a sixfold rather than eightfold series, the more common calculation in the commentary *catena*:[22]

1:7-17	Four horsemen report on their patrol
2:1-4 (Eng 1:18-21)	Four horns and four blacksmiths
2:5-9 (2:1-5)	The man with the measuring line
5:1-4	The flying scroll

21. Albert T. Olmstead, *History of the Persian Empire: Achaemenid Period* (Chicago: University of Chicago Press, 1948) 135-41. Olmstead's reconstruction of the history as it affected Judah at that time, while often insightful, is in some respects out of date and should be read alongside more recent studies.

22. Otto Eissfeldt, *The Old Testament: An Introduction* (New York: Harper & Row, 1965) 430; Hinckley G. Mitchell, "Haggai, Zechariah," in Mitchell, J. M. Powis Smith, and Julius A. Bewer, *A Critical and Exegetical Commentary on Haggai, Zechariah, Malachi, Jonah* (ICC; New York: Scribner, 1912) 84; Beuken, *Haggai-Sacharja 1–8,* 115-18; Rudolph, *Haggai — Sacharja 1–8 — Sacharja 9–14 — Maleachi,* 71-126, and many others.

5:5-11	The female figurine in a basket
6:1-8	Four charioteers going out on patrol

All open in the same formulaic way — "I raised my eyes and saw" — except the first, which begins "in the night I saw . . .," and the fifth, where the *angelus interpres* uses an adapted form — "raise your eyes and see." This opening formula is not found elsewhere in chs. 1–8. An interesting feature of the visions is the interactivity between the seer and characters in the visions. In the first, the patrols report that the whole earth is at peace. In the historical context this means that the rebellious provinces of the Persian Empire had been "pacified" by Darius — not good news for Judah and Jerusalem, or at least not for those Judeans who saw in the numerous revolts of the previous two years an opportunity for the restoration of national identity and the native dynasty. The complaint of the angel in the vision on hearing the report, coming as it did only two months after Haggai's prediction, can therefore be read as a lament for the nonfulfillment of that prophecy. The lament is answered by an assurance of future fulfillment, including a prediction that the temple will be rebuilt. As for the rest of the night visions, it will suffice for the present purpose to say that, in different ways and with widely different imagery, they repeat and reinforce this reassurance about an eventual positive outcome.[23]

The close links between Haggai and Zechariah 1–8, detectable in the first vision of the series, are even more apparent in passages intermediate between the visions in which Zerubbabel is either named (Zech 4:6-10) or referred to indirectly. Unfortunately, these passages, of crucial importance for understanding Zerubbabel's role, carry no date and speak in an arcane symbolic code which has not proved easy to decrypt. The attempt to do so which follows is therefore necessarily hypothetical, and space permits only a presentation in broad outline. The passages in question are the following:

An urgent summons to leave Babylon (Zech 2:10-13[Eng 6-9])
Joshua, high priest designate, and the presentation of "Branch" (3:1-8, 9b-10)

23. In the final vision (6:1-8) it is unclear what meaning to attach to the sentence *hēnîḥû ʾet-rûḥî bĕʾereṣ ṣāpôn* (v. 8), whether in the sense that Yahweh's anger at Babylon has now been assuaged (cf. Ezek 5:13; 16:42), therefore something like "they have assuaged my spirit in the north country," or in the sense that Yahweh's spirit is now present there and its presence assures a positive outcome. The coronation scene which follows (Zech 6:9-15), made possible by arrivals from "the north country," i.e., Babylon, supports a preference for the latter.

The stone with seven eyes (3:9a; 4:4-5, 10b, 6-10a)
The menorah and the two olive trees (4:1-3, 11-14)
The secret coronation of "Branch" (6:9-15)

We shall deal with these in turn.

An Urgent Summons to Leave Babylon (Zechariah 2:10-13[6-9])

The seer exhorts the Jewish Diaspora community in Babylon to leave the city, and the urgency of the message is reinforced by a brief oracle predicting an imminent catastrophic event which will bring about a radical redistribution of power on the political scene. Like the parallel prediction in Hag 2:20-23, this event will spell disaster for hostile nations and a change of fortune for Judah. It therefore calls for Judean expatriates to leave Babylon without delay. The passage reads as follows (later interpolations in parentheses):

> Away, away, flee from the north country! {Word of Yahweh.}
> [I scattered you abroad like the four winds of the sky;
>   Word of Yahweh.]
> Away, people of Zion! Escape, you who dwell in Babylon!
> For this is what Yahweh of the hosts has said [after the glory had
> sent me] concerning the nations which have plundered you [for
> whoever touches you touches the apple of his eye]: "I wave my hand
> over them; they will be plundered by those they had enslaved."
> Then you will know that Yahweh of the hosts has sent me.

Strictly speaking, the oracle occurs only in 2:13(Eng 9), the penultimate sentence in inverted commas. The lead-up to it shows signs of heavy editing, but the essential lines are clear. The expatriate Judean community in Babylon[24] is given an oracle warning of an imminent divine intervention, the consequences of which they are to escape by emigrating to Judah. The return to Zion will coincide with a radical reversal of fortunes and redistri-

---

24. On the term "the north country," see W. H. Schmidt, "ṣāpôn," *TLOT* 3 (1997) 1093-98. In spite of the parallelism between the north country in v. 10(6) and Babylon in v. 11(7), the expression *bat-bābel*, lit., "daughter Babylon," is of a type conventionally designating a city, e.g., Sidon (Isa. 23:12), Dibon (Jer. 48:18), and of course Jerusalem/Zion. The city can also stand for the nation as a whole.

bution of power, and when this happens the authority of the prophetic word will be confirmed.

The identification of scribal additions, indicated above, is to some extent speculative, but supported by what is known about the form and structure of this kind of prophetic saying, and even more so by evident syntactic disjunctions and irregularities. The first addition — "I scattered them abroad to the four winds of the sky" — intrudes between the parallel imperatives which in this type of saying always follow immediately one after the other.[25] In addition, the statement explains not why they should leave but how they got there in the first place.[26] The next insertion has caused the commentators no end of trouble and has given rise to numerous hypotheses.[27] Perhaps the glossator, prompted by the mention of the divine glory in the saying immediately preceding (2:9b[Eng 5b]), wanted to make the point that the prophetic mission originated in the presence of the same glory witnessed by Ezekiel in the vision of the chariot-throne (Ezek 1:28; 3:23; 10:4). According to Hag 2:7, this glory will fill the temple once it is completed. Absent these three words, the lead-up to the actual oracle continues smoothly by identifying those against whom the imminent intervention of Yahweh will be directed, namely, the nations which have plundered Judah in the past and continued to do so at the time the or-

---

25. Examples: Isa. 48:20; 52:11; 62:10; Jer. 50:8; 51:6, 45. Robert Bach, *Die Aufforderungen zur Flucht und zum Kampf im alttestamentlichen Prophetenspruch* (WMANT 9; Neukirchen-Vluyn: Neukirchener, 1962) 19, assigns our passage to the genre "summons to flight or fight," but this does not correspond to the context of the passage: those addressed here are not summoned to battle or to flee after defeat. See further on this point, Beuken, *Haggai — Sacharja 1-8*, 317-19.

26. LXX "I will gather you from the four winds of the sky," is quite different from MT. The verb *prś* more commonly means "spread out" (wings, Jer 48:40; 49:22; sails, Isa 33:23; fishing nets, Isa 19:8) rather than "scatter," but see Ps 68:15(Eng 14), "when Shaddai scatters kings," and Ezek 17:21, "the survivors of Zedekiah's army shall be scattered to all the winds," both with the same verb. Since the insertion makes sense as it stands, it is probably better not to emend *kĕʾarbaʿ* to *lĕʾarbaʿ*, implying that the deportees were dispersed to all points of the compass, as in Jer 49:36: "I will scatter them (Elamites) to all these winds."

27. Including Mitchell, *Haggai, Zechariah*, 141, who took "glory" to refer to the three visions immediately preceding; Ernst Sellin, *Das Zwölfprophetenbuch übersetzt und erklärt* (KAT 12; 3rd ed., Leipzig: Scholl, 1930) 491-92, who emended *ʾahar* to *ʾăšer* ("whose glory sent me"); Theodorus C. Vriezen, "Two Old Cruces," *OtSt* 5 (1948) 88-91, who read *ʾahar kābôd* as an editorial note indicating that v. 12 should follow v. 9. Robert B. Y. Scott, "Secondary Meanings of אַחַר," *JTS* 50 (1949) 178-79, translated *ʾahar* "with" instead of "after" as in Ps 73:24; Eccl 12:2. Joyce Baldwin, *Haggai, Zechariah, Malachi* (TOTC; Downers Grove: IVP, 1972) 109, took *kābôd* in the alternative sense of "weight" and translated "with insistence."

acle was delivered. There is one final insertion — "Whoever touches you touches the apple of his eye" — which, unlike the rest of the saying, is not in divine *oratio recta*, and therefore is not part of the oracle.[28] Perhaps this last addition was suggested by nothing more than assonance between *bĕbābat* and *bat-bābel* in the previous verse.

In its reconstructed original form, therefore, the prophetic injunction reinforced by the oracular prediction opens with the call for attention, perhaps modeled on an earlier summons in Isa 52:11 to leave the same city before its fall to the Persians and their allies about two decades earlier. The summons in Zech 2:10-13(6-9) is not dated, but belongs probably within the chronological parameters of Haggai and Zechariah 1–8, the period from August 520 in the second regnal year of Darius I Hystaspes (Hag 1:1) to December 518 in the fourth regnal year of the same monarch (Zech 7:1).[29] This was a time of turmoil for Jewish communities in Judah and abroad. Prophetic-eschatological agitation in Judah and the eastern Diaspora focused on aspirations for the rebuilding of the temple, the resumption of its cult, and the restoration of the native dynasty in the person of Zerubbabel. Haggai's announcement of an imminent upheaval which would overturn the existing political order, proclaimed on 18 December 520 (Hag 2:20-23), could have reached the Babylonian expatriate community, which had its own history of nationalistic-prophetic protest, in the following spring. Disseminated in Babylon and elsewhere, it would have reinforced similar predictions followed by calls to return to Judah of the kind represented by Zech 2:10-13(6-9).

The period covered by the dates in Haggai and Zechariah 1–8, from

---

28. Unless one takes *ʿênô* ("his eye") as *reverential tiqqun* for *ʿênî* ("my eye"; cf. Vulgate: *pupillam oculi mei*). On the expression, see Edward Robertson, "The Apple of the Eye in the Masoretic Text," *JTS* 38 (1937) 56-59. Use of the hapax legomenon *bābâ* rather than *ʾišôn* for the pupil of the eye (Deut 32:10; Ps 17:8; Prov 7:2, 9) may have been intended as a punning and presumably prejudicial allusion to *bat-bābel*, but the point escapes us. Another suggestion is T. J. Finley, "The Apple of His Eye *(bābat ʿênô)* in Zechariah ii 12," *VT* 38 (1988) 337-38.

29. Darius seized power by deposing and murdering Bardiya (Gaumata) in September 522 B.C.E., hence the dating sequence in Haggai — Zechariah 1–8 begins towards the end of Darius's second regnal year. For a chronological table of events during the period 522-518, see M. A. Dandamaev, *Persien unter den ersten Achämeniden (6. Jh. v. Chr.)* (Wiesbaden: Reichert, 1976) 255-56; *A Political History of the Achaemenid Empire*, trans. W. J. Vogelsang (Leiden: Brill, 1989) 103-40; Pierre Briant, *Histoire de l'Empire perse de Cyrus à Alexandre* (Paris: Fayard, 1996) 1:119-50; Eng. trans. *From Cyrus to Alexander: A History of the Persian Empire*, trans. Peter T. Daniels (Winona Lake: Eisenbrauns, 2002) 107-38.

August 520 to December 518 B.C.E., is poorly documented and the chronology sometimes uncertain. In the first vision dated to February 519, the horse patrols sent out to range over the earth reported that "the whole world is quiet and at peace" (1:10-11), in agreement with Darius's account of the pacification of rebellious provinces and suppression of local dynasties in the Bisitun Inscription. It will be obvious, however, that this document, no less than the Cyrus Cylinder, is propagandistic. It makes no mention of defeats or setbacks which could not have been lacking, witness the fact that several of the centers of rebellion — Armenia, Media, Elam, Babylon, especially Babylon — revolted more than once. It would therefore not be surprising if the fires had not all been put out by the time the inscription and sculpture had been carved out of the side of the Bisitun (Behistun, Bagastana) mountain, sometime in 521. Two later rebellions, led respectively by Atamaita of Elam and Skunkha of the Saka people of Central Asia, in fact required the addition of a fifth column to the Bisitun Inscription, and a ninth figure at the end of the line of captives had to be hacked out of the rock.[30] The inscription also records the suppression of a revolt in Egypt, listed after the defeat of Nidintu-Bēl (col. II ll. 5-8), but of uncertain date. Later still, Darius mandated the codification of Egyptian laws, an important contribution to pacification.[31] These notices show that unrest continued at least sporadically into 519, and we know that Darius was not in a position to carry out his reorganization of the empire until the following year. In sum: we do not have the means to place the prophetic summons to leave Babylon and the Zerubbabel episode precisely within contemporary events. We can, however, begin to view it within the context of a broadly based movement of nationalist-dynastic resistance to empire, which seems to have been especially intense within the Babylonian-Trans-Euphratene satrapy, to which Judah belonged, during the crucial early years of the reign of Darius I.

30. The sculpture accompanying the inscription depicts Darius with his foot on Gaumata's stomach and facing him, roped together at the neck, nine of the defeated insurgents. The last, easily recognized by the Scythian pointed cap, is Skunkha, the one added after the original sculpture had been completed. The inscription accompanying the sculpture identifies the second-last as Frada of Margiana (cf. IV. 24-25) and the third-last as Arkha the Armenian, leader of the second Babylonian insurrection (cf. IV. 29-30).

31. Dandamaev, *A Political History of the Achaemenid Empire*, 141-46. More on Darius's activities in Egypt in Georges Posener, *La première domination perse en Égypte* (Cairo: Institut français d'archéologie orientale, 1936) 1-16, 178-90; Richard A. Parker, "Darius and His Egyptian Campaign," *AJSL* 58 (1941) 373-77; George G. Cameron, "Darius, Egypt, and 'the Lands beyond the Sea,'" *JNES* 2 (1943) 307-13; Edda Bresciani, "Egypt, Persian satrapy," in *CHJ*, 1: *Introduction; The Persian Period* (1984), 358-72.

Joshua, High Priest Designate, and the Presentation of "Branch" (Zechariah 3:1-8, 9b-10)

Practically all commentators agree that the order in which events are recorded in Zechariah chs. 3 and 4 has undergone dislocation and rearrangement, but there is disagreement as to the original order. I have followed with some minor modifications the rearrangement of the text in REB, which seems to me to keep to the narrative logic throughout these two chapters. But even if some other arrangement is preferred, this approach will at least serve to isolate and concentrate our attention on the separate but interconnected narrative themes embedded in these chapters. This second intercalatory episode (Zech 3:1-8) begins when the angel admits the seer to the unfolding drama.[32] Zechariah asks questions about what he sees, gets answers from the angel-guide within the drama,[33] and on one occasion has to be aroused from his catatonic state in order to continue observing and recording what he sees (Zech 4:1). Though these scenes are formally different from the vision sequence, they are characterized by the same level of interactivity. The present scene also has themes and features in common with the throne vision of Isaiah (Isa 6:1-13): ritual uncleanness, a purification ritual, the removal of guilt, and, possibly, the participation of the prophet in the proceedings.

The scenario is, however, a court of law rather than the heavenly throne room of Isaiah's vision. Joshua, high priest designate, is discovered facing the angel of Yahweh as judge, and the prosecutor, the satan, is accusing him — of what, we are not told. It appears, in fact, that the seer has been admitted as observer only towards the end of the trial, but in time to hear the case dismissed by the judge on the grounds that the defendant is "a brand snatched from the fire." This image, borrowed from Amos (Amos 4:11), compares survival of exile in a land polluted with idolatry with passing through fire, recalling the description of the escape from Egypt as being pulled out of the iron furnace (Deut 4:20; 1 Kgs 8:51; Jer 11:4). The accusation is not stated. It is possible that Joshua had been involved in non-Yahwistic cults in Babylonia. The trial now over, there follows the investi-

---

32. Christian Jeremias, *Die Nachtgesichte des Sacharja* (FRLANT 117; Göttingen: Vandenhoeck & Ruprecht, 1977) 201-2, 223, points out the distinctive character of the *Grundschema* of Zech 3:1-7 but leaves it in the widely accepted eight-vision series.

33. According to MT Zech 3:5, he becomes an actor in the unfolding drama by proposing that they put a turban on Joshua's head, though it is also possible that *wā'ōmar* should either be emended to third person or omitted with LXX, Syriac, and Vulgate.

ture of Joshua and his installation in office as the high priest designate of the future temple. His filthy rags are removed, he is clothed in festal vestments,[34] and a clean turban is placed on his head in keeping with the traditional priestly dress code (Exod 28:4; 39:28). The admonition which follows (3:6-7), delivered by the angel, may correspond to a regular feature of the rite of installation into the office of the high priesthood. Joshua thus officially assumes the office of full control of the temple and its precincts, a privilege contingent on his faithful adherence to the high moral standards associated with that office and his conscientious discharge of the duties of the high priesthood. On this condition, he will have access among "those standing here," meaning the angelic beings in attendance on Yahweh (vv. 4 and 5) as distinct from Joshua's priestly associates who are seated (v. 8). This is not simply access to the heavenly court, but to the divine presence in the inner sanctum of the temple which he will enter once a year on behalf of the entire community, a unique prerogative of the high priest (Exod 30:10; Lev 16:17-19).[35]

The following statement is addressed to Joshua and his priestly associates seated around him who are described as "an omen of things to come." An omen can, of course, portend something unwelcome or disastrous (e.g., Deut 28:46), but this can hardly be the case in the present context. Perhaps the closest parallel is the reference in Isa 8:18 to Isaiah's children who are "signs and portents in Israel." The children in question, Shear Yashub and Maher-shalal-hash-baz (Isa 7:3; 8:1),[36] are given symbolic names which, while insinuating present misfortune, point to eventual good fortune. In the scene here described, the good fortune promised is

---

34. David Winton Thomas, "A Note on *mhlswt* in Zechariah 3:4," *JTS* 33 (1931-1932) 279-80, suggested that the Hebrew term, which appears only here and at Isa 3:22 where it refers to festal robes (NRSV) or fine dresses (REB) worn by women, is to be understood, on the basis of Arabic and Akkadian cognates, as "ritually pure garments." See also Meyers and Meyers, *Haggai, Zechariah 1-8*, 190. Independently of this linguistic point, the ceremony includes a frequent feature of purification rituals, i.e., the changing or washing of garments (cf. Gen 35:2; Lev 14:8-9; Num 8:21).

35. On the rare term *maḥălāṣôt*, see Rudolph, *Haggai — Sacharja 1-8 — Sacharja 9-14 — Maleachi*, 93. Rudolph, however, holds that the assurance of a hearing on those occasions when the high priest presents the community's concerns to God has taken the place of the unique prerogative of entry into the holy of holies (p. 97). But why must we have to choose between these priestly functions?

36. The reference is not to disciples of the prophet, as Bernhard Duhm proposed in *Das Buch Jesaja* (HKAT 3/1; 4th ed., Göttingen: Vandenhoeck & Ruprecht, 1922) 85. Disciples are referred to as *bānîm* ("sons") but never as *yĕlādîm* ("children").

the restoration of temple worship beginning, as in Haggai (2:9, 18-19), with the dedication of the temple to be rebuilt.

The statement itself reads as follows: "I am about to bring my servant 'Branch' . . . and in a single day I shall wipe out the guilt of this land" (3:8b, 9b). The term *ṣemaḥ*, cognate with the verbal stem *ṣāmaḥ* ("sprout," "germinate"), refers to something growing from the ground. The translation "branch" is not very satisfactory, but no better term (shoot, sprout, slip, sprig, offshoot?) has been proposed. As an organic metaphor, *ṣemaḥ* takes its place with the range of terms indicating organic growth in the opening verse of the Isaian poem about the peaceful kingdom under an ideal ruler (Isa 11:1):

> A shoot *(ḥōṭer)* shall come out from the stump *(gēzaʿ)* of Jesse,
> and a branch *(nēṣer)* shall grow out of his roots *(šārāšâw)*.
>
> (NRSV)

Used as a code name, *ṣemaḥ* has therefore a certain congruity with the name Zerubbabel, derived from Akkadian *zēr bābili* ("seed of Babylon"), but its use here was most likely suggested by the "righteous branch" or "branch of righteousness" in Jeremiah, terms for the future ruler whose reign will bring justice, security, and salvation (Jer 23:5-6; 33:15). There can scarcely be any doubt that, in this statement to Joshua and his colleagues, *ṣemaḥ* refers to Zerubbabel, absent from the scene but closely associated with Joshua the high priest in all our sources. Moreover, "Branch" is the designated builder of the temple in Zech 6:12, and the same is said of Zerubbabel in Zech 4:9.[37]

The Stone with Seven Eyes (Zechariah 3:9a, 4:4-5, 10b, 6-10a)

The next scene, tentatively reconstructed, reads as follows:

> [3:9a]Here is the stone I have set before Joshua. On this one stone are seven eyes. I shall engrave its inscription. [Word of Yahweh of the hosts]. [4:4]I asked the angel who talked with me, "What are these, sir?"

---

37. The LXX translation of *ṣemaḥ* in Jer 23:5; Zech 3:8; 6:12 with *anatolē* makes the transition from an organic to an astronomical metaphor, i.e., from a plant rising from the soil to a star in its ascendancy. In that form, *anatolē* came to serve as a messianic title, as in Matt 2:2 (the star of the Magi) and Luke 1:78. Jerome in his Vulgate likewise translated *ṣemaḥ* in Zechariah as *Oriens*.

4:5The angel who talked with me replied, "Don't you know what these are?" "No, sir," I replied. 4:10b"These are the eyes of Yahweh which range over the whole earth." 4:6Then he said to me, "This is the word of Yahweh to Zerubbabel: 'Neither by violence nor by power but by my spirit' says Yahweh of the hosts.' 4:7Who are you, great mountain? Faced with Zerubbabel you will become a flat surface. He will bring out the stone of foundation amid shouts of 'Blessings, blessings on it!'" 4:8Then the word of Yahweh came to me: 4:9"The hands of Zerubbabel have laid the foundations of this house, and it is his hands that will finish it." Then you will acknowledge that Yahweh of the hosts sent me to you. 4:10Who were the ones who despised the day of small achievements? They will rejoice when they see the plummet in the hands of Zerubbabel.

One attempt to elucidate the far from smooth sequence of thought in this passage and, at the same time, justify the proposed rearrangement of the text, might begin with the prophet's request for an explanation of something and the angel's reply (4:4-5, 10b). The association in the reply between the eyes of Yahweh and Yahweh's surveillance or oversight ranging over the earth has suggested to authors both ancient and modern an analogy with the seven planets (lit., "wanderers") that range over the sky.[38] Many other proposals about the eyes on the stone have been advanced,[39] to which I may be permitted to add one more. The idea of eyes ranging over the earth may have been suggested by a category of agents employed by the imperial Achaemenid court known to Greek authors as "the eyes and ears of the king" or, more simply, "the eyes of the king" (*ophthalmoi basileōs*), perhaps corresponding to the Persian *spasaka*.[40] The function of

38. See esp. Hermann Gunkel, *Schöpfung und Chaos in Urzeit und Endzeit: Eine religionsgeschichtliche Untersuching über Gen. 1 und Ap. Jon 12* (Göttingen: Vandenhoeck & Ruprecht, 1895) 126-27; Eng. *Creation and Chaos in the Primeval Era and the Eschaton*, trans. K. William Whitney Jr. (BRS; Grand Rapids: Eerdmans, 2006) 85-86.

39. Some find a secondary meaning for *'ênayim* as "facets," as NRSV and Petersen, *Haggai and Zechariah 1-8*, 211-12. Edouard Lipiński, "Recherches sur le livre de Zacharie," *VT* 23 (1970) 26, suggests "springs of water." More often the eyes are given a symbolic interpretation, with reference either to the stone or the menorah. See Mitchell, *Haggai, Zechariah*, 157-58; Albert Petitjean, *Les Oracles du Proto-Zacharie* (EBib; Paris: Gabalda, 1969) 161-206; Beuken, *Haggai — Sacharja 1-8*, 287-88; Rudolph, *Haggai — Sacharja 1-8 — Sacharja 9-14 — Maleachi*, 101-2; Jeremias, *Die Nachtgesichte des Sacharja*, 185-88; Meyers and Meyers, *Haggai, Zechariah 1-8*, 208-9.

40. Herodotus, *Hist.* 1:114; Xenophon, *Cyr.* 8:6, 16; cf. *Cyr.* 8:2, 10-12: "They say, the king

these officials was to range over the Persian Empire checking on local officials and occasionally acting as agents provocateurs to test their loyalty to the emperor. Precisely the same activity is attributed to the Satan in the book of Job, a member of Yahweh's cabinet who explains that he has been ranging over the earth and walking back and forth upon it, using the same verb as here (Job 1:7).

If the connection with the foundation stone of the rebuilt temple is accepted, we may go on to note an interesting if somewhat oblique parallel in the fourth vision, the flying scroll whose proportions, gigantic for a scroll, correspond to those of the porch of Solomon's temple (Zech 5:1-4; cf. 1 Kgs 6:3). Both the stone and the scroll are inscribed, and the scroll, like the eyes of Yahweh, ranges over the face of the entire earth. The text on the stone is not given (3:9b) but the airborne scroll, inscribed on both recto and verso, contains a curse, metonymic for covenant. The point of the comparison is that both the foundation stone and the scroll are associated with the temple. It is from the temple, the dwelling of Yahweh, that everything that happens on earth, including political events, is visible, and it is from the temple that the moral demands of the covenant are promulgated and enforced.

The inscribed stone therefore bears a design representing divine oversight of the earth in the form of seven eyes, seven indicating totality. The eye symbol is by no means uncommon in antiquity. Well-known examples would be the numerous eye images in humanoid form from Nagar-Tell Brak in northeast Syria and the Eye of Horus from ancient Egypt. The identity of the stone has long been discussed,[41] with several commentators viewing it as an element in the high priestly vestments, associated either with the pectoral or turban.[42] Though it is well represented, I believe this reading is less plausible than the alternative proposed here, since the em-

---

has a thousand eyes." See C. Authrun, "L'Oeil du Roi: concept politico-administratif commun à l'Iran, à la Chine, et à l'Hellade," *Humanitas* 3 (1950-51) 287-91; Jack Martin Balcer, "The Athenian episcopos and the Achaemenid King's Eye," *AJP* 98 (1977) 252-63; *Sparda by the Bitter Sea* (BJS 52; Chico: Scholars, 1984) 120-21. To date, I have found this political metaphor exploited only by A. Leo Oppenheim, "The Eyes of the Lord," *JAOS* 88 (1968) 173-80.

41. For an older summary, see Beuken, *Haggai — Sacharja 1-8*, 284-90; Petitjean, *Les Oracles du Proto-Zacharie*, 173-84; more recently Samuel Amsler, André Lacocque, René Vuilleumier, *Aggée, Zacharie, Malachie* (CAT 11C; Neuchâtel: Delachaux & Niestlé, 1981) 83-86.

42. Many in the modern period have followed Mitchell, *Haggai and Zechariah*, 157-58, in embracing one or another form of this interpretation including, among English-language scholars, Petersen, *Haggai and Zechariah 1-8*, 211-12; and James C. VanderKam, "Joshua the High Priest and the Interpretation of Zechariah 3," *CBQ* 53 (1991) 553-70. Meyers and Meyers, *Haggai, Zechariah 1-8*, 204-11, think that the stone may be deliberately ambiguous.

phasis in the passage is on Zerubbabel as founder of the new temple, and therefore a person of royal status, rather than on the high priest and his vestments and priestly accessories. The stone is introduced immediately after the presentation of Branch and is set *before* Joshua, not on his person. Its introduction is also followed at once by the removal of the guilt of the land and therefore of its current miseries, which reversal is to come about, according to Haggai (2:9, 18-19), with the dedication of the temple by Zerubbabel. The stone brought out by Zerubbabel, accompanied by the enthusiastic reaction of those present (Zech 4:7b), cannot be the top stone (NRSV; German: *Schussstein, Giebelstein*), since work on the temple was not yet finished as Zech 4:9 explicitly states. In fact, the temple was completed no less than two years after the date assigned to Zechariah's visions (Ezra 6:15). In the rearranged text as presented here it would be natural to assume that this stone is identical with the stone placed before Joshua (Zech 3:9a), and therefore a foundation stone. The euphoria which characterized the scene is also reminiscent of the laying of the foundations of the temple in Ezra 3:10-13, though there the event is set in the reign of Cyrus II rather than that of Darius I.

This account which, as I have argued, describes the laying of the temple foundation stone, is obscure, disjointed, and not necessarily in chronological sequence, but it can be summarized as follows. The foundation stone is exhibited in the presence of Joshua as the newly appointed high priest. Since laying the foundation stone of a temple is traditionally a royal prerogative, this symbolically important act is assigned to Zerubbabel, scion of the Davidic dynasty. The act itself, with all its implications and all that follows from it including, it was hoped, the reestablishment of the native dynasty, would come about not by the usual exercise of political and military power but by the spirit of Yahweh, the same spirit which inspired Zerubbabel and Joshua to undertake the work in the first place (Hag 1:14). The mountain which will disappear as a result of Zerubbabel's efforts may represent anticipated opposition to the project, but it may also simply indicate the mountain of rubble and fallen masonry which must be removed in order to recover and put in place the foundation stone or foundation deposits from Solomon's temple.

Viewed in this way, the incident falls into a pattern of temple construction familiar in Mesopotamia and elsewhere from time immemorial. Sacred tradition, which would be carried over from temple to synagogue construction, required that a newly rebuilt temple be located on the site of the previous one. Hence Nabonidus, last king of Babylon, rebuilt the temple of the god Sīn at Harran on the same site as the previous temple destroyed by the Medes.[43] After restoring the temple of the goddess Anunītum at Sippar destroyed by Sennacherib, the same monarch placed an inscription in the rebuilt temple requesting any future restorer not to change it but to place it with his own inscription in its proper place.[44] Many other examples could be cited from the cuneiform archive.[45] Not surprisingly, therefore, Cyrus, in his edict to the Jewish elders, ordained that the temple in Jerusalem be rebuilt "in its (original) place" (Ezra 5:15), and the governors of Judah and Samaria likewise stipulated that the Jewish temple in Elephantine, destroyed in a pogrom, be rebuilt "on the site where it was before."[46] Hence the need for continuity not only in the high priestly office and the sacred vessels, but also in the location of the temple.[47]

After the oracular message for Zerubbabel is delivered (4:6-7), there comes the statement that the essential first stage, the laying of the foundation stone, has been accomplished, that construction will proceed under the direction of Zerubbabel, that it will be completed to general rejoicing,[48] and that when this happens the truth of the prophetic message will be con-

---

43. *ANET*, 311.

44. Paul-Alain Beaulieu, *The Reign of Nabonidus, King of Babylon, 556-539 B.C.* (New Haven: Yale University Press, 1989) 210-12.

45. See Ellis, *Foundation Deposits in Ancient Mesopotamia*.

46. Arthur E. Cowley, *Aramaic Papyri of the Fifth Century B.C.* (1923; repr. Osnabrück: Zeller, 1967) 123 (AP #32 line 8) = Bezalel Porten and Ada Yardeni, *Textbook of Aramaic Documents from Ancient Egypt*. Vol. 1: *Letters* (Jerusalem: Hebrew University, 1986) 76 (#A4.9).

47. The importance of continuity is also apparent in that Joshua/Jeshua, high priest designate, was the grandson of Seraiah, the last high priest to function in Solomon's temple (2 Kgs 25:18-21). On the temple vessels, see Ezra 1:7-11; 5:14-15 and the comments of Peter R. Ackroyd, "The Temple Vessels — A Continuity Theme," in *Studies in the Religion of Ancient Israel* (VTSup 23; Leiden: Brill, 1972) 166-81. On the matter of location, mention should be made of Galling's proposed emendation of *hā'eben hārō'šâ* (Zech 4:7b, "the top stone," NRSV) to *hā'eben hā'ašrâ*, a putative Hebrew cognate of Akkadian *ašru* and Aramaic *'ătar*, giving the meaning "the stone of the (previous) place." See Galling, *Studien zur Geschichte Israels im Persischen Zeitalter*, 143.

48. The final word addressed to the discouraged and the doubters in Zech 4:10 (cf. Hag 2:3) assures them that they will rejoice when they see something called the *'eben habbĕdîl* in Zerubbabel's hand (4:10). Since a stone made of tin or slag, the usual meanings assigned to *bĕdîl*, does not make good sense and "the stone called Separation" (REB), presumably with reference to the Urim and Thummim, does not seem to fit the context, we may accept provisionally the usual translation "plummet," understood as a building instrument to determine horizontality; cf. the equally problematic *'ănak* of Amos 7:7-8.

firmed. That this actually turned out as predicted is by no means clear, however. According to the Aramaic source in Ezra, Tattenai, governor of the Trans-Euphrates province, mentions only Jewish elders in reporting to Darius on the building activity in Jerusalem (Ezra 5:9). The reply of the elders, addressed to both Tattenai and Darius, refers only to an unnamed "governor of the Jews" together with the elders (6:7), and the Aramaic source concludes by noting that the Jewish elders, encouraged by Haggai and Zechariah, completed the rebuilding in the sixth year of Darius, that is, 516/515 B.C.E. Zerubbabel is conspicuously absent from this report.

The Lampstand and the Two Olive Trees (4:1-3, 11-14)

It is not difficult to understand why the vision of the temple menorah and the two "sons of oil" would have brought to mind the close association between Joshua and Zerubbabel throughout this entire sequence of *tableaux vivants* and, more particularly, have been linked with the theme of temple dedication in the scene just described. As reconstructed, therefore, this fourth intercalatory scene reads as follows:

> The angel who talked with me came back and aroused me, as one is aroused from sleep. He asked me, "What do you see?" I replied, "I see a lampstand all of gold with a bowl on top of it. There are seven lamps on it, with seven metal spouts for the lamps [which are on top of it].[49] Beside it there are two olive trees, one to the right of the bowl and one to its left. . . . Then I asked him, "What are these two olive trees, to the right of the lampstand and to its left?" I then asked him a second question, "What are the two clusters of olive which discharge the flow (of oil)[50] by means of the two golden ducts?" He said to me, "Don't you know what they are?" "No, sir," I replied. "These," he said, "are the two anointed ones who attend the Lord of all the earth."

The prophet is aroused from the catatonic state into which he had fallen, understandably in view of the rapid succession of vivid, confusing, and

---

49. *'ăšer 'al-rō'šô* is difficult to fit into the visual image; it may be a dittographic repetition of *'al-rāy'šāh* earlier in the same verse.

50. MT reads "which discharge the gold" *(hamĕrîqîm . . . hazzāhāb)*. I have accepted the emendation of Rudolph, *Haggai — Sacharja 1-8 — Sacharja 9-14 — Maleachi*, 104, reading *hazzāb*, "the flow," for the second *hazzāhāb* of v. 12.

mysterious images and scenarios to which he had been exposed. The description of the lampstand, its cylindrical base for the seven lamps (the bowl), and the means by which they are supplied with oil (the spouts and the ducts) has occasioned a vast amount of commentary which it is not to our present purpose to document.[51] In addition, the occurrence of several obscure technical terms makes for difficult visual reconstruction, not to mention translation. Most commentators agree that the second question in v. 12 has been added, perhaps as a corrective to the first or to explain how the lamps were supplied with oil.[52] The lampstand itself represents a combination of elements from the menorah in the wilderness sanctuary, made of pure gold (Exod 25:31-40, etc.), with a type of domestic ceramic lamp great numbers of which have come to light from Iron Age sites. Also relevant is the well-attested iconographic tradition in seal impressions of a deity represented by a cult symbol signifying light, often sun, moon, or other astral body, flanked to the right and left by attendants.[53]

In answering the question put to him at the beginning of the scene, the prophet draws attention to the two olive trees, and it is about these that he inquires further in his first question. The angel-intermediary's reaction to the question suggests that the prophet, and perhaps also we the readers, should by now be in a position to decode the meaning of the symbolism. Be that as it may, the two olive trees are the two "sons of oil" who "stand by," that is, attend on, the Lord of all the earth. One conclusion we may draw from this is that, according to the angel's interpretation, the lampstand is a symbol for the deity. This accords well with the iconographic tradition, noted a moment ago, which represents the deity surrounded by attendants, one on each side, often in the form of stylized trees.[54] Like the hosts of

51. For basic information on the lampstand, see, in addition to the commentaries, Lawrence E. Toombs, "Lampstand," *IDB* 3 (1962), 64-66; Carol L. Meyers, "Menorah," *IDBS* (1976), 586-87; and for an interpretation of the iconography, Othmar Keel, *Jahwe-Visionen und Siegelkunst: Eine neue Deutung der Majestätsschilderungen in Jes 6, Ez 1 und 10 und Sach 4* (Stuttgart: Katholisches Bibelwerk, 1977) 274-320; Keel and Christoph Uelinger, *Gods, Goddesses, and Images of God in Ancient Israel,* trans. Thomas H. Trapp (Minneapolis: Fortress, 1998) 305-6.

52. Perhaps the interpolator was concerned that the two olive trees perform no function and therefore wished to make the point that they provide oil for the lamps. The addition of the second question is discussed by Rudolph, *Haggai — Sacharja 1-8 — Sacharja 9-14 — Maleachi,* 109-10.

53. Examples in Keel and Uehlinger, *Gods, Goddesses, and Images of God,* 305-6, 402-3.

54. One example from the Neo-Babylonian period is the representation of the god Sîn as the crescent moon flanked by two worshippers. Sîn's temple at Harran was restored by

heaven attendant on Yahweh to the right and the left in Micaiah's vision (1 Kgs 22:19) and the seraphim in Isaiah's throne vision (Isa 6:2), the scene draws on the familiar theme of the heavenly court. This does not, however, preclude the presence of human actors, as in the tableau of the investiture of the high priest discussed earlier (Zech 3:1-10).

Most commentators have therefore had no difficulty in drawing the conclusion that the two olive trees represent Zerubbabel and Joshua.[55] But why olive trees, and why "sons of oil"? It is well known that this type of idiomatic expression would, in this instance, indicate some association between the individuals in question and olive oil. Many possibilities come to mind in the abstract, but in the present context it is difficult to avoid the conclusion that anointing is intended. An objection to this conclusion has been raised on the grounds that the two Hebrew terms for olive oil, *šemen* and *yiṣhār*, do not have precisely the identical meaning and that, more to the point, the oil used in anointing is always *šemen*, never *yiṣhār* as here. In terms of biblical usage, however, the difference between the two terms is not so clearly in evidence. The term for freshly expressed olive oil, *yiṣhār*, occurs often, associated with grain and wine, to suggest fertility and well-being (Deut 7:13; 11:14; 2 Kgs 18:32, etc.), but olive oil *(šemen)* is also found in similar contexts and with similar implications.[56] The latter is certainly used exclusively in accounts of the anointing of kings, no doubt because it indicates more precisely oil prepared for use, but it also occurs in common usage, occasionally linked with *dešen*, connoting fatness, fullness, prosperity. It is therefore inconceivable that Zechariah's angelic interlocutor would have described the two attendants on Yahweh, no matter how identified, as two *běnê-šemen*.

To summarize: the exchange between the seer and his angelic interlocutor places before the reader a symbolic representation of the God of Israel flanked by attendants, his human attendants Zerubbabel and Joshua, who are to be the instruments of his purpose for his people. The menorah with its seven lamps, corresponding to the seven eyes (4:10b), does not therefore represent the temple either past or future, except indirectly in the

---

Nabonidus after its destruction by the Medes. See Keel and Uehlinger, *Gods, Goddesses, and Images of God,* 146, 305.

55. Including Mitchell, *Haggai and Zechariah,* 165-66; Galling, *Studien zur Geschichte Israels im Persischen Zeitalter,* 117; Beuken, *Haggai — Sacharja 1-8,* 282; Rudolph, *Haggai — Sacharja 1-8 — Sacharja 9-14 — Maleachi,* 107-9; Jeremias, *Die Nachtgesichte des Sacharja,* 183-84, 217-18.

56. Deut 8:8; 32:13; Isa 61:3; Jer 40:10; 41:8, etc.

sense that it is Yahweh's house and a light shining from a house indicates presence. Yahweh is here described as "the Lord of all the earth,"[57] in keeping with the intense interest of Haggai and Zechariah in international affairs and the uncertain future of Jewish communities in the Persian Empire at the time of composition. Though the seer would have been well aware of tensions between priests and civil authorities, and he himself probably belonged to a family of priests,[58] no distinction is made in status or honor between the two attendants. Nevertheless, throughout Haggai and Zechariah 1–8 the main concern is with the rebuilding of the Jerusalem temple and the reestablishment of its cult, an essential precondition for a viable and flourishing community. Since, however, the temple, planned by David, built by Solomon, and maintained by successive members of the dynasty, was primarily the responsibility of the ruler, the role of Zerubbabel, current representative of the native dynasty, was crucial. The question remaining to be answered was whether Zerubbabel would assume responsibility for the task as client of the imperial overlord, a role Sheshbazzar is said to have assumed under Cyrus, or whether he would do so in his own right as autonomous ruler, accepting the unforeseeable consequences of such a decision.

The Secret Coronation of Zerubbabel (Zechariah 6:9-15)

The fifth and final scene involving Zerubabel ends with the spirit of Yahweh coming to rest on Babylon, the land of the north (Zech 6:8). One outcome of this spiritual awakening in the eastern Diaspora is now presented: the arrival in Jerusalem of three delegates bringing gifts for the temple. The same point is reiterated at the conclusion of this scene, where we are told that those who are far distant will come and take part in the rebuilding of the temple (6:15a). It is important to note that what is described here is an event in real time, not a visionary experience. The scene falls into a familiar and simple pattern as in the sign-acts performed by prophets (e.g., Isa 20:1-6; Jer 27:1-7): an action followed by an oracular utterance explanatory of the action. The scene concludes with the by now familiar

57. Also Josh 3:11, 13; Mic 4:13; Ps 97:5. Similar titles at Isa 54:5; Ps 47:3(Eng 2); 83:19(18); 97:9.

58. He is either son or grandson of Iddo (Zech 1:1; Neh 12:16), a familiar priestly name, e.g., the Iddo who presided over the cult establishment at Casiphia in southern Mesopotamia (Ezra 8:17).

assurance of fulfillment. The text presents many problems and has given rise to a great deal of emendation. Making such adjustments as would seem necessary, it may be read as follows:

> The word of Yahweh came to me: "Accept the gifts[59] from the Diaspora, from Heldai, Tobiah, and Jedaiah who have arrived from Babylon,[60] and that same day go to the house of Josiah son of Zephaniah. Take the silver and gold, make a crown,[61] and place it on the head of the high priest, Joshua son of Jehozadak. Say to him: 'This is what Yahweh of the hosts has said: Here is a man whose name is Branch. He will "branch out" from his place and will rebuild the temple of Yahweh. It is he who will rebuild the temple of Yahweh, and it is he who will assume royal dignity, sit on his throne and rule. There will be a priest by his throne, and there will be peaceful coexistence[62] between them.' The crown will serve as a memorial for Helem, Tobiah, Jedaiah, and Hen son of Zephaniah in the temple of Yahweh. Those far distant will come and take part in rebuilding the temple of Yahweh. Then you will acknowledge that Yahweh of the hosts has sent me to you. It will come about if you diligently pay heed to the voice of Yahweh your God.'"

It is important, in the first place, to keep in mind the connection between the action which the seer is commanded to perform and the oracular utterance which explains its point and purpose. The action begins with the visit of the three named Judeo-Babylonians, and the wording suggests that they are delegates from the Diaspora bringing gifts for the temple including gold and silver, comparable to the reports of similar visits and similar donations in Ezra 1:3-4, 6; 7:15-16. Since these are gifts from expatriate Judeans, there is no hint of the "despoiling the Egyptians" motif to which

---

59. "The gifts," or perhaps "the silver and gold," is required since *lāqôaḥ*, infinitive absolute as imperative, has no object.

60. "Who have arrived from Babylon," in the plural, is out of place after "Josiah son of Zephaniah."

61. Reading *'ăṭeret* sing. for MT *'ăṭārôt* pl. here and v. 14 with some codices of LXX, Syriac, and Targum. Lipiński, "Recherches sur le livre de Zacharie," 34-35, suggested that the word may be a Phoenician-type singular, like *ḥokmôt* (Prov 1:20; 9:1; 24:7); cf. Job 31:36, in which the plural also occurs where clearly only one crown is called for. The decision between singular and plural also depends, of course, on how one interprets the context as a whole.

62. Reading *'ăṣat šālôm*, lit., "a counsel of peace," as hendiadys.

appeal is sometimes made. The awkward wording in MT may suggest that Josiah son of Zephaniah was the fourth member of the delegation. If, however, the event took place in Jerusalem, as most commentators assume, the fact that he has his own house and is living in it renders this unlikely. The names of the delegates suggest that they were specially chosen for this task. The name Heldai has associations with Davidic lore (1 Chr 11:30; 27:15) and with Bethlehem and Netophah, Davidic territory (Ezra 2:22; 1 Esd 5:18). Tobiah was probably a member of the distinguished Transjordanian family which some years later entertained ambitions to control the temple and its considerable assets (Neh 13:4-9; Josephus, *Ant.* 12:160-236). Jedaiah was probably a priest, since the name is closely associated with the priesthood, even with the house to which Joshua, the high priest designate, belonged (Ezra 2:36 = Neh 7:39). Josiah son of Zephaniah, owner or occupant of the house where the action takes place, bears the name of the last significant king of Judah, and his father that of a high-status priest executed by the Babylonians after the fall of Jerusalem (2 Kgs 25:18-21 = Jer 52:24-27). The fact that two of the names in 6:14 — Helem and Hen son of Zephaniah — are different strengthens the suspicion that this notice about the later disposal of the crown, as a memorial in the temple, was added by an editorial hand, perhaps with the idea of showing that the gold and silver served the purpose for which they were originally intended after all.

The relation between the act the seer is to perform — having the crown made and placing it on the high priest's head — and the oracular utterance explaining its significance is the key to the interpretation of this scene.[63] The focus of the oracle is on a person bearing the sobriquet *ṣemaḥ,* the same person encountered in Zech 3:8 described as *'abdî ṣemaḥ* ("my servant Branch"), meaning a descendant of David prophetically foretold (Jer 23:5-6; 33:15). What is said of this individual here — that he will rebuild the temple and sit on the throne and rule, in other words, restore the native dynasty in his own person — is said of Zerubbabel in Haggai's fifth and last discourse (2:20-23). Hence, according to the oracular pronouncement, it is clear that the prediction is about the future destiny of Zerubbabel and the direction which his "branching out" is to take.

This conclusion leaves us, however, with the problem of the role of

63. I therefore disagree with Gerhard Wallis, "Erwägungen zu Sacharja VI 9-15," *Congress Volume, Uppsala 1971*, VTSup 22 (1972) 232-37, who stipulated two distinct texts dealing, respectively, with the manufacture of diadems for the high priest and their later deposition in the temple and an eschatological, messianic oracle about "Branch." He held that the problems of interpretation arise from the combination of these two texts.

the high priest to whom the oracle is addressed and on whose head the crown is to be placed. The close association between Zerubbabel and Joshua is not in itself problematic. In all of our sources they are mentioned together, with Zerubbabel generally named before Joshua. This is simply a function of the intimate association between dynasty and temple, the role of the king as temple-builder, and the as yet unsolved issue of the future status of the temple, whether as an indispensable element of restored national identity or another instrument of imperial control.

What Happened in the House of Josiah ben Shephaniah?

It is unfortunate that the description of the action which the prophet is told to perform is more than usually obscure. MT *ʿăṭārôt* ("crowns") has induced some commentators to postulate the manufacture of two crowns, one for the high priest, the other either for Zerubbabel or for a future messianic figure.[64] The problem with this reading of the event, in any of its several variations, is that only in the Hellenistic period did the Jerusalem temple priesthood assume political control as the local agent of the hegemonic power of the day. During the two centuries of Achaemenid rule the province of Yehud (Judah) remained under the control of a governor. We must wait even longer, to the Hasmonaean period, for the union of high priesthood and royal rule, and even then it was a case of a king taking on the dignity of the high priesthood rather than the reverse. Also, as we have just heard (Zech 3:5), the high priest wore a turban not a crown.

We shall never know for certain what happened that day in the house of Josiah son of Zephaniah, but the most plausible of the many hypotheses proposed still starts out with the replacement of the name of Zerubbabel with that of "the high priest Joshua son of Jehozadak" (Zech 6:11). The de-

---

64. Rudolph, *Sacharja 1–8*, 127-33, defends MT and assigns one crown to Joshua and the other to a messianic ruler of the last days. He argued that Zerubbabel was disqualified since he was born in Babylon (cf. the "birther controversy" over President Obama's credentials at this writing!), interpreting *mitaḥtâw* as "aus seinem eigenen Boden" in spite of the future *yiṣmaḥ*. Ackroyd, *Exile and Restoration*, 194-200, agrees that a ceremonial crowning of Zerubbabel is meant, but interprets 6:13 as referring alternatively to Zerubbabel and Joshua, so that each is assigned a throne. For similar views, putting Joshua on an equal or higher level than Zerubbabel, see Petersen, *Haggai and Zechariah 1–8*, 272-81; Ralph L. Smith, *Micah–Malachi* (WBC; Waco: Word, 1984) 215-19; Meyers and Meyers, *Haggai, Zechariah 1–8*, 336-75.

liberate alteration would have been in reaction to the disconfirmation of the predictions of both Haggai and Zechariah concerning Zerubbabel, and it would not have seemed unreasonable in view of the great increase in political power of the Jerusalem priestly aristocracy in the early Hellenistic period. If this is accepted, the following reconstruction of the event may be proposed. Under prophetic prompting, some of the bullion from the Babylonian Diaspora destined for the future temple was diverted to finance the symbolic and secret coronation of Zerubbabel, governor of the province and current representative of the Davidic line. This incident may have been seen as a sequel to Haggai's equally secret summons to Zerubbabel to restore the eclipsed dynasty (Hag 2:20-23), somewhat after the manner of the secret anointing of Saul by Samuel (1 Sam 9:27–10:1). The ceremony took place in the presence of the high priest–designate of the new temple. To what extent Zerubbabel, in taking part in this symbolic ritual, shared the dangerously radical political views of Haggai, Zechariah, and no doubt other prophets, spiritual heirs of those Judeo-Babylonian martyr-prophets executed by Nebuchadnezzar (Jer 29:21-22), we do not know. The Persian authorities tended to support temples as instruments of imperial control, and we hear that the Jerusalem temple was completed with imperial approval and even subsidized from the imperial treasury in the sixth year of Darius's reign, namely, 516 B.C.E. (Ezra 6:15). But plotting to set up an independent kingdom under a native dynast was an entirely different matter, especially shortly after the violent suppression of two major dynastic revolts in Babylon.[65]

How it ended we do not know, but if the information provided by Ezra 6:14-15, that only Jewish elders were involved with the completion of the temple in 516 B.C.E., is accepted, Zerubbabel must have disappeared from the scene by that time, under what circumstances we do not know. It now remains to be seen how the Davidic-messianic hope was sustained in Jewish communities throughout the remainder of Persian rule and the Hellenistic kingdoms, to flare up once again under the Roman Empire.

---

65. The revolt of Nidintu-Bel (Nebuchadnezzar III) lasted from October to December 522, and that of Arkha (Nebuchadnezzar IV) from August to November 521. On the chronology of the revolts, see the "Chronologische Übersicht" in Dandamaev, *Persien unter den ersten Achämeniden*, 255-56.

CHAPTER SIX

From Zerubbabel to Nehemiah and Beyond

It is reported among the nations that you and the Jews intend to rebel;
that is why you are building the wall. According to this report, you wish
to become their king.

Nehemiah 6:6

From Zerubbabel to Nehemiah

For the two centuries of Persian imperial rule, from the reign of Darius I
and the Zerubbabel episode to the conquests of Alexander and the defeat
of Darius III, information from biblical sources about Jewish communities in general and Davidic messianism in particular is in short supply
and, where available, more often than not of uncertain date and interpretation. None of the Greek historians who cover the period so much as
mentions Jews and Judaism. Josephus, our principal source apart from
biblical texts, is not well informed on the Persian period and makes things
worse by a tendency to conflate the three rulers named Darius and the
three named Artaxerxes, thus drastically reducing the duration of Persian
rule. This chronological shrinkage is compounded in later Jewish sources,
for example, in the Tannaitic treatise *Seder Olam Rabba*, which reduces
the two centuries of the Achaemenid Empire to thirty-four years. Where
available, archaeological excavations, surveys, and artefacts of different
kinds which have come to light (coins, seals, seal impressions, jar impressions, etc.) make a valuable contribution, but are no less subject to con-

flicting interpretations than the written sources. Looking ahead, this un-satisfactory state of affairs is not much better for the period from Nehemiah in the mid-fifth century B.C.E. all the way to the accession of Antiochus IV Epiphanes in 175 B.C.E., a fateful moment in the history of the Jewish people.

To return to the beginning of this period: Once Darius I had over-come the numerous revolts which followed his succession in 522 B.C.E. and reorganized the empire, Judah became part, a very small part, of the Babylon-Trans-Euphrates satrapy which corresponded in extent to the Neo-Babylonian Empire and constituted, as Herodotus reports, one of twenty-two satrapies in the vast Persian Empire (*Hist.* 3:89). After the sup-pression of revolts in Babylon early in the reign of Xerxes (486-465), the Trans-Euphrates region *(eber nāri)* may have been put under separate ad-ministration; the evidence is not clear. There were, in any case, officials re-sponsible for the administration of this vast area west of the Euphrates, among whom was Tattenai, described in Ezra 5:3 as "governor of the prov-ince Beyond the River." The province of Judah *(yĕhûd mĕdînâ)*, lying within this jurisdiction, was administered by governors appointed by the court in Susa, as were Jewish communities in Mesopotamia, Egypt, and elsewhere. Samaria may have been a local administrative center, but the hypothesis of Albrecht Alt, according to which Judah was ruled from Sa-maria until Nehemiah succeeded in establishing its relative autonomy within the Persian Empire, can no longer be sustained. Both Sheshbazzar and Zerubbabel are identified as governors of Judah prior to Nehemiah, Malachi refers to but does not name a governor of the province (Mal 1:8), and Nehemiah himself alludes to governors who preceded him (Neh 5:15).[1] Whether Judeans or Persians, these appointees represented the imperial court in Susa, and some scholars believe it possible to reconstruct a list of Persian-period governors with the help of extrabiblical data. One attempt to do so reads as follows:

Sheshbazzar (Ezra 5:14)
Zerubbabel (Hag 1:1, 14)
Elnathan (bulla and seal)

---

1. Albrecht Alt, "Die Rolle Samarias bei der Entstehung des Judentums," in *Kleine Schriften zur Geschichte des Volkes Israel* (Munich: Beck, 1953), 2:316-37. One of the few to de-fend the hypothesis in more recent years was Sean E. McEvenue, "The Political Structure in Judah from Cyrus to Nehemiah," *CBQ* 43 (1981) 353-64.

Yeho'ezer (jar impression from Ramat Raḥel)
Ahzai (jar impression from Ramat Raḥel)
Nehemiah (Neh 5:14; 12:26)
Bagohi/Bigvai/Bagoas (Elephantine papyrus AP 30:1)
Yehezqiyah (coins from Beth-zur and Tell Jemme)[2]

With the sole exception of Bagohi, all these names are Jewish, and among them that of Nehemiah is certainly the most familiar. The only one of these names which appears in the Chronicler's Davidic genealogy is Zerubbabel (1 Chr 3:19-24).

On the assumption that "the twentieth year of King Artaxerxes" in which Nehemiah was given leave to go to Jerusalem refers to Artaxerxes I, the year in which Nehemiah's story begins would be 445 B.C.E. (Neh 2:1; cf. 1:1).[3] According to his own memoir Nehemiah was appointed governor in the same year, continued in that office for twelve years (Neh 5:14), returned to the court at Susa, and, after a brief absence, resumed his tenure of office in Jerusalem and continued in it for an unknown period of time, but at any rate not beyond 424/423, the year of the death of Artaxerxes I (Neh 13:6-7). Some commentators have suggested that Nehemiah was recalled to explain allegations that his rebuilding of the city wall was a prelude to rebellion. This is quite uncertain, but it is not surprising that his refortification of Jerusalem aroused the suspicion of hostile neighbors, principally Sanballat governor of Samaria, the Kedarite-Arab chieftain Gashmu (Hebrew: Geshem), and Tobiah the Ammonite prince. After work on the wall was finished, Sanballat sent Nehemiah an unsealed letter with the following message: "It is reported among the nations, and Gashmu also is saying it, that you and the Jews are planning to rebel, and it is for this reason that you are rebuilding the wall. To judge by these reports you are to be their

---

2. Nahman Avigad, *Bullae and Seals from a Post-Exilic Judean Archive* (Qedem 4; Jerusalem: Hebrew University Institute of Archaeology, 1976) 35. The chronology, and therefore the order of governors, is uncertain. For relevant observations apropos of the list of governors, see Frank Moore Cross, "Aspects of Samaritan and Jewish History in Late Persian and Hellenistic Times," *HTR* 59 (1966) 201-11; "Samaria and Jerusalem in the Era of the Restoration," in *From Epic to Canon: History and Literature in Ancient Israel* (Baltimore: Johns Hopkins University Press, 1998) 173-202; John W. Betlyon, "The Provincial Government of Persian Period Judah and the Yehud Coins," *JBL* 105 (1986) 633-42; Hugh G. M. Williamson, "The Governors of Judah under the Persians," *TynBul* 39 (1988) 59-82.

3. On the date, see my *Ezra-Nehemiah* (OTL; Philadelphia: Westminster, 1988) 205-6, 213.

king, and you have even set up prophets to proclaim in Jerusalem, 'There is (once again) a king in Judah!' — this with reference to yourself" (Neh 6:5-7). Nehemiah naturally dismissed these charges as fabrications, which they probably were. There is no evidence that he was of Davidic descent. His name does not appear in any royal genealogy, and neither his allusion to his ancestral sepulchers in Jerusalem nor his confession of the sins of his ancestor's house warrants this conclusion (Neh 1:6; 2:3).[4] This being so, it is doubtful that the prophets alleged by Sanballat to be proclaiming Nehemiah's kingship in Jerusalem (Neh 6:7), and to whom Nehemiah refers disparagingly at the end of his account of this incident (6:14), would have supported a claimant not of Davidic descent. This episode was therefore not a repeat of the enthusiasm surrounding Zerubbabel, also a governor, about seventy-five years earlier.

The accusation was nevertheless not, in itself, implausible. Revolts by satraps and governors of provinces were by no means unknown to the Persian imperial administration. A few years before Nehemiah's arrival in the province, Megabyzus, satrap of *eber nāri,* had rebelled, and in the following century the "Great Revolt of the Satraps" reported by Diodorus of Sicily (XV. 93.1) caused Artaxerxes II a great deal of trouble.[5] Revolts also occurred in city-states like Tyre and Sidon which had a long history of dynastic rule. Evagoras, ruler of Salamis in Cyprus, even succeeded in founding a dynasty while nominally subject to Persian authority, one which survived for a time even after the Macedonian conquest of Persia.[6] An especially interesting case is the Hecatomnid dynasty founded by Mausolus son of Hecatomnus, satrap of Caria in western Asia Minor in the first half of the fourth century B.C.E. Mausolus described himself in inscriptions as satrap, but acted in all respects like a king, endowing and en-

---

4. The argument for Nehemiah's Davidic descent was presented by Ulrich Kellermann, *Nehemia: Quellen, Überlieferung und Geschichte* (BZAW 102; Berlin: Töpelmann, 1967) 21-23, 154-59. The contrary position is held by Loren W. Batten, *A Critical and Exegetical Commentary on the Books of Ezra and Nehemiah* (ICC; Edinburgh: T. & T. Clark, 1913) 253-54; Wilhelm Rudolph, *Esra und Nehemia samt 3. Esra* (HAT 20; Tübingen: Mohr, 1949) 135; W. Th. In der Smitten, "Erwägungen zu Nehemias Davidizität," *JSJ* 5 (1974) 41-48; Hugh G. M. Williamson, *Ezra, Nehemiah* (WBC 16; Waco: Word, 1985) 256-57; Blenkinsopp, *Ezra-Nehemiah,* 268-70.

5. Pierre Briant, *Histoire de l'Empire perse de Cyrus à Alexandre* (Paris: Fayard, 1996) 1:675-94; Eng. trans. *From Cyrus to Alexander: A History of the Persian Empire,* trans Peter T. Daniels (Winona Lake: Eisenbrauns, 2002) 656-59.

6. On Evagoras I and his successors, see Vassos Karageorghis, *Cyprus, from the Stone Age to the Romans* (London: Thames & Hudson, 1982) 162-70.

larging the local Zeus sanctuary, establishing and repopulating a new capital at Halicarnassus, and engaging in ambitious building projects, especially a splendid mausoleum for himself and his descendants.[7]

Genealogical Continuity

The accusation directed against Nehemiah, a figure comparable to Mausolus in ambition and achievements, at least provides evidence that the revival of the national dynasty could still be contemplated in the middle years of the fifth century. The preservation of the genealogy of David's descendants by the author of Chronicles, or of 1 Chronicles 1–9 for those who consider it a separate text (1 Chr 3:1-24), demonstrates that for some of Nehemiah's contemporaries hope for the restoration of the dynasty had not faded. The postexilic section of this genealogy (3:17-24) is beset by textual problems, and even more so by the author's own casual way of presenting a lineage. The problem is especially acute with the sons of Hananiah, himself grandson of Zerubbabel (1 Chr 3:21). It is unclear from the wording whether all six named after Hananiah are his sons or whether Pelatiah is the only son named — in other words, whether these six names are to be read horizontally or vertically, or, in yet other words, whether we are to count ten generations from Zerubbabel to Anani, the last named in the genealogy, or six. The formal features of the genealogy would suggest a preference for the longer count, since in all other cases of three or more sons the number (5, 6, 3, 7) is given. On the other hand, since the maximum length of a generation in antiquity is about thirty years,[8] ten generations counting from Zerubbabel would take the Davidic genealogy down as far as the late third century B.C.E. This would be late for the composition of Chronicles but might favor those who maintain that 1 Chronicles 1–9 is a prologue added at a later point in time to the narrative which follows.[9]

A stronger argument for a short genealogy is the mention of Hattush,

7. Stephen Ruzicka, *Politics of a Persian Dynasty: The Hecatomnids in the Fourth Century B.C.* (Norman: University of Oklahoma Press, 1992).

8. See above, p. 39.

9. On the place of 1 Chronicles 1–9 in the book and the unity-disunity issue see Hugh G. M. Williamson, *1 and 2 Chronicles* (NCBC; Grand Rapids: Eerdmans, 1982) 12-15, 39-40; Sara Japhet, *I & II Chronicles* (OTL; Louisville: Westminster/John Knox, 1993) 5-7; Marshall D. Johnson, *The Purpose of the Biblical Genealogies* (SNTSMS 8; 2nd ed., Cambridge: Cambridge University Press, 1988) 44-55.

descendant of Shecaniah, of Davidic descent, as one of the leaders of Ezra's caravan en route from southern Mesopotamia to Palestine (Ezra 8:2). In the genealogy (1 Chr 3:22) Hattush, grandson of Shecaniah, is certainly the same individual, and, according to the short count, he is located in the third or fourth generation from Zerubbabel. This places him in the late decades of the fifth century or somewhat earlier, in other words, in the same time frame as the earlier date for the arrival of Ezra in the province, i.e., the seventh year of Artaxerxes I (465-424 B.C.E.). This conclusion is reasonable, but there is so much uncertainty about the interpretation of Chronicles and Ezra-Nehemiah that, in the present state of our knowledge, or rather ignorance, no conclusion can be considered definitive. Also to be considered is the fragility of textual transmission where lists of names are involved and the well-attested fact that genealogies often omit or add generations for one reason or another, especially in their middle reaches. As historical source material, the Davidic genealogy should therefore be treated with reserve.[10]

In respect to the dynastic theme during the Persian period, an interesting point emerges when we compare the leadership of the original immigrant group listed in Ezra 2 and Nehemiah 7 and dated to the beginning of the reign of Cyrus with the much briefer list of those who accompanied Ezra on his arrival in Judah almost a century later under Artaxerxes, probably the first of that name. In the former, Zerubbabel, scion of the house of David, is listed first followed by Jeshua, high priest designate (Ezra 2:2), but by the time of Ezra the precedence has passed to representatives of the priesthood who are named first in the list of immigrants followed by Hattush, a descendant of David (Ezra 8:1-2). Furthermore, the priests are now of the family of Aaron rather than of the Zadokite line to which Jeshua belonged. Gershom and Daniel who arrived with Ezra are descendants of Phineas and Ithamar, respectively, both Aaronids (Ezra 8:2; Leviticus 10), while the Zadokite connections of Jeshua show up in the name of his father Jehozadak (Hag 1:1, etc.). This small difference between the lists may be taken to illustrate the growing political power and influence of the temple priesthood as local representatives of the imperial court vis-à-vis the civic authorities and, within the ranks of the priesthood, the increasing eminence of the Aaronid faction.

10. See Robert R. Wilson, "The Old Testament Genealogies in Recent Research," *JBL* 94 (1975), 169-89; Wilson, *Genealogy and History in the Biblical World* (Yale Near Eastern Researches 7; New Haven: Yale University Press, 1977).

The creation of genealogies, amply attested in Chronicles and Ezra-Nehemiah, is the standard way of affirming continuity with the past. It fuses the memory of origins into the collective consciousness of the community which transmits the genealogy. It gives expression, whether oral or written, to an immersion in the past which, for ancient societies and those which continue to cherish tradition, confers substance, solidity, and identity. We see, for example, how the charming story of Ruth's marriage to Boaz achieves resonance beyond that moment in time by being grafted onto the genealogy of the house of Judah (Ruth 4:18-22; cf. 1 Chr 2:1-17). But genealogy is only one way of creating and maintaining links with a cherished past. Something was said earlier about Josiah as a second David and how, in the decades immediately preceding or following the Macedonian conquest, the deeds and death of this last great king of Judah were still being commemorated by rhapsodists (2 Chr 35:24b-25). It was further suggested that there may be an allusion to Josiah's death in the enigmatic passage about the Pierced One in Zech 12:10-14. Later still, Jesus ben Sirach extols the memory of Josiah "as sweet as honey to every mouth" (Sir 49:1-4). About the same time, the author of 1 Esdras opened his account of the return from exile and restoration of community life in Judah not with the decree of Cyrus, as in Ezra 1:1-4, but with the great Passover of Josiah, the first and last under the monarchy (2 Kgs 23:22). Josiah, last great descendant of David to occupy the throne, is therefore not just the end of the old but the beginning of the new, the essential link in the chain of continuity with the past.

David and the Levites

According to one strand in the skein of tradition about David — warlord, armor-bearer, shepherd — he was assigned the role of the Hebrew Orpheus. Like Orpheus, he was a skilled performer on the lyre, his music could control and exorcise evil spirits, and his psalms, like the Orphic hymns, were read or sung as a source of inspiration, esoteric knowledge, and prophecy. Anointed by Samuel and possessed by the spirit, he is recruited as a skilled performer on the lyre to play for Saul (1 Sam 16:12-14, 23). His playing calmed Saul's troubled spirits, though sometimes it had the opposite effect (1 Sam 18:10-11; 19:8-10). During the procession of the ark from Kiriath-jearim he led the people in sacred dance accompanied by an orchestra of musical instruments (2 Sam 6:5). He also composed and performed laments, and in a late version of "Last Words of David" (2 Sam 23:1-7), he is memorialized as "the singer of Israel's psalms" or perhaps "the favorite (object) of Israel's songs."[11] Like Orpheus, first in a ten-generation lineage leading to Homer, David also came to be regarded as the founder of the guilds of liturgical musicians who passed on their skills to those who came after them.

In keeping with this profile, a prominent aspect of the David of Chronicles and Ezra-Nehemiah is therefore as founder and organizer of temple personnel, among temple personnel especially Levites and, among Levites, especially liturgical musicians and their assistants. Already in Dtr we find David composing psalms (2 Samuel 22; cf. Ps 18), and his musical gifts are in the service of divine worship. But this aspect of the David tradition comes to full expression in Chronicles and, indirectly, in Ezra-Nehemiah. Both have a stronger emphasis on and predilection for Levites than for priests and, among Levites, for liturgical musicians. This group has a special place in the evolution of Davidic messianism and traditions about David in general which deserves our attention.

We know little about liturgical personnel and liturgies performed in Solomon's temple, but it is certain that sacred music composed and performed by professional male musicians played an important part.[12] Like other professionals, these musicians were organized in guilds, each taking its turn in the temple service, some during the night hours.[13] More is known about the temple service and its personnel in the second temple, especially with regard to music. Guilds of professional musicians who composed and performed sacred music cherished the traditions about David and adopted him as their founder and patron. They thereby served as a channel for the transmission and further evolution of Davidic messianism, an especially efficacious channel in view of the iterative nature of liturgy and the emotive power of song accompanied by dramatic representation. According to the author of Chronicles, for whom the composition and

11. Depending on the disputed meaning of *nĕ'îm zĕmirôt yiśrā'ēl* (23:1b). On David's laments, see 2 Sam 1:17-27; 3:33-34.

12. There is no evidence for female officiants, musicians, or singers in temple worship. In Amos 8:3 *hêlîlû šîrôt hêkāl* ("the songs of the temple/palace wail") should probably read *hêlîlû šārôt hêkāl* ("female singers" rather than "songs") since wailing is done by people not songs, but in that case the *hêkāl* would be the royal palace not the temple. There were professional female singers, especially in mourning rituals (*hākāmôt, mĕqônĕnôt;* Judg 11:39-40; Jer 9:16-19; Zech 12:11-14; 2 Chr 35:25), but none of these were temple personnel.

13. 1 Chr 9:33-34; Ps 92:3(Eng 2); 119:62; 134:1-3.

rendition of liturgical music appears to have been the most important of the functions assigned to Levites, David as founder established guilds of temple musicians named for their respective leaders: Heman, Asaph, and Merari.[14] Without attempting to unravel the complicated genealogy of Levi in Chronicles, we can say that new names would have been added and older names would have dropped out with the passing of time.[15] One indication is the attribution of ten psalms to Korahite Levites (Ps 42, 44–49, 84, 85, 87) and one to Ethan (Ps 89), listed as a singer and performer on the cymbals in 1 Chr 15:17, 19, who seems to have displaced Jeduthun to whom Ps 39 and 77 are attributed. The Chronicler also mentions a certain Levite named Chenaniah, a famous precentor.[16]

These liturgical musicians originally operated independently but were eventually incorporated, together with gatekeepers, into the ranks of the Levites. Musicians and singers are still distinct from Levites in the census of those who first returned from Babylon[17] and who accompanied Ezra on his mission (Ezra 7:7), but by the time of the Chronicler they were incorporated into the Levitical order. The author's preferential option for these Levitical musicians is in evidence to such an extent as to justify the suspicion that he himself belonged to their ranks. He wrote at a disturbed time for Jewish communities, a few decades either before or after the Macedonian conquest. The Chronicler was not messianic in the general sense of the expression, much less apocalyptic in his thinking. Terms such as "utopian" and "programmatic" would perhaps describe his work better. It is noticeable that the term "anointed," "messiah" *(māšîaḥ),* occurs only twice in his work, both times in citations from psalms (1 Chr 16:22; 2 Chr 6:42). There was a place in his ideal polity for a restored Davidic kingship but only if it met the needs of the community for which he wrote and sup-

---

14. 1 Chr 6:16-32(Eng 31-47); 16:4-6, 37-42; 25:1-8.

15. On Second Temple Levitical musicians, see Helmut Gese, "Zur Geschichte der Kultsänger am Zweiten Tempel," in *Abraham unser Vater: Juden und Christen im Gespräch über die Bibel,* ed. Otto Betz, Martin Hengel, and Peter Schmidt (AGSU 5; Leiden: Brill, 1963) 222-34; Sigmund Mowinckel, *The Psalms in Israel's Worship,* trans. D. R. Ap-Thomas (1967; repr. BRS; Grand Rapids: Eerdmans and Livonia: Dove, 2004) 2:53-73; David L. Petersen, *Late Israelite Prophecy* (SBLMS 23; Missoula: Scholars, 1977) 60-62; Joseph Blenkinsopp, *A History of Prophecy in Israel* (2nd ed., Louisville: Westminster/John Knox, 1996) 222-26.

16. 1 Chr 15:22, 27; 26:29. The title *śar hammaśśā'* assigned to Chenaniah at 1 Chr 15:27 and translated "precentor" by REB, was taken by Mowinckel, *The Psalms in Israel's Worship,* 2:56, to mean "master of the oracles" based on a common meaning of *maśśā'* and the immemorial association between music and prophetic inspiration.

17. Ezra 2:40-41, 70; Neh 7:43-44, 73.

ported the operation of the temple cult on which, for the author, everything else depended.

In order to meet these needs the author of Chronicles set about constructing his own image of David as founder and patron of the guilds with the greatest freedom from the constraints of tradition. The David thus reconstructed established the Levitical guilds and assigned them their tasks, and did so on his own authority and initiative.[18] As recipient of the overall plan of the temple and its appointments (*tabnît*, 1 Chr 28:19), he was on the same level as Moses, who received from God the *tabnît* of the wilderness sanctuary (Exod 25:9, 40). While certainly acknowledging the preeminence of Moses as lawgiver, the Chronicler's David claimed for himself an authority which was prophetic in origin, resting as it did on divine revelation about the temple and its personnel delivered to him *in writing* (1 Chr 28:11-19). This authoritative text remained available down to the time of Josiah (2 Chr 35:4), perhaps even to the time of Nehemiah, who mentions "a commandment from the king" *(miṣwat hammelek)* concerning the Levitical musicians (Neh 11:23).

For the Chronicler, the composition and rendition of liturgical music was also a prophetic activity in which David himself shared as presiding over "the leaders in inspired prophecy to the accompaniment of lyres, lutes and cymbals" (1 Chr 25:1). All three guild leaders during his reign are described as seers *(ḥōzîm)*.[19] Affinity between music and prophetic inspiration, encapsulated in the mantic and shamanistic figure of Orpheus, was a commonplace of the ancient world. In Israel it may be traced back to the cultic prophets active in the first temple. In the Historian's account of Josiah's reign, the participants in his covenant included "the priests and the (cultic) prophets" (2 Kgs 23:2), but in the Chronicler's version of the same event "Levites" substitutes for "prophets" (2 Chr 34:30).[20] It was, at any rate, among the members of these guilds that the tradition of David as a prophetic figure, and the psalms as mantic texts composed by David and his Levitical associates originated. The tradition persisted into the Roman period and beyond. The Qumran Psalms scroll (11QPs[a]) assigns to David 4,050 hymns which he composed by virtue of his prophetic gift

18. 1 Chr 6:16-33(Eng 31-48); 15:16-24; 16:4-6, 37-42; 23:2-23; 25:1-31.
19. 1 Chr 25:5; 2 Chr 29:30; 35:15.
20. Aubrey R. Johnson, *The Cultic Prophet in Ancient Israel* (2nd ed., Cardiff: University of Wales Press, 1962) 70-71. A standard work on cultic prophecy, though in some respects now out of date, is the same author's *The Cultic Prophet and Israel's Psalmody* (Cardiff: University of Wales Press, 1979).

(něbû'â),[21] and among the first Christians the psalms were read as prophecies of Christ and his mission (Acts 1:16; 2:25-31, 34).

The collection of canonical psalms — the Psalter — is the *chef d'oeuvre* of these guilds of religious poets, musicians, and singers. The notations attached to most of the 150 psalms assign thirty to members of the guilds, in particular Asaphites and Korahites, and seventy-two to David. Several of the latter are associated with incidents in his life drawing on a narrative tradition by that time much as we have it today in 1-2 Samuel. The emphasis is on his struggles with Saul and other enemies, and there is one which gives expression to his repentance for his adultery with Bathsheba and murder of her husband (Ps 51). Since David was himself engaged with the Levitical musicians in this inspired activity (1 Chr 25:1-8), the much-debated *lĕdāwîd* at the head of several of these psalms can indicate the belief that David was both their author and subject. In pragmatic and realistic terms, the David of Chronicles and Ezra-Nehemiah represents an accommodation to the increased importance of the temple and its personnel during the Persian and early Hellenistic periods. Ultimately, however, it made it easier to incorporate the dynastic theme into a broader and richer vision of the future.

---

21. James A. Sanders, *The Psalms Scroll of Qumrân Cave 11 (11QPs*ᵃ*)* (DJD 4; Oxford: Oxford University Press, 1965) 137-39.

CHAPTER SEVEN

The Dynastic Theme in Eschatological Prophecy

The great line of the centuries begins anew. Now the Virgin returns, the reign of Saturn returns, now a new generation descends from heaven on high.

Virgil, *Fourth Eclogue*

Rereading, Reinterpreting, and Expanding Prophetic Books

The idea that biblical prophecy is essentially about the future is widespread and understandable, but can be misleading when we are dealing with the kind of biblical prophecy which achieved its own distinctive, canonical status in book form. To take an example: there is agreement that the prophecies of Amos, from the middle decades of the eighth century B.C.E., focus predominantly on the present and the immediate future. They begin with denunciation of neighboring states for unprovoked aggression, war atrocities, and selling prisoners of war into slavery. They then move on to a scathing condemnation of social injustice, the oppression of the poor by the ruling classes, and widespread commercial and economic cheating and fraud in Israelite society, all covered with a veneer of religious devotion which Amos rejects with bitter scorn. There are other forms of prophecy in this book and in the other nine books in "Latter Prophets" which date from the time of the kingdoms, but this concentration on the contemporary scene is characteristic of all of them. Max Weber could therefore say, with some exaggeration, that "the preexilic prophets from Amos to Jeremiah and Ezekiel, viewed through the eyes of the contemporary outsider, appeared to be, above all, political demagogues and, on occasion, pamphleteers."[1]

The judgment that these preexilic prophets pass on their contemporaries is predicted for the immediate future, to be inflicted more often than not through the agency of foreign nations, whether Assyrians or Babylonians. Prospects for the more distant and imagined future are to be sought, for the most part, in additions to the collections resulting from reading, reflection, and reinterpretation in the light of later events and situations unknown to and unanticipated by the original prophetic authors. Among these events the most important and cataclysmic were, of course, the fall of Jerusalem, the eclipse of the national dynasty, and subsequent deportations. For most of these expansions the future state, the end time, is envisaged as a return to an idealized past — a *restitutio in integrum,* an instantiation of the restorative and utopian messianism as described by Gershom Scholem.[2] For many of these addenda, the ideal past is the time when David ruled over a united and prosperous Israel free from foreign inroads and subjection to the rule of the great empires.

Since our concern is with the dynastic theme, we begin by noting the almost uniformly negative view of the monarchy in the original prophetic deposit. With the exception of Obadiah, Nahum, and Habakkuk, books concerned exclusively with foreign nations (respectively, Edom, Assyria, and Babylonia), the preexilic prophets, to a greater or lesser degree of intensity, denounce current rulers and ruling classes. These same books are also the ones which contain, to a greater or lesser degree, expansive commentary provoked by these denunciations. The commentary comes for the most part in the form of a projection into the future of a reconstituted and reunited people under an ideal ruler modelled on a David who was already at that time the stuff of legend. This dictates what must be done in the present chapter before going any further. The task is to survey from this specific perspective some of the more significant examples of additions to and expansions of prophetic texts in the light of later situations, often situations of crisis, in which David, or a Davidic dynast, is to play a decisive role. The texts in question are taken from the following books: Isaiah, Jere-

1. Max Weber, *Ancient Judaism,* trans. and ed. Hans H. Gerth and Don Martindale (Glencoe: Free Press, 1952) 267. On Weber's views on prophecy, see also his *Economy and Society,* ed. Guenther Roth and Claus Wittich (Berkeley: University of California Press, 1978) 1:439-68.

2. Gershom Scholem, *The Messianic Idea in Judaism* (New York: Schocken, 1971) 1-36.

miah, Ezekiel, Amos, Hosea, Micah, and Zephaniah. At the outset, caveats are in order. First, most, but not all, scholars agree that the passages in question are additions to the original prophecies; second, it is not always possible to determine the time of composition of the additions; third, it will bear repeating that our investigation is limited to *Davidic* messianism and does not call for venturing into the vast hinterland of messianic movements and messianism in general, on which an enormous amount has been, and continues to be, written.[3]

Jeremiah and Ezekiel

According to the superscript of the book which bears his name, Jeremiah was active from sometime before the death of Josiah in 609 B.C.E. to sometime after the flight into Egypt following the assassination of Gedaliah, an event which, as stated earlier, probably took place in 582. Ezekiel's commissioning for the prophetic office is dated to the fifth year of King Jehoiachin's exile, therefore to 593 (Ezek 1:2), and the final vision, about the new temple (Ezekiel 40–48), occurred in the twenty-fifth year of the exile, halfway to the fifty-year Jubilee, therefore in 572 (Ezek 40:1). This last section, though well enough integrated into the structure of the book as a whole, is, in its final form, a product of Ezekiel's disciples and followers.[4] Since it bears the stamp of Ezekiel's own theological thinking and style, there is no reason to deny him a part in its production. Ezekiel was therefore a some-

---

3. For one recent exploration in the hinterland, see Adela Yarbro Collins and John J. Collins, *King and Messiah as Son of God: Divine, Human, and Angelic Messianic Figures in Biblical and Related Literature* (Grand Rapids: Eerdmans, 2008).

4. A major thematic link is the departure of the divine *kābôd* ("glory," "effulgence") from the east gate of the temple before its destruction (10:18-19) and its return by the same gate in the vision narrated in chs. 40–48 (43:1-5). At an earlier stage of the formation of the book, the vision of the new temple probably followed immediately Ezek 37:26-28, the promise of God's perpetual presence in the sanctuary, before the insertion of the apocalypse about Gog in the land of Magog (chs. 38–39). A survey of issues in the editorial history of Ezekiel can be found in Ronald E. Clements, "The Ezekiel Tradition: Prophecy in a Time of Crisis," in *Israel's Prophetic Tradition: Essays in Honour of Peter Ackroyd*, ed. Richard Coggins, Anthony Phillips, and Michael Knibb (Cambridge: Cambridge University Press, 1982) 119-36. The reader might also consult the most recent commentaries at this time of writing: Paul M. Joyce, *Ezekiel* (LHB/OTS 482; New York: T. & T. Clark, 2007); Karl-Friedrich Pohlmann, *Ezechiel: Der Stand der theologischen Diskussion* (Darmstadt: Wissenschaftliche Buchgesellschaft, 2008); Steven Tuell, *Ezekiel* (NIBCOT; Peabody: Hendrickson, 2009).

what younger contemporary of Jeremiah, about whom we hear nothing after his preaching to an unreceptive public in Egypt where presumably he died (Jeremiah 44). The oracles and discourses of both were subjected to editorial expansion, Jeremiah's more than Ezekiel's, and there are some indications of reciprocal influence. One example: Ezekiel's condemnation of venal and self-serving shepherds (i.e., rulers), whose sheep have been scattered far and wide (Ezek 34:1-10), either draws on the passage about "shepherds" in Jer 23:1-8 or both derive from the same source.[5] Both books convey the sense of a world which has come to an end and a groping for a new beginning. Both are concerned with the question how the disaster of 586 could have happened and what might be the necessary conditions for the restoration of a meaningful religious life in its aftermath.

An indication that the editorial activity apparent in Jeremiah and Ezekiel began soon after the floruit of the two prophets is the close literary connection between condemnation of current Judean rulers and predictions of a radically different future. Jeremiah's condemnation of worthless shepherds (23:1-4), the Judean kings named in the previous passage (22:11-30), is followed immediately by the prediction of a future righteous ruler of David's lineage (23:5-6).[6] Likewise Ezekiel, whose promise of a future good shepherd, "my servant David" (34:23-24), follows an extended allegory about worthless shepherds and abandoned sheep in the present (34:1-19). This expansive comment in both books then gave rise to a further rereading in a famously obscure passage about shepherds and sheep in Zechariah 11, which will be discussed in the following chapter. The condemnation in Jer 17:19-23 of Judean kings for nonobservance of Sabbath is likewise countered with the prediction that, if the Sabbath law is observed, "there shall enter by the gates of this city kings who occupy the throne of David, riding in chariots and on horses" (Jer 17:24-25), a promise repeated in practically identical words later in the book (22:4). This prediction of the triumphant entry into Jerusalem of a Davidic ruler may, in its turn, have prompted the vision of the royal *parousia* in Zech 9:9-10, but in that case of a ruler who will reject chariots and war horses and enter riding on a donkey. The Zech-

---

5. See John Wolf Miller, *Das Verhältnis Jeremias und Hesekiels sprachlich und theologisch untersucht* (Assen: Van Gorcum, 1955), and the commentaries on Ezek 34:1-10 listed in the previous note; also Clements, "The Ezekiel Tradition," 119-26.

6. The title *YHWH ṣidqēnû* ("Yahweh our righteousness") assigned to the future ruler of David's lineage may be an ironic allusion to the name of Judah's last king, Zedekiah (*ṣidqiyyāhû*) who, in the view of the Dtr Historian, was conspicuously unrighteous.

ariah text, finally, will shape the account of the entry of Jesus, Son of David, into Jerusalem in the last week of his life (Matt 21:1-11 and parallels).

One aspect of the formation of the book of Jeremiah, in progress throughout the Second Temple period, is the significant difference in extent between MT and the LXX, the latter being shorter than the former by about an eighth. Jer 23:5-6, the passage about the righteous future ruler, which corresponds to the shorter Greek text, has a close parallel in Jer 33:14-16, which is the longer variant of the Masoretic Text (MT Jer 33:14-26). This longer and later version betrays an interesting development in attitude towards the dynasty. In the first place, it avoids using the word "king" *(melek),* referring instead to the future dynast as "a man seated on the throne of the house of Israel" (33:17). It also substitutes "Jerusalem" for "Judah," and the title "Yahweh our righteousness" *(YHWH ṣidqēnû)* is transferred from the future Davidic ruler to Jerusalem. While predicting a righteous king of the line of David, it therefore focuses as much on Jerusalem as on the ruler. Even more significant is the introduction in the longer version of the Levitical priesthood alongside the dynasty and the Levitical covenant alongside the Davidic covenant, both of which are guaranteed perpetuity (33:17-22). The later version therefore reflects the growing power of the priesthood vis-à-vis civic rulers in the later Second Temple period. This important development is anticipated in the Deuteronomistic ideal polity, including "the law of the king," which postulates something close to a constitutional monarchy under the law administered by the Levitical priesthood (Deut 17:14-20).

The same tendency is displayed in schematic fashion in Ezekiel's vision of the ideal temple state, "a kingdom of priests, a holy nation" (Exod 19:6), in chs. 40–48. Throughout this section of the book the future civic authority is referred to as *nāśî'* ("prince," "leader"), never as *melek* ("king").[7] The land allotted to the civic leader in this visionary cartography is less central topographically and symbolically than that of the priesthood (Ezek 45:7-8; 48:21-22). His principal duty appears to be the provision of abundant subventions in species and kind to the temple cult (45:13-25; 46:4-7, 13-15), and his liturgical functions are set out in some detail (44:3; 46:2, 8, 10, 12). He is reminded of his obligation to obey the law and avoid abuses such as the expropriation of property for his own purposes (45:9-12). Since this is the record of a visionary experience, whether real or purely literary, it could

---

7. The term *melek* occurs only where the seer's angelic guide speaks of the idolatry and ritual transgressions of Judah's kings in the past (Ezek 43:6-9).

afford to lay out a future prospect and agenda strongly in favor of the class to which Ezekiel himself belonged, namely, the priesthood (Ezek 1:3). The relation between Zerubbabel the governor and Jeshua the high priest in the early Persian period exhibits a similar but more friendly and cooperative balance between the civil and religious authority.

This balance of power between monarchy and priesthood, royal palace and temple seems to point to more chastened political expectations for the restoration of the Davidic dynasty and the tendency for the dynastic theme to become part of a more complex eschatological scenario. In Ezekiel 37, which seems to have been originally the final chapter of the first part of the book,[8] the David theme takes its place in the vision of the future together with a return to the land (vv. 12, 21, 25), the reunion of north and south, Ephraim and Judah (vv. 15-23), endowment with the spirit (v. 14), and the divine indwellng (v. 27). Since the priest had long been considered the custodian of the law, this tensive relationship between ruler and the temple clergy represented a movement away from the idea that the ruler was the epitome and embodiment of the law, the *lex animata,* and the principal agent of its promulgation and implementation. The temple priesthood, or at least the temple priestly aristocracy under Persian rule, and more unambiguously under Ptolemaic and Seleucid dominion, therefore grew in power, influence, and wealth, but their theocratic ideal was never free of the shadow of David and the memory of a past that one day might become a present.

Amos, Hosea, Micah, Zephaniah

Though Hosea comes first in the Book of the Twelve *(Dodekapropheton),* Amos has chronological priority. The title of his book places him in the mid-decades of the eighth century B.C.E., during the relatively prosperous

---

8. Consistent with the solemn, recapitulatory nature of the material, including the Valley of Dry Bones and the Two Sticks Made One. The chapter concludes with the promise of Yahweh's sanctuary in the midst of his people (37:27-28), an appropriate introduction to the Temple Vision of chs. 40-48, with the Gog in the Land of Magog apocalypse inserted at a later date, as many commentators have argued, e.g., G. A. Cooke, *A Critical and Exegetical Commentary on the Book of Ezekiel* (ICC 21; Edinburgh: T. & T. Clark, 1936) 407-8; Walther Zimmerli, *Ezekiel 2,* trans. James D. Martin (Hermeneia; Philadelphia: Fortress, 1983) 302-4 (attribution to Ezekiel no more than possible). On these issues connected with the formation of the book, see the variety of opinion in the most recent commentators.

and successful reign of Jeroboam II in Samaria. He was therefore an older contemporary of Hosea who lived through the last days of the kingdom of Samaria but apparently did not witness the fall of the city to the Assyrians in 722.[9] No more than three years after the death of Jeroboam, the Assyrian emperor Tiglath-pileser III embarked on a deliberate program of expansion reaching as far west as the Aegean, with a view to establishing an imperial system of subject provinces involving the displacement of entire populations. This was a fateful moment for Israel, Judah, and neighboring small and mid-size states, and although Assyria is not mentioned in the book of Amos,[10] its shadow lies threateningly over it.[11]

In its final form, the book of Amos is of Judean origin, having been subjected to more than one Judean redaction both before and after 586 B.C.E.[12] The book opens with indictments of foreign nations composed in a

---

9. Hosea's namesake, the last ruler of the kingdom of Israel/Samaria, rebelled against Shalmaneser V, was captured, imprisoned, and perhaps put to death before the fall of the city (2 Kgs 17:3-6; Hos 13:10-11). For the historical background, see J. Maxwell Miller and John H. Hayes, *A History of Ancient Israel and Judah* (2nd ed., Louisville: Westminster/John Knox, 2006) 383-88; A. A. Macintosh, *A Critical and Exegetical Commentary on Hosea* (ICC; Edinburgh: T. & T. Clark, 1997) lxxxiii-vii.

10. Amos 3:9 LXX reads *en assyriois* ("among the Assyrians") for MT *bĕʾašdôd* ("in Ashdod"), but emendation is not called for.

11. Amos 6:1-3 invites the ruling class in Jerusalem and Samaria to inspect the sites of Calneh, Hamath, and Gath to get an idea of what is in store for them. That Calneh (or Calno) and Hamath were conquered by Tiglath-pileser in 738 B.C.E. has persuaded some commentators, most recently D. F. Strijdom, "Reappraising the Historical Context of Amos," *OTE* 24 (1911) 221-54, that Amos must have been active after the Assyrian campaign of that year. But the fact that this passage is addressed in the first place to "those that are at ease in Zion," taken with the Assyrian boast of having conquered the two cities in Isa 10:9; 36:19, suggests the likelihood that this saying is of Judean origin.

12. Advocates of multiple redactions include Robert B. Coote, *Amos Among the Prophets: Composition and Theology* (Philadelphia: Fortress, 1981); Theodor Lescow, "Das nachexilische Amosbuch: Erwägungen zu seiner Kompositionsgeschichte," *BN* 99 (1999) 69-101 (at least five redactions from the early seventh century B.C.E. to the Hellenistic period); Reinhard Gregor Kratz, "Die Worte des Amos von Tekoa," in *Propheten in Mari, Assyrien und Israel,* ed. Matthias Köchert and Martti Nissinen (FRLANT 201; Göttingen: Vandenhoeck & Ruprecht, 2003) 54-89 = Kratz, *Prophetenstudien* (FAT 74; Tübingen: Mohr Sieback, 2011) 310-43; *Die Propheten Israels* (Munich: Beck, 2003) 63-69. The most radical and revisionist thesis is that of Christoph Levin, "Das Amosbuch der Anawim," *ZTK* 94 (1997) 407-36 = *Fortschreibungen: Gesammelte Studien zum Alten Testament* (BZAW 316; Berlin: de Gruyter, 2003) 265-90, according to whom the book reflects an apocalyptic *Weltanschauung* and its social criticism must be understood against the conditions obtaining during the Achaemenid and Hellenistic periods.

formulaic style which, surprisingly, include Judah and Israel (Amos 1:3–2:8). No one doubts that Israel was added to the original list to make the point, repeated throughout the book, that Israel, meaning in this context the kingdom of Samaria, has forfeited its special relationship with Yahweh on account of religious infidelity and immorality and is now on the same level as the other foreign nations mentioned. Read in this way, the indictment of Israel serves as introduction to the entire book. It is equally apparent that the Judah saying is a later addition (2:4-5). The charge of neglecting the law *(tôrâ)* and the statutes reflects the point of view of Deuteronomy and postdisaster Deuteronomistic scribes whose activity can be detected elsewhere in the book.[13] A particularly interesting case occurs in the gnomic poem about the irresistible force of divine inspiration couched in a series of rhetorical questions (Amos 3:3-8). The seventh and last of these, which runs: "If disaster strikes a city, has not Yahweh brought it about?" provoked the scribal comment which follows, to the effect that "Yahweh God does nothing without revealing his secret to his servants the prophets." "His servants the prophets" is the standard way of referring to prophets in Dtr and related writings, and since the reader in the postdisaster era would inevitably identify the city with Jerusalem, the gloss would have had the purpose of justifying Yahweh's action in bringing about its destruction.[14] What is only hinted at here is stated explicitly in the Historian's reflections on the unheeded warnings of "his servants the prophets" which hastened the fall of Samaria one hundred and thirty-six years earlier (2 Kgs 17:13).

There is some uncertainty about the original status of the indictments against Tyre (Amos 1:9-10)[15] and Edom (1:11-12),[16] but it is arguable

---

13. Two examples: the synchrony of northern and southern reigns in the titles of Amos and Hosea corresponds to the same practice in the introduction to individual reigns in Dtr beginning at 1 Kgs 15:1 and ending with 2 Kgs 18:1; the appeal to "seek Yahweh" or "seek what is good" (Amos 5:4, 6, 14-15) corresponds to the Deuteronomistic plea, addressed to Judean expatriates, to seek Yahweh in repentance, prayer, and worship (Deut 4:29; Jer 29:13; 50:4).

14. See the discussion of this passage above, pp. 56-57.

15. Tyre was never part of David's "empire." The toponym *mibṣār-ṣōr* appears in the account of David's census of his subjects (2 Sam 24:7), but this "Fort Tyre" was probably a site on the Phoenician-Israelite border, as suggested by P. Kyle McCarter, Jr., *II Samuel* (AB 9; Garden City: Doubleday, 1984) 510.

16. Many commentators regard the Edom oracle as "secondary" on account of the hostility towards Edom in texts from the postdisaster period (Obad 10-14; Lam 4:21-22; Ps 137:7; Isa 34:5-17; 63:1-6), but hostility towards Edom did not begin then (see, e.g., 1 Kgs 11:14-22; 2 Kgs 8:20-22; 14:7-10), and there is nothing in Amos 1:11-12 specific to that later time.

that behind the present text there lies a core group of five[17] — Syria, Philistia, Edom, Ammon, and Moab — all neighbors, which is to say enemies of Israel, and all nations subdued by David (2 Sam 8:12). The same names of relatively small western states which, according to tradition, belonged to the "Greater Israel" of David appear frequently in psalms, hymns, and celebratory prose.[18]

Corresponding to the indictment of these five nations at the beginning of the book is the prediction of their future reincorporation into the "Davidic empire" at its end. The relevant passage (Amos 9:11-12) reads as follows:

> On that day
> I shall restore the fallen[19] booth of David,
> I shall repair the gaps in its walls and restore its ruins,
> rebuilding it as it was ages ago;
> so that they may possess what is left of Edom,
> and all the nations once called by my name.[20]
> An oracle of Yahweh who will bring this about.

A *sukkâ,* usually translated "booth" as here, is a structure which, unless temporary like the one Jonah put up to shade himself from the sun (Jonah 4:5), is made of solid materials, especially wood. It can be a guard post in a vineyard (Isa 1:8; Job 27:18), a shelter for cattle (Gen 33:17), or a temporary army headquarters when on campaign (1 Kgs 20:12, 16). It can also have religious connotations, most obviously in connection with the Festival of *Sukkôt,* but also as a supernatural protective covering in the depiction of the eschatological Jerusalem in Isa 4:5-6. In our passage, the vocabulary strongly suggests a building, or buildings, and since it is David's *sukkâ,* and in ruins, most probably Jerusalem in the aftermath of the Babylonian conquest.[21]

---

17. Pentads are frequent in Amos: five visions (7:1-3, 4-6, 7-9; 8:1-3; 9:1-4), five reproaches each concluding with the complaint "yet you did not return to me" (4:6-11), five indictments (2:6-8), and five verdicts (5:13-15). Compare the fivefold Torah and the fivefold division of Psalms.

18. E.g., Zech 2:4-11(Eng 1:21–2:6); Ps 60:9-11(7-9); 83:7-8(6-7).

19. The temporal sense of the participle *nōpelet* can be present, imminent future, or past (GKC §116d). Here the best option is past, as in LXX, Vulg, and Tg *(dĕnāpĕlat).*

20. The idiom signifies possession; see Kurt Galling, "Die Ausrufung des Namens als Rechtsakt in Israel," *TLZ* 81 (1956) 65-70; Shalom M. Paul, *Amos* (Hermeneia; Minneapolis: Fortress, 1991) 292.

21. See, *inter alios,* Kenneth E. Pomykala, "Jerusalem as the Fallen Booth of David,

This prediction of the restoration of the "Greater Israel" of the Davidic-Solomonic epoch and the rebuilding of Jerusalem can be situated with a good degree of probability during the late Neo-Babylonian or early Achaemenid period. Its language and themes have their counterpart in the later stages of the Isaian literary tradition, including the so-called Trito-Isaiah (chs. 56–66) which, however, does not refer explicitly to David. The point may be made by citing two passages from that section of the book:[22]

> Some of your people will rebuild the ancient ruins,
> you will build on foundations laid long ago;
> you will be called repairer of the breach,
> restorer of ruined dwellings.
>
> (Isa 58:12)

> They will rebuild the ancient ruins,
> restore the places long desolate,
> repair the ruined cities
> desolate for ages past.
>
> (Isa 61:4)

The idea of restoration or "raising up" in Amos 9:11 is of frequent occurrence in late-Isaian texts with reference to the desolate sites left in the wake of the Babylonian conquest. The repair of the gaps or breaches in the walls of ruined cities, especially of course Jerusalem, is equally frequent (Isa 58:12; cf. Ezek 13:5; 22:30). This work of restoration, repairing, and rebuilding looks back to the way it was "ages ago, in the days of old" (cf. Isa 51:9; 63:9, 11). Repairing the ruins was one of the tasks with which Cyrus was

---

Amos 9:11," in *God's Word for Our World*. Vol. 1: *Biblical Studies in Honor of Simon John De Vries*, ed. J. Harold Ellens *et al.* (JSOTSup 388; London: T. & T. Clark, 2004) 1:275-93. Max E. Polley, *Amos and the Davidic Empire: A Socio-Historical Approach* (New York: Oxford University Press, 1989), argues on the basis of Amos 9:11-12, which he regards as a saying of Amos, that the prophet's goal was the reunion of the two kingdoms under the Davidic dynasty. Klaus Koch, *The Prophets*. Vol. 1: *The Assyrian Period* (Philadelphia: Fortress, 1983 [German ed. 1978]) 69-70, also assigns 9:11-12 to Amos, even though he regards Amos as originating not in Judean Tekoa but in a Galilean town of the same name, one unattested in the Hebrew Bible. John Barton, *Amos' Oracles against the Nations: A Study of Amos 1.3–2.5* (SOTSMS 6; Cambridge: Cambridge University Press, 1980), holds that both the Edom and Tyre oracles are editorially added. He deals for the most part with social-ethical issues.

22. The translations are from my *Isaiah 56–66* (AB 19B; New York: Doubleday, 2003) 8, 13.

charged by the God of Israel (Isa 44:26-28; 45:13), and his failure to do so is apparent in the mood of disillusionment expressed in the later stages of the tradition in Isaiah 40–66. The emphasis on Edom in Amos 9:12 (". . . in order that they may possess what is left of Edom") is also understandable in view of Judean-Edomite hostility during and after the Babylonian conquest, well attested in biblical texts from that time.[23]

This vision of a restored dynasty in a rebuilt Jerusalem with its former territories continues and concludes as follows:

> The time is coming, says Yahweh,
> when the one who ploughs will catch up with the one who reaps,
> and the one who treads the grapes with the one who sows the seed.
> The mountains will drip sweet wine, and every hill flow with it.
> I shall restore the fortunes of my people Israel;
> they will rebuild their ruined cities and live in them;
> they will plant vineyards and drink the wine from them,
> cultivate orchards and eat the fruit from them.
> I shall plant them on their own soil,
> no more will they be uprooted from the soil I have given them.
> This is the word of Yahweh your God.
>
> (Amos 9:13-15)

The close connection in ancient societies between the ruler and the well-being of the governed, especially the fertility of the womenfolk, fields, and domestic animals, hardly calls for documentation. Several of the ways in which the association is expressed in this passage are familiar from prophetic texts from the postdisaster period: the mountains dripping with freshly pressed wine (Joel 4:18[Eng 3:18]), planting vineyards and orchards and living to enjoy their produce (Isa 62:8-9; 65:21-22), and a return to the miraculous fertility of the golden age (Isa 65:21-25). The cities laid in ruins by the Babylonians, which Cyrus was expected to restore but did not (Isa 44:26-28; 45:13), will be rebuilt. These projections of a future quite differ-

---

23. Obad 10-14; Lam 4:21-22; Ps 137:7, and esp. the virulent anti-Edomite oracles in Isa 34:5-17; 63:1-6. The reference to "what is left of Edom" *(šĕʾērît ʾĕdôm)* in Amos 9:12 may be an indirect allusion to the takeover of much of the territory of the former kingdom of Edom by the Kedarite Arabs throughout the period of Neo-Babylonian and Achaemenid imperial rule. See Anselm C. Hagedorn, "Edom in the Book of Amos and Beyond," in *Aspects of Amos: Exegesis and Imagination,* ed. Hagedorn and Andrew Mein (LHB/OTS 536; London: T. & T. Clark, 2011) 41-57.

ent from the unsatisfactory present are well attested in biblical texts and are summed up in the succinct Hebrew expression *šûb šĕbût,* which is practically untranslatable but signifies a change from bad to good fortune as, for example, from captivity to freedom (9:14). It encapsulates, especially in Deuteronomy and prophetic texts, the idea of the restoration of an idealized past.[24] It does so by playing on the ambiguities of the Hebrew verb *šûb,* meaning "return," but with the further connotations of "a return to the past," "restoration," "repentance," "return from exile" — this last reinforced by assonance with the verb *šābâ,* "take captive."

This last prophecy in Amos may be read as a visionary reaction to the disappointment of hopes in the restoration of the Davidic line. One of the most persistent ways of reacting to disaster, decline, or powerlessness is nostalgia for an imagined great age in the past, often at the beginnings of the national or ethnic group, and more often than not in the form of the recovery of political and military power and influence. After the fall of Jerusalem, attempts were made to preserve links with that past by the direct route of restoring the dynastic succession cut off with the public execution of the sons of Zedekiah (2 Kgs 25:7). But after the failed coup of Ishmael, the failure of Jehoiachin to return as king after thirty-seven years of exile (2 Kgs 25:27-30), the failure of the Babylonian revolts to prevent the consolidation of the Persian Empire in the early months of the reign of Darius I, and the disappointment of expectations placed on the elusive figure of Zerubbabel, the restoration of the Davidic dynasty in the present or immediate future gave way to visions, aspirations, and dreams of a restoration of the past in a future only dimly discerned.

Implicit in the envisaged future restoration of the Davidic "empire" in Amos 9:11-12 is the reunion of Ephraim, the kingdom of Israel, and Judah, north and south, under one of David's lineage and therefore the restoration of a perceived common origin. This feature is more clearly in evidence in editorial additions to Hosea, not all from the postdisaster period.[25] It will continue to be an essential element in prophetic restora-

---

24. Deut 30:3; also Hos 6:11; Joel 4:1(3:1); Zeph 3:20; and frequently in Jeremiah 30-31, a section of the book which is full of restorative imagery. Peter Weimar, "Der Schluss des Amos-Buches: Ein Beitrag zur Redaktionsgeschichte des Amos-Buches," *BN* 16 (1981) 60-100, argues that Amos 9:11, 14-15 is a restorationist-messianic text from the time of Haggai, Zechariah 1–8, and Zerubbabel.

25. Methods and results in scholarly opinion on the editorial history of the book of Hosea differ widely. Contrast, e.g., the rather minimal position of James Luther Mays, *Hosea* (OTL; Philadelphia: Westminster, 1969) 15-17; and Macintosh, *Commentary on Hosea,* lxv-

tion scenarios, especially in additions to Jeremiah, some sections of which seem to have been strongly influenced by Hosea. The belief in a common origin of north and south is part of the subtext of the following comment added to the figurative history of Hosea's marriage and his three children with which the book of Hosea opens:

> The number of the people of Israel will be like the sand of the sea which can neither be measured nor counted. In the place where it was said of them, "You are not my people," they will be addressed as "sons of the Living God." The people of Judah and the people of Israel will be gathered together, they will appoint for themselves one leader, and they will flourish in the land, for great will be the day of Jezreel. You are to say to your brothers "You are my people" and to your sisters "You are loved." (Hos 2:1-3[Eng 1:10–2:1])

In this passage the Davidic dynast is referred to obliquely as "one leader," but in another description of the prospect for the future the restoration of a united Israel under a descendant of David is more explicit.

> For a long time the people of Israel will remain without king or prince, without sacrifice and sacred pillar, without ephod and teraphim. Afterwards, the people of Israel will once again seek Yahweh their God and David their king, and they will revere Yahweh and his goodness in the latter days. (Hos 3:4-5)[26]

The allusion in this prediction to the goodness or bounty of Yahweh recalls the vision of future well-being and abundance following on the restoration of Israel's fortunes in Amos 9:13-15. The point is made in a rather more recondite manner in a rare case of a gloss on a gloss in Hos 6:11. After one more denunciation of Israel (the kingdom of Samaria) by Hosea in the previous verse, a Judean scribe has added, probably shortly after the fall of Samaria, a brief admonition about the danger of Judah sharing the same

---

lxxiv, with the multilayered editorial history of Thomas Naumann, *Hoseas Erben: Strukturen der Nachinterpretation im Buch Hosea* (BWANT 7/11; Stuttgart: Kohlhammer, 1991); and Martti Nissinen, *Prophetie, Redaktion und Fortschreibung im Hoseabuch: Studien zum Werdegang eines Prophetenbuches im Licht vom Hos 4 und 1* (AOAT 231; Kevalaer: Butzon & Bercker and Neukirchen: Neukirchener, 1991).

26. It seems to me more probable that the entire passage is editorial rather than just the phrase "and David their king" (*wě'ēt dāwid malkām*).

fate: "For you too, Judah, a harvest is appointed" (v. 11a). This is an ominous warning, and "a harvest" is to be understood as "a harvest of reckoning" (REB). But then a later Judean glossator chose to understand "harvest" in a positive sense, as was perfectly normal, and added to the existing gloss the qualification "when I restore the fortunes of my people" (6:11b). This too is reminiscent of Amos 9:13-15 and uses the same shorthand idiom, *šûb šĕbût*, the restoration of good fortune.

Micah, the most radical critic of contemporary society among the prophets, even more so than Amos, was a contemporary of Isaiah (mid- to late 8th century B.C.E.), and his book has enough in common with the book of Isaiah to justify the proposal that the two collections were edited together.[27] The description of a corrupt Jerusalem doomed to destruction is in stark contrast to the vision in Mic 4:1-7 of the ideal Zion to which the dispersed sons and daughters of Israel will return under the guidance of Yahweh and in which Yahweh will reign as king, clearly a later addition to the book. Unlike Amos and Isaiah, however, Micah has little to say about David and his dynasty. At a time of deprivation and disorientation, Zion is told that the former dominion and sovereignty will return, but David is not named (Mic 4:8-10). Even more recondite is the prediction of a ruler from Bethlehem (Mic 5:1-4a[Eng 2-5a]):

From you, Bethlehem Ephrathah,
one of the least among the clans of Judah,
there shall come forth for me a ruler over Israel,
one whose origins are from old, from ancient times.[28]
Therefore he shall give them up until the time
when she who is pregnant gives birth.

27. Among indications of a shared editorial history are the following: "I will go barefoot and naked" (Mic 1:8), which brings to mind Isaiah's sign-act of walking naked and barefoot on the occasion of Sargon's campaign against Philistine Ashdod in 711 B.C.E. (Isa 20:1-6); the approach of an enemy from the southwest (Mic 1:10-16), close to a similar scenario in Isa 10:27b-32; the vision of the eschatological Zion in Mic 4:1-5, a variant of Isa 2:2-5; and the description of a land full of idols, cult objects, and sorcery in Mic 5:9-14(Eng 10-15), which has much in common in content and style with Isa 2:6-22.

28. In the phrase *môṣā'ōtâw miqqedem*, "his origins (are) from old," the rare word *môṣā'â*, from the verbal stem *yṣ'*, "to go out," could perhaps, like the similar substantive *môṣā'* in Ps 19:7(6), refer to the ascendancy from the horizon of the sun or a planet. In keeping with this possibility, Aage Bentzen, *King and Messiah* (London: Lutterworth, 1955) 17, gave the alternative meaning "east" to *qedem* (reference in Delbert R. Hillers, *Micah* [Hermeneia; Philadelphia: Fortress, 1984] 65), but this does not make a good fit with the context.

> Then the rest of their kin will return
> to the people of Israel.
> He will rise up and tend the flock
> in the strength of Yahweh,
> in the majesty of the name of Yahweh his God.
> They will dwell in security
> for then his name will be great to the ends of the earth.
> Then there will be peace.

The language is deliberately arcane in keeping with its oracular content, in this respect not unlike the last of Balaam's oracular utterances in which the astronomical or astrological allusion is explicit:

> I see him, but not now,
> I behold him, but not near:
> a star will come forth out of Jacob,
> a comet will arise from Israel.

(Num 24:17)

Both sayings may have drawn on much older, oracular material. In the Micah passage the ruler originates in Bethlehem, David's town, and belongs to the Ephrathites, David's clan (1 Sam 17:12; Ruth 1:2; 4:17). These humble origins, expressed in conventional language — "one of the least among the clans of Judah" (cf. Gideon in Judg 6:15 and Saul in 1 Sam 9:21) — are in deliberate contrast with Jerusalem, corrupted by its current leadership and doomed, according to Mic 3:12, to be destroyed. It is not clear whether this is the eschatological language of *David redivivus,* the king now hidden who will return, or a prediction of a change of fortune in real time with the birth of a new ruler who will bring back those dispersed abroad, be solicitous for his subjects — the familiar "good shepherd" motif — and have the power and prestige to ensure security and peace. The language and themes are close enough to the Isaian prediction of the birth of the wonderful child (Isa 7:14-16; 9:1-6[Eng 2-7]) to permit the conclusion that Mic 5:1-4a(2-5a) is another instance of redaction and transmission shared with Isaiah.[29] In both books, in any case, predictions about a more immediate fu-

---

29. See Theodor Lescow, "Das Geburtsmotiv in den messianischen Weissagungen bei Jesaja und Micha," *ZAW* 79 (1967) 172-207; and on the passage in general, Hillers, *Micah,* 64-67.

ture event — a royal pregnancy and birth — could have been given a different and more ample scope once the Davidic dynasty had passed from the scene.

The superscript of Zephaniah places his prophecies in the reign of Josiah (640-609 B.C.E.), but some are certainly later, beginning with the apocalyptic threat of total destruction with which the prophecies open (Zeph 1:2-3). The vividly described future projection in Zeph 3:8-20, featuring the assembly of the nations for judgment (cf. Joel 4:1-3, 11-15[Eng 3:1-3, 11-15]), the universal worship of Israel's God (cf. Isa 19:24-25), the purified remnant of Israel (cf. Mic 2:12-13), and the establishment of Yahweh's reign in Zion (cf. Ps 99:1-5), is certainly postexilic. There are, in addition, problems involved in matching Zephaniah's description of conditions under Josiah with the account of the reign of Josiah in Dtr (2 Kgs 22–23). The threat of divine punishment directed against the king's sons (Zeph 1:8) is difficult to place during the reign of a ruler only eight years old at his accession (2 Kgs 22:1). The denunciation of the Baal cult and its priests, Assyrian astral deities, and the national deity of Ammon (Zeph 1:4-6), together with the condemnation of the royal court, the religious sceptics ("Yahweh will do nothing, neither good nor bad," 1:12), and the entire political and religious elite in a city defiled by idolatry (1:7-13; 2:1-3; 3:1-5), is also problematic. If all this is from Josiah's reign, it must correspond to the situation preceding the religious reforms, dated in Dtr to Josiah's eighteenth year, that is, 622 (2 Kgs 22:3). In that case, however, questions arise about the role of the politically and religiously traditionalist ʿam hāʾāreṣ who, having put Josiah on the throne, would probably have had a strong, possibly controlling influence on policies pursued at the court during his minority.

The four prophetic books briefly surveyed for clues to the afterlife of the Davidic-dynastic theme cover the period of the high tide and the sudden collapse of Assyrian imperialism: according to the superscripts, Amos and Hosea during the reign of Uzziah (785-760), Micah under the reign of Jotham (759-744), and Zephaniah during the reign of Josiah (640-609). They have enough in common, chronologically and in some other respects, to suggest that they may have constituted an early stage in the redaction of the Book of the Twelve.[30] One thing all four, and in fact all the

---

30. James Nogalski, *Literary Precursors to the Book of the Twelve* (BZAW 217; Berlin: de Gruyter, 1993) 278-80; Rainer Albertz, "Exile as Purification: Reconstructing the 'Book of the Four,'" in *Thematic Threads in the Book of the Twelve*, ed. Paul L. Redditt and Aaron Schart (BZAW 325; Berlin: de Gruyter, 2003) 232-51; Jakob Wöhrle, *Die frühen Sammlungen des Zwölfprophetenbuch: Entstehung und Komposition* (BZAW 360; Berlin: de Gruyter, 2006).

units in the *Dodekapropheton,* have in common is a dominant eschatological perspective. This conclusion results from a close reading of the Twelve, but can also be deduced from broader structural features, beginning with the number of books in the collection. It seems that some reconfiguration and rearrangement was necessary in order to come up with and maintain the number twelve. The collection ends with three units roughly equal in length and with the identical superscript, "an oracle; word of Yahweh" (*maśśāʾ, dĕbar YHWH:* Zech 9:1; 12:1; Mal 1:1). The third of these, Malachi, has been assigned an obvious pseudonym, taken as it is from Mal 3:1 (*mal'ākî* = "my messenger"), with reference to a future "messenger of the covenant."[31] Then, in order to avoid exceeding the number twelve, the other two were appended to Zechariah 1–8.

If we go on to ask why these readjustments were considered necessary, the answer that comes to mind is that the collection is intended to represent twelve-tribal Israel and, in view of the direction of the editing of the book, the eschatological twelve-tribal Israel, the Israel which plays such a dominant role in end-time scenarios, including the New Testament book of Revelation. Confirmation is at hand in the concluding statement in Malachi, and therefore in the Book of the Twelve, which identifies the "messenger of the covenant" in Mal 3:1 with Elijah, who is to return before the great and terrible Day of Yahweh (Mal 3:23-24[Eng 4:5-6]). In his eulogy on Elijah, Jesus ben Sira takes a similar view:

> You who are ready at the appointed time, it is written,
> to calm the wrath of God before it breaks out in fury,
> to turn the heart of the father to the son,
> and to restore the tribes of Israel.
>
> (Sir 48:10)

This statement is clearly not about family values, a subject on which the author has much to say elsewhere, but rather about the eschatological reunion and reintegration of divided Israel, a powerful theme present throughout the *Dodekapropheton.* The theme of reunification is also expressed in Ben Sira's prayer for the deliverance of Israel:

31. Malachi may not be the only example of a pseudonym created to fill out or maintain the number twelve. Obadiah, the shortest "book" in the Hebrew Bible, may have been created ad hoc out of the anti-Edomite oracle in Jer 49:7-11 of which it is a variant. In this respect it is worth noting that the name Obadiah in the shorter form (*'ōbadyâ*) occurs only in Chronicles and Ezra-Nehemiah.

Gather all the tribes of Jacob,
and give them their inheritance, as at the beginning.

(Sir 36:13, 16)[32]

Reading the Book of the Twelve in this way, with those who left it as we today find it, the number twelve is a clue to its basically eschatological intent. Numerological symbolism of this kind will be suspect to many, often justifiably so but not, I believe, in this instance. Consider the parallel case of the fivefold division of the Psalter. Since there was nothing inevitable about this feature, it makes good sense to view it as replicating the fivefold Torah *(ḥamišê ḥumšê ha-tôrâ)*, especially in view of the first psalm, which invites the reader to the study and practice of Torah.[33] The eschatological theme of the Twelve is encapsulated in two of the most frequently recurring motifs throughout it: the Day of Yahweh *(yôm YHWH)*[34] and Reversal of Fortune *(šûb šĕbût)*.[35] These key terms encapsulate a wide but converging range of themes: the restoration of an idealized past, reunion of north and south, repatriation, the pure worship of God, judgment on hostile nations, and secure existence for Israel on its land. These goals are attainable only by the establishment or restoration of stable institutions which means, in the first place, a dynastic monarchy. Neither in Israel nor anywhere else in the ancient Near East and Levant was there any alterna-

32. The David figure is not eschatologized in Ben Sira's eulogy of David (Sir 47:1-11), but the following paragraph on Solomon states that David will have a root and remnant from his own family in spite of Solomon's failings (47:22b). On the reference to the horn of David which will arise from his house in the Hebrew text following 51:12, see Emil Schürer, *The History of the Jewish People in the Age of Jesus Christ (175 B.C.–A.D. 135)*, rev. and ed. by Geza Vermes, Fergus Millar, and Matthew Black (Edinburgh: T. & T. Clark, 1979) 2:498-500.

33. On the last section of Latter Prophets, see my *Prophecy and Canon: A Contribution to the Study of Jewish Origins* (Notre Dame: University of Notre Dame Press, 1977) 120-23.

34. The expression is of frequent occurrence: Joel 1:15-16; 2:1-2, 11; 3:3-5(Eng 2:30-32); 4:14-15(3:14-15); Amos 5:8, 18, 20; Ob 15; Zeph 1:7-8, 14-16, 18; 2:3; Mal 3:19-24(4:1-6). We should also take into account such terms as *bayyôm hahû'* or *bĕ'aḥărît hayyāmîm*, referring to a decisive future divine intervention. See Richard H. Hiers, "Day of the Lord," *ABD*, 2:82-83; Rolf Rentdorff, "'Alas for the Day!': 'The Day of the Lord' in the Book of the Twelve," in *God in the Fray: A Tribute to Walter Brueggemann*, ed. Tod Linafelt and Timothy K. Beal (Minneapolis: Fortress, 1998) 186-97; Jean-Daniel Macchi, "Le thème du 'jour de YHWH' dans les XII petits prophètes," in *Les prophètes de la Bible et le fin des temps: XXIIIᵉ Congrès de l'Association Catholique Française pour l'étude de la Bible,* ed. Jacques Vermeylen. (LD 240; Paris: Cerf, 2010) 141-81.

35. Hos 6:11; Joel 4:1(Eng 3:1); Amos 9:14; Zeph 3:20.

tive to some form of monocracy, elements of which even survived in Athenian democracy of the fifth and fourth centuries B.C.E.[36] It happens, however, that the Davidic dynastic as an explicit theme is by no means prominent throughout the Twelve. David himself is mentioned only twice in the four books surveyed — as the ruler of a future reunited Israel (Hos 3:5) and of those neighboring peoples condemned in the indictments at the beginning of the book (Amos 9:11-12).[37] The theme of reunion was probably relatively short-lived, in the first place on account of the Assyrian policy of cross-deportation resulting in a foreign settlement around Samaria (2 Kgs 17:24); then in view of increasing hostility at the time of Nehemiah between Judah and Samaria ruled by the Sanballat family; then, finally, with the definitive rupture between the Jerusalemite and Samaritan communities. Beginning with the reintegration under a future David, or Davidic descendant, of the neighboring countries subdued by David (Amos 9:11-12), the territorial theme tended to spin off into mythic fantasies of ever-expanding boundaries: Dan to Bethsheba, from the river of Egypt to the Euphrates (Gen 15:18), from the southern wilderness to the Lebanon range, from the Euphrates to the Mediterranean, hence covering the territory of the entire Transeuphrates satrapy under Persian rule (Deut 1:7-8; 11:24), and, finally, from sea to sea and from the Euphrates to the ends of the earth (Ps 72:8; Zech 9:10).

Isaiah

The Isaian collection, built up around the sayings of the prophet Isaiah active in Jerusalem in the latter half of the eighth century B.C.E., is the richest and most diverse of prophetic books. This was no doubt due to the initial impetus given to the *traditio* by Isaiah himself, together with the prestige of the city of which he was to become the prophet laureate. The primary emphasis in the book is, in fact, on the city and its temple as focal points of an envisaged future, more so than on the Davidic theme. The temple is to be the destination for people from all nations — perhaps an allusion to proselytes — who will gladly receive moral instruction which, as always, it

36. Francis Oakley, *Kingship: The Politics of Enchantment* (Oxford: Blackwell, 2006) 46-47.

37. *kĕdāwîd*, Amos 6:5, where the ruling classes in Jerusalem and Samaria either improvise on musical instruments or invent them "like David," is either a textual error or an inappropriate or at least unhelpful gloss.

is the duty of priests to impart (Isa 2:2-5). The term *ṣemaḥ*, "branch," more commonly associated with a Davidic-messianic figure beginning with Zerubbabel, as we have seen, occurs in a brief postexilic adjunct to an Isaian saying, but with reference not to David or the Davidic lineage but to the future purified remnant of the people resident in Jerusalem (Isa 4:2-6). In one of the high points of Proto-Isaiah (chs. 1–39), the future inauguration of Yahweh as king and the revelation of his glory in Jerusalem, followed by the messianic banquet, will mark the end of sorrow and weeping and will even cross the ultimate boundary with the abolition of death (Isa 24:21-23; 25:6-8).

Many of the future-oriented sayings in these chapters from which the dynastic theme is absent have their counterparts in Isaiah 40–66 in which, with the one exception discussed earlier (55:3),[38] the name David does not appear. Yet the prophet himself was directly involved with two rulers, Ahaz (Jehoahaz) and his son Hezekiah, at moments of deadly crisis for the Judean state. In the first of these, in the year 734 B.C.E., the prophet gave comfort and assurance to Ahaz faced with the prospect of an imminent attack on Jerusalem by a coalition of Aram (Damascus) and the kingdom of Israel (Isa 7:1-17). This event is more fully described in 2 Kgs 16:5-20 and probably alluded to in Hos 5:8–6:6.[39] Isaiah offered a sign to back his reassurance; the offer was declined but was given anyway. The sign was a young woman who is pregnant and will give birth in the near future to a son whose name will be Immanuel (Isa 7:14). Since the consoling word, so prominent in early Christianity and Christian liturgies, was addressed in the first instance to the current ruler in the line of David, it is probable that the young woman was his wife and the message to Ahaz was that the dynasty would survive in the person of his son Hezekiah.[40] About three decades later this son of Ahaz faced an even greater threat from the Assyrian

---

38. See above, pp. 61-62.

39. For the Syro-Ephraimite war, the background to this episode, see Miller and Hayes, *A History of Ancient Israel and Judah*, 378-83.

40. The earliest interpretation of the much-debated *'almâ* ("young woman") in Isa 7:14 speaks of a threatened Assyrian attack on Immanuel's land, which in all probability refers to Sennacherib's punitive expedition in 701 B.C.E. (8:8). This reinforces the identification of the child to be born with Hezekiah rather than another son of Ahaz and also militates against the opinion that Immanuel is the prophet's son. Hezekiah is Immanuel; he is also the child born for us, the son given to us of Isa 9:5(Eng 6); he is even the Messiah, the One to Come, in a famous saying of Johanan ben Zakkai in *b. Ber.* 28b. For more detailed discussion and references on this and related issues, see my *Isaiah 1–39* (AB 19; New York: Doubleday, 2000) 227-45.

punitive expedition under Sennacherib as described in Isaiah 36–37. Here, too, Isaiah intervenes and offers assurance of survival reinforced by a sign (37:30-32). Following the fulfillment of his prediction of the Assyrian retreat from before Jerusalem, he heals the king in the name of "Yahweh, God of David your ancestor," and predicts fifteen years more life for him, a prediction reinforced by another sign, this time a miraculous one (Isa 38:1-22). Proto-Isaiah then ends with Isaiah's final intervention on the occasion of the visit of a delegation to Hezekiah from Babylon (39:1-8).[41] The message is that attacks by hostile forces will not succeed and that the dynasty will survive at least for some time to come.

If Isaiah's announcement of the birth of a son to Ahaz gave assurance that the dynasty would not be extinguished by the threat from Judah's northern neighbors, and the sign given Hezekiah provided assurance of surviving the fury of the Assyrian empire, the field of vision in the prediction of a branch from the stump of Jesse in Isa 11:1-9 is amplified and deepened to take in an open-ended future. The passage reads as follows:

> A shoot will grow from Jesse's stump,
> a sprig will spring from its roots.
> On him the spirit of Yahweh will rest,
> a spirit of wisdom and understanding,
> a spirit of counsel and strength,
> a spirit of knowledge and the fear of Yahweh.
> (His delight will be in the fear of Yahweh.)[42]
> He will not judge by appearances,
> he will not decide by hearsay,
> but with righteous judgement he will judge the poor,
> and with equity defend the lowly of the earth.
> He will strike the violent with the rod of his mouth,
> with the breath of his lips he will kill the wicked.
> Justice will be the belt around his waist,
> truth the band around his middle.

41. For more detailed discussion of Isaiah 39, see my "Hezekiah and the Babylonian Delegation: A Critical Reading of Isaiah 39:1-8," in *Essays on Ancient Israel in Its Near Eastern Context: A Tribute to Nadav Na'aman*, ed. Yairah Amit *et al.* (Winona Lake: Eisenbrauns, 2006) 107-22.

42. Several commentators take this half-verse to be an insertion into the poem, perhaps to make the point that the fear of Yahweh is not inconsistent with delight. The options are discussed by Willem A. M. Beuken, *Jesaja 1–12* (HTKAT; Freiburg: Herder, 2003) 302.

The wolf will share its lodging with the lamb,
the leopard will lie down beside the goat,
the calf and the lion cub will feed together,
even a little child will lead them.
The cow and the bear will share their pasture,
their young lying side by side;
the lion will eat hay like the ox,
the infant will play at the cobra's hole,
the child barely weaned will put its hand over the viper's lair.
No longer will they hurt or destroy in all my holy mountain;
for the earth will be full of the knowledge of YHWH
as the waters cover the sea.

There have always been scholars who defended the Isaian authenticity of this magnificent poem, from Duhm who regarded it as Isaiah's *Schwannengesang* (swan song) to more recent commentators including Wildberger and Beuken.[43] I find this view unpersuasive for the following reasons. The language of the poem, beginning with the plant metaphors in the opening verse, is characteristic of the postexilic period.[44] Moreover, the image conjured up in this first verse is the stump of a tree which has been cut down but yet may put out new shoots, as sometimes happens with tree stumps; cf. Job 14:8, which refers to the stump of a tree *(gēzaʿ)* lying dead on the ground. The allusion is therefore to the dynasty, now extinct, which may nevertheless be revived in a future only dimly discerned.

---

43. Bernhard Duhm, *Das Buch Jesaja* (HKAT; 4th ed., Göttingen: Vandenhoeck & Ruprecht, 1922) 36; Gerhard von Rad, *Old Testament Theology. Vol. 2: The Theology of Israel's Prophetic Traditions*, trans. D. M. G. Stalker (New York: Harper & Row, 1965) 169-70; Hans Wildberger, *Isaiah 1–12*, trans. Thomas H. Trapp (CC; Minneapolis: Fortress, 1991) 467-69; Beuken, *Jesaja 1–12*, 299-315. According to Jacques Vermeylen, *Du Prophète Isaïe à l'Apocalyptique: Isaïe I–XXXV* (EBib; Paris: Gabalda, 1977) 1:269-70; *The Book of Isaiah/Le Livre d'Isaïe: les oracles et leurs relectures* (BETL 81; Leuven: Leuven University Press and Peeters, 1989) 271; and Marvin A. Sweeney, "Jesse's New Shoot in Isaiah 11: A Josianic Reading of the Prophet Isaiah," in *A Gift of God in Due Season: Essays on Scripture and Community in Honor of James A. Sanders*, ed. Richard D. Weis and David M. Carr (JSOT 225; Sheffield: Sheffield Academic, 1996) 103-18, the poem was composed in connection with hopes and expectations placed on the young Josiah some sixty or seventy years later.

44. *ḥōṭer* ("shoot") occurs elsewhere only at Prov 14:3; *gēzaʿ* ("stump") only at Isa 40:24 and Job 14:8; and *nēṣer* ("sprig") at Isa 14:19, in a poem about the king of Babylon, and Dan 11:7. "My holy mountain" *(har qodšî)* in the final verse is characteristic of Trito-Isaiah (Isa 56:7; 57:13; 65:11, 25; 66:20). All of these texts are postexilic.

The spirit-endowment or charisma of the future Davidic ruler will no longer be demonstrated by the performance of heroic deeds, as in the early days, but in the possession of God-given qualities essential for wise and just government, especially in protecting the poor and those of low estate and executing justice on the violent and lawless.

It was inevitable that the second half of the poem (vv. 6-9) would be read as a later addition, the purpose of which was to place the first half (vv. 1-5) in an eschatological-restorationist context. There seems, however, to be no good reason to draw this conclusion.[45] As in Amos 9:11-15 discussed earlier, ideal governance inaugurates an era of security, fertility, and abundance and can even include the eschatological horizon of the abolition of war. As in the first creation, the transformation will reach into the animal world. This *apokatastasis,* the restoration to the primeval state of perfection in the first creation, is an ancient and well-attested theme. It appears in a fragmentary Mesopotamian prophecy predicting the future coming of a prince whose reign, after a period of disaster and death, will bring fertility, well-being, and general rejoicing.[46] Then, many centuries later, after another period of disaster and death, it is heard once again in Virgil's famous *Fourth Eclogue:*

> *Magnus ab integro saeclorum nascitur ordo.*
> *Iam reddit et Virgo, redeunt Saturnia regna;*
> *iam nova progenies caelo demittitur alto.*[47]

It is hardly surprising if, from time to time, readers have caught echoes of Isaian prophecy in this iconic text.[48]

---

45. As Hermann Barth, *Die Jesaja Worte in der Josiazeit: Israel und Asshur als Thema einer produktiven Neuinterpretation der Josiaüberlieferung* (WMANT 48; Neukirchen: Neukirchener, 1977) 60-63; Jacques Vermeylen, *"L'Unité du Livre d'Isaïe,"* in *The Book of Isaiah — Le Livre d'Isaïe,* 275-76.

46. The text is entitled "A Prince will arise" (*ANET,* 451-52).

47. For the translation, see the epigraph at the head of this chapter. The translation is that of Rushton Fairclought, revised by G. P. Gould, in *Virgil, Eclogues, Georgics, Aeneid I-VI* (LCL 63. Rev. ed., Cambridge, MA: Harvard University Press, 1999) 48-49.

48. Jewish influence on the *Fourth Eclogue* has occasionally been suggested. According to Simon Hornblower and Antony Spawforth, eds., *The Oxford Classical Dictionary* (3rd ed., Oxford: Oxford University Press, 1996) 1604, "The influence of Jewish messianic writing on the poem is nowhere a required hypothesis, but is not in itself unlikely." The earliest Christian appropriation of the *Eclogue* is in the *Address of Constantine to the Holy Assembly (oratio ad sanctum coetum,* 19-21) appended by Eusebius of Caesarea to his *Life of Constantine.*

CHAPTER EIGHT

Davidic Messianism in the Later Zechariah Tradition

On that day I shall pour out on the house of David and the inhabitants of Jerusalem a spirit of grace and supplication, so that they will look to me concerning the one whom they pierced through; they will lament over him like the lamenting over an only child, and will grieve bitterly over him like the bitter grieving for the firstborn son.

Zechariah 12:10

The Historical Background

The Persian Empire of the Achaemenid dynasty, like other empires before that time and since, assumed for most contemporaries an air of permanence. It seemed no more likely to fall than that the stars would fall from the sky. No previous empire was as extensive, none as competently administered, and even in its final decades it did not seem to be at all in decline; yet within the four years between Alexander of Macedon's victory at the Granikos River and the assassination of Darius III, last of the Persian-Achaemenid line, it had ceased to exist. The appearance of new imperial overlords was no improvement and must have opened up uncertain and disquieting prospects for Jewish communities in Judah and the Diaspora. The transition could also be expected to provoke reaction in the form of dynastic resistance and apocalyptic visions of the future, and not only in Jewish communities.[1] Such vi-

---

1. Examples from Persia and elsewhere in Samuel K. Eddy, *The King Is Dead: Studies*

sion accounts, never unrelated to situations of political crisis, are of frequent occurrence in the Hellenistic and Roman periods. They include the fourth kingdom and the fourth beast of the book of Daniel (Dan 2:40; 7:7), the fourth kingdom of the fourth *Sibylline Oracle* (*Sib. Or.* 4:88-101), and the third phase of history featuring the twenty-three shepherds in Enoch's second dream vision (*1 En.* 90:2-5). All of these have reference to Alexander and the Diadochoi, the rulers who divided up his empire between them after his death.[2] The question now arises how Jewish communities reacted to a new form of imperial rule during the early Hellenistic period, which we can conveniently define as from Alexander (332 B.C.E.) to the accession of the Seleucid monarch Antiochus IV Epiphanes (175), an event which was to have fateful consequences for Jews in Judea and elsewhere and change the course of their history. A few biblical texts have been dated with some plausibility to this century and a half, among which the most important for our purpose, and far and away the most obscure, is Zechariah 9–14, consisting in the two addenda to Zechariah 1–8 known as Deutero-Zechariah (chs. 9–11) and Trito-Zechariah (chapters 12–14). Since both have themes in common with Proto-Zechariah (chs. 1–8), in the first place David and the Davidic dynasty, taken together they may be said to constitute the Zechariah prophetic tradition.

Before taking a closer look at these texts, it may be helpful to begin with a short summary of events and personalities during the period in question. We have seen that Josephus, a major source for the history of Judaism during the Hellenistic and Roman periods, is not well informed on the Persian period in general and the second century of Persian rule with the transition to the Hellenistic kingdoms in particular. After recording the death of Nehemiah at an advanced age after a meritorious life (*Ant.* 11:181), Josephus launches into a long and detailed paraphrase of Greek Esther, which he took to be chronologically the last biblical book, not excluding the book of Daniel (*Ant.* 11:184-296). At this point he seems to run out of source material with the exception of a few disedifying anecdotes about

---

in the Near Eastern Resistance to Hellenism, 334-31 B.C. (Lincoln: University of Nebraska Press, 1961).

2. On the four kingdoms theme in Daniel, see the detailed discussion in John J. Collins, *Daniel* (Hermeneia; Minneapolis: Fortress, 1993) 166-70, 297; *The Scepter and the Star: Messianism in Light of the Dead Sea Scrolls* (2nd ed., BRS; Grand Rapids: Eerdmans, 2010) 42-46; for the *Enoch* text, see E. Isaac in *OTP*, 1:69; and for the *Fourth Sibyl*, see David Flusser, "The Four Empires in the Fourth Sibyl and in the Book of Daniel," *IOS* 2 (1972) 148-75.

the temple priesthood, one of his favorite topics.[3] This brings him to Alexander the Great and the dealings of the Macedonian conqueror with Judah and Samaria (*Ant.* 11:304-47). It is at this point that Josephus reproduces, or invents, the legend of Alexander's visit to Jerusalem, his deference to Jaddua, the high priest, his offering of sacrifice in the Jerusalem temple, and the oracular dream-vision in which the God of Israel approves his conquests.

For events on the broader international stage we are dependent principally on Diodorus of Sicily (XVI. 40.3–45.9), author in the first century B.C.E. of a universal history in forty volumes, substantial fragments of which have survived. In covering the period in question, however, Diodorus at no point refers to Jews or Judah. We can summarize the main events as follows. The failure of the first attempt by Artaxerxes III Ochus (359-338) to subdue independent Egypt in 350 led to revolt in the Phoenician cities led by Tennes, ruler of Sidon, supported by Pharaoh Nectenabo and opposed by Belesys, satrap of the Trans-Euphrates region. This marked the beginning of a long period of disruption and disaster for the people of Syria and Palestine. Artaxerxes eventually succeeded in bringing Egypt back into the Persian Empire, if only for about a decade (343-332). Meanwhile, Philip II of Macedon was putting together the formidable fighting machine which, under his son Alexander's leadership, would soon subdue the last of the Achaemenids in a series of battles ending with the decisive victory at Gaugamela on the upper reaches of the Tigris in October 331.

After the death of Alexander in Babylon in June 323 B.C.E., the satrapies of the vast Persian Empire — while still part of one entity under the nominal rule of Alexander's insignificant brother Philip and the actual control of Perdiccas, regent of the empire — were assigned to his most outstanding generals. This set the scene for a long and costly scramble for territory, in the course of which Syria and Palestine were contested between Seleucus in Babylon and Ptolemy in Egypt in an endless series of cam-

---

3. On the high priests under the last Achaemenids, ending with Jaddua, contemporary of Alexander, see James C. VanderKam, *From Joshua to Caiaphas: High Priests after the Exile* (Minneapolis: Fortress, 2004) 54-85. On the history of the later Persian period in general, consult Pierre Briant, *From Cyrus to Alexander: A History of the Persian Empire*, trans. Peter T. Daniels (Winona Lake: Eisenbrauns, 2002) 681-90, 769-871; and, more succinctly, J. M. Cook, *The Persian Empire* (New York: Schocken, 1983) 222-31. Relevant reading is available also in some of the essays in Oded Lipschits, Gary N. Knoppers, Rainer Albertz, eds., *Judah and the Judeans in the Fourth Century B.C.E.* (Winona Lake: Eisenbrauns, 2007).

paigns, with mercenary armies traversing the country from end to end and living off the land. Josephus states the outcome as follows:

> As these quarreled and fought jealously with one another, each for his own kingdom, the result was that continual and prolonged wars arose, and the cities suffered through their struggles and lost many of their inhabitants, so that all of Syria [which included Palestine] at the hands of Ptolemy, the son of Lagus, who was then called *Soter* (Saviour), suffered the reverse of that which was indicated by his surname. (*Ant.* 12:3)

1 Maccabees sums up the situation more succinctly. Speaking of Alexander's successors the author states that "they all put on crowns after his death, and so did their descendants after them for many years, and they caused many evils on the earth" (1 Macc. 1:8-9). Ptolemy was one of these successors who wasted no time in assuming the kingship as the new pharaoh in Egypt and, following traditional Egyptian policy, in controlling Palestine and the crucial route northward along the Mediterranean coast (the Via Maris). By 320 B.C.E. he had succeeded after much fighting in occupying the wealthy Phoenician cities with their ports and fleets. After the defeat and death in 301 of a major rival, Antigonus Monophthalmos ("One-Eyed Antigonus"), one of Alexander's most successful and ambitious generals who laid claim to Syria, Ptolemy captured Jerusalem, by guile according to Josephus,[4] thereby initiating a long period of Ptolemaic rule of Judah.

The century during which the Ptolemies controlled Palestine, Syria, most of the Phoenician cities, and Cyprus was for the most part peaceful. It is also poorly documented. Josephus fills in with a long and somewhat tedious account of the translation of the Jewish Torah into Greek commissioned by Ptolemy Philadelphus (285-246 B.C.E.), successor to Soter (*Ant.* 12:11-128). Shortly afterwards he digresses once again with the much more lively account, in the so-called "Tobiad Romance," of the adventures and misadventures of the wealthy Tobiad tax collectors, Joseph and Hyrcanus (*Ant.* 12:160-236), thus illustrating a way of being Jewish at that time very different from that of Ezra and Nehemiah. The Ptolemaic system of state capitalism and, incidentally, the relatively peaceful state of the country are

---

4. He is said to have entered the city unopposed by the residents on the Sabbath, on the pretext of offering sacrifice (*Ant.* 12:4-6; *C. Ap.* 1:209-12). Josephus relates this incident on the authority of Agatharchides, a second-century B.C.E. historian and geographer, who found the conduct of the Jerusalemites on this occasion ridiculous, a view not shared by Josephus.

illustrated by the archive of Zenon, agent of Apollonius, finance minister of Ptolemy, who traversed Palestine, Syria, and Phoenicia from end to end in 259-258, assessing real estate for tax purposes and checking on the vast holdings of his master.[5] Ecclesiastes, whose author has much to say about the folly of accumulating great wealth, may have been written during this period, but betrays no interest in eschatological speculations of any kind. The religious interests of Ben Sira, more properly, Yeshua ben El'azar ben Sira (Sir 50:27), also dated by most scholars to this period, focus primarily on the temple and its personnel. In his encomium on the great figures of the past (44:1–50:24) he assigns almost three times as much space to Aaron as to Moses (44:23–45:22) and concludes his moral treatise with a eulogy on the high priest Simon II, recently deceased (50:1-24). He is familiar with Nathan's oracle to David (2 Sam 7:4-17) and alludes to the perpetuity of David's dynasty under the figure of the root (Sir 47:22) and the horn of David, the latter in the thanksgiving psalm inserted into the Greek text of ch. 51, but does so without emphasis. In his eulogy of David (47:1-11), he praises him as liturgical musician and performer and as solicitous for temple worship, after the manner of the David of the book of Chronicles, but there is no *David redivivus* in Ben Sira and he entertains no lively expectation of a revival of the dynasty.

The *pax ptolemaica* came to an end with the accession to the Seleucid throne in 223 B.C.E. of Antiochus III, known to history as Antiochus the Great. In retrospect, this turned out to be the opening chapter in a history of three and one-half centuries of almost constant disruption and warfare for the Jewish population of Judea. Antiochus revived the Seleucid claim to the Trans-Euphratine part of the Seleucid — and formerly Babylonian — Empire, and after a series of mostly unsuccessful campaigns in Syria, Phoenicia, and Palestine, finally won a decisive victory at Paneas (Banyas) at the headwaters of the Jordan which gave him control of Palestine (201). The Jewish leadership favored the Seleucids and assisted Antiochus in his campaigns and in return were granted significant tax relief, help in rebuilding the temple damaged in the course of the hostilities,[6] subventions

5. On the Zenon papyri, see Victor Tcherikover, *Hellenistic Civilization and the Jews,* trans. S. Applebaum (New York: Atheneum, 1975) 60-73 and references 427 n. 53; Martin Hengel, *Judaism and Hellenism: Studies in Their Encounter in Palestine during the Early Hellenistic Period,* trans. John Bowden (Philadelphia: Fortress, 1974) 1:35-47.

6. Josephus's transcription of the edict of Antiochus III to the governor of Syria lists benefits to be conferred on the Jews, the first of which was the restoration of Jerusalem "destroyed by the hazards of war" (*Ant.* 12:139).

for the sacrificial cult, and freedom to live according to their laws and practices. The decrees in which these favors were granted designate the Jewish political leadership as the *gerousia,* the council of elders, composed of the leading members of the priestly and lay aristocracy.[7]

In the latter part of his reign, Antiochus's expansionist policies brought him into direct and hostile contact with Rome, the beginning of a process which would end, more than a century later, with Judea a province of the Roman Empire. After the defeat by a Roman army of Philip V of Macedon, to whom Antiochus was bound by treaty, he led an army into Thrace, thence into Greece, where he too was defeated by the Romans at Thermopylae and then, after retreating into Asia Minor, decisively at Magnesia in Lydia by an army of the Roman Republic under Scipio Africanus (190 B.C.E.). By the treaty of Apamea two years later Antiochus lost all his territories in Asia Minor north of the Taurus mountains, had to surrender his war-elephants and most of his fleet, and pay a huge indemnity of twelve thousand talents within a period of twelve years. This last requirement can be viewed, in retrospect, as the most ominous. It would lead Antiochus and his successors, Seleucus IV and Antiochus IV, to set their sights on the wealth of the many temples within their domains. Antiochus III himself met his death ignominiously attempting to rob the treasures of the temple of Bel at Elymais in southwestern Iran (187). Taking advantage of a dispute between Simon, an important temple official, and the high priest Onias III, his successor Seleucus sent his prime minister Heliodorus to confiscate the temple treasure. Heliodorus set out to fulfil his task, but 2 Maccabees 3 reports that he was prevented by supernatural intervention from doing so and had to be carried out of the temple on a stretcher. Antiochus IV Epiphanes went much further, despoiling the temple of its treasure, sacred vessels, golden lampstands, and anything he could get his hands on (*Ant.* 12:248-50). The furious reaction to this sacrilegious despoliation led to what was, in effect, the proscription of the Jewish religion, the first "final solution of the Jewish problem," which in turn provoked the ultimately successful Maccabean Revolt and everything that followed from it.

7. On the decrees of Antiochus with respect to the Jews, see Josephus, *Ant.* 12:138-53, and, on their authenticity, the Appendix of Ralph Marcus in Josephus, *Jewish Antiquities VII: Books XII-XIV* (LCL 365; Cambridge, MA: Harvard University Press, 1933) 743-66. On the inscription from Hephzibah near Scythopolis (Beth Shean), consisting in six edicts in the form of letters from Antiochus to Ptolemy governor of Syria, see Martin Hengel, in *CHJ,* 2: *The Hellenistic Age* (1989) 72, 74-75.

Davidic Messianism in Zechariah 9:1-8

Our brief historical survey will suggest that this was a time of almost constant upheaval calculated to arouse in Jewish communities desires and dreams for the restoration of an imagined, ideal past of peace, prosperity, and immunity from foreign rule. This is what we find in Deutero-Zechariah, which may have been attached to Proto-Zechariah because it was perceived to deal with a later incident, or perhaps later incidents, in the episodic history of the dynastic theme analogous to the Zerubbabel episode in Proto-Zechariah. In both sections an eschatological perspective is combined with a focus on a historical individual, Zerubbabel in Proto-Zechariah, at least one unnamed individual presented under the image of shepherd in Deutero-Zechariah, but both in the line of David. Eschatological and apocalyptic movements are always in reaction to historical situations of crisis; we do not have to choose between the historical and the eschatological. The intense interest in a specific individual in the Davidic line, one who might resume the broken succession in a critical situation, would tend to generate eschatological fervor. This was obviously the case with Zerubbabel, as we have seen, and, in spite of the much greater obscurity, the same appears to have been the case in Zechariah 9–11. The case will be argued in the following section of the chapter.

Deutero-Zechariah opens with a prophetic oracle directed against countries and cities to the north and west of Judah (Zech 9:1-8). They fall into three groups: (1) Aram (Syria) and Hamath, Aramaean states to the north of Israel with their cities: Damascus in Syria, Hadrach in Hamath to the north of Syria;[8] (2) Tyre and Sidon, the most powerful of the Phoenician cities; (3) Ashkelon, Gaza, Ekron, and Ashdod, four of the five confederate Philistine cities. Since all of these are said to belong to Yahweh and therefore to be under the same jurisdiction as "all the tribes of Israel" (9:1; cf. 9:7), and all except the Phoenician cities had actually been under Davidic control for a time, the theme is clearly the restoration of the "Greater Israel" of David's time.[9]

---

8. Hadrach is mentioned only here in biblical texts, but the stela of Zakir (or Zakkur) king of Hamath and Lu'ash refers to the siege of Hadrach (Hatarikka) by Ben-Hadad III of Aram, and the annals of Tiglath-pileser III name Hadrach as a district of Hamath (*ANET*, 282-83, 501-2).

9. Wilhelm Rudolph, *Haggai — Sacharja 1–8 — Sacharja 9–14 — Maleachi* (KAT 13/4; Gütersloh: Mohn, 1976) 171, describes the theme as "die Wiederherstellung des davidischen Grossreichs."

A further conclusion, easily missed, is that the oracle in Zech 9:1-8 is a deliberate appropriation of the claim on behalf of the God of Israel to "all the nations called by my name" at the end of Amos (9:11-12), corresponding to the foreign nations censured at the beginning of the book (Amos 1:3–2:3).[10] In the course of time there were of course changes on the international scene; new nations emerged and some older ones ceased to exist. Aram,[11] Tyre, and the Philistine cities are common to both Amos and Zechariah, with Hamath and Hadrach added. Sidon, an important autonomous administrative and naval center under the Persian Empire, is now, in Zech 9:2, linked with Tyre, practically destroyed in the siege by Alexander's army. The same four Philistine cities as in Amos 1:6-8 (also Zeph 2:4) are present. Gath is absent from both texts, perhaps because it had long ceased to exist (see 2 Chr 26:6); the Philistine pentapolis is therefore reduced to a tetrapolis.[12] The most conspicuous absentees from Zech 9:1 8, however, are the Transjordanian kingdoms Edom, Ammon, and Moab. This may be because they had ceased to exist as recognizable political entities by the time of writing, but there may also be a theological explanation for their omission, on the grounds that they were never promised to Israel in the first place.[13] In sum: Zech 9:1-8 envisages the same consummation as Amos 9:11-12, the restoration of the "Greater Israel" of David's time, and may be directly dependent on the Amos text.

10. See above, pp. 121-28.

11. With most commentators I emend *'ēn 'ādām* (lit., "eye of a man") to *'ārê 'ārām*, "the cities of Aram/Syria" (9:1b). Other proposals in E. Zolli, "Eyn 'Adam (Zach IX.1), *VT* 5 (1955) 90-92; M. Dahood, "Zecharia 9:1, 'En 'Adam," *CBQ* 25 (1963) 123-24. "Because the eye of man belongs to Yahweh," a literal translation of MT by Ralph L. Smith, *Micah — Malachi* (Waco: Word, 1984) 250, does not make satisfactory sense in the context.

12. Ashdod's "mongrel people" (*mamzēr*, 9:6) brings to mind Nehemiah's angry encounter with Jews who had married Ashdodite women and whose children spoke *'ašdôdît* instead of Hebrew (*'ibrît*, Neh 13:23-27).

13. A suggestion of Rudolph, *Haggai — Sacharja 1-8 — Sacharja 9–14 — Maleachi*, 176. On this point see Deut 2:4-5 (Edom); Deut 2:8-9 (Moab); Deut 2:19 (Ammon). If this line of argument is correct, Zech 9:1-8 cannot be from the Neo-Assyrian period, as proposed by Abraham Malamat, "The Historical Setting of Two Biblical Prophecies on the Nations," *IEJ* 1 (1950/51) 149-59; and Benedikt Otzen, *Studien über Deuterosacharja* (ATDan 6; Copenhagen: Munksgaard, 1964) 42-45.

The King Who Is to Come (Zechariah 9:9-10)

This first intimation of a return to the heroic and, by now, mythical age of David and Solomon is followed by an apostrophe to Zion-Jerusalem bidding her participate with joy in the advent of her king (Zech 9:9-10):

> Daughter Zion, rejoice! rejoice!
> Daughter Jerusalem, shout for joy!
> See, your king is coming to you,
> victorious over his foes[14]
> yet humble, mounted on a donkey,
> on a colt, foal of a donkey.
> He will banish the chariot from Ephraim,
> the war horse from Jerusalem.
> He will banish the battle bow
> and dictate peace to the nations.
> His dominion is from sea to sea,
> from the River to the ends of the earth.

In the call to Jerusalem to rejoice, familiar from other postexilic texts,[15] we may be hearing echoes of a *parousia*, the solemn entry of a ruler into his city after victory in battle, combined with memories of an ancient ceremony of anointing and coronation, especially in evidence in the language of universal domination. The last verse of the poem reproduces the same territorial boundaries as Ps 72:8, a composition some have identified as a coronation ode. If "from sea to sea" means from the Mediterranean in the west to the Arabian Sea in the east, we would then expect a matching south to north direction, in which case the River would be "the River of Egypt," later Wadi el-Arish, and the "ends of the earth" somewhere in the far north, the direction least familiar to inhabitants of Palestine. But in most texts of this kind *the* River is the Euphrates, the river *par excellence*. The Euphrates is the ideal eastern boundary of David's

---

14. In this semistich, *hû wĕnôšā* *ṣaddîq*', I take the epithets together as hendiadys. The verbal stem *ṣdq* connotes "salvation" in addition to "righteousness," including salvation in war, i.e., victory, as, e.g., in Isa 1:27; 56:1; 59:9, 16-17; 61:10. The passive form *nôšā* > *yš*', normally "saved," can also connote by extension "saved by winning a victory," hence "victorious," e.g., Ps 33:16, *'ên-hammelek nôšā bĕrāb-ḥāyil*, "no king is victorious on account of the size of his army." Cf. Zech 9:9 REB: "his cause won, his victory gained."

15. Isa 52:1-2; 54:1-3; 66:10-11; Zeph 3:14-20.

"Greater Israel,"[16] also, not coincidentally, the eastern boundary of the Trans-Euphratene province of the Persian Empire.

The king's mount, which plays an important role in the messianic entry of Jesus into Jerusalem,[17] is contrasted with the war horse and other symbols of martial pomp and circumstance including chariots, bows, swords, and other warlike paraphernalia. In antiquity the donkey did not have the reputation as a stubborn and stupid animal which it undeservedly has for many today. In the absence of horses, not native to Palestine, it was the traditional means of transport and portage for everyone, of high and low estate, in the premonarchic period. This tradition was continued by David (2 Sam 16:1-2) but abandoned reprehensibly by Absalom (2 Sam 15:1) and, on a massive scale, by Solomon.[18] In this respect, too, Israel is not to be a nation like all the nations round about, and this conviction is appropriately reflected in the coming of the future king riding on a donkey rather than a horse. On his arrival in Jerusalem, the king will impose universal disarmament, leaving a monopoly of violence in the hands of the ruler to be deployed in imposing a just order, punishing the unrighteous, and bringing an end to war. The abolition of warfare, together with the manufacture and possession of weapons of war, is, in many of these visions of an ideal future, the ultimate, eschatological horizon and one of the great themes of Hebrew prophecy.[19]

One of the most common procedures in Zechariah 9–14 is the appropriating, updating, and rewriting of earlier prophecies. We have just seen, for example, how Zech 9:1-8 draws on and updates Amos 9:11-12. Now, in this poem immediately following (9:9-10), the prophet takes inspiration from the oracle about Judah pronounced by Jacob on his deathbed (Gen 49:8-12):

> Judah, your brothers praise you,
> your hand is on the neck of your enemies;
> your father's sons bow down to you in homage.
> Judah is a lion's whelp,

16. Gen 15:18; Deut 1:7; 11:24; Josh 1:4; 2 Sam 8:3; 1 Kgs 4:21; Ps 72:8.

17. Matt 21:1-11; Mark 11:1-10; Luke 19:29-38; John 12:12-19. See below, pp. 176-78.

18. The mount of choice for the "judges" was the donkey: Judg 5:10; 10:4; 12:14. For Solomon's accumulation of war-horses and chariots, see 1 Kgs 5:6, 8(Eng 4:26, 28); 10:25, many imported from Egypt (1 Kgs 10:28-29). The rule for the king in Deut 17:14-20 forbids the acquisition of many horses and the trade in horses with Egypt (v. 16).

19. See esp. Isa 2:4; 9:4(Eng 5); 11:6-9; 60:18; 65:21-25; Mic 4:3-4.

> you are back from the kill, my son!
> When he crouches or stretches like a lion,
> or like a lioness, who dares arouse him?
> The scepter will not pass from Judah,
> nor the staff from between his feet,
> until Shiloh comes,[20] to whom the peoples offer submission.
> He ties his colt to the vine,
> his donkey's foal to the red vine.
> He washes his clothing in wine,
> his robe in the blood of grapes.
> His eyes are darker than wine,
> his teeth whiter than milk.

The affinity of Zech 9:9-10 with the Judah oracle is apparent. Both antici-pate one who is to come who will have universal dominion — the submis-sion and obedience of the peoples — and both appear riding the same mount. It is equally clear in the Judah oracle that the one whose coming is anticipated is David, founder of the Judean monarchy. This has been ac-cepted from the earliest stages of the vast amount of commentary lavished on these verses. It can be seen in the Targum tradition: all four Targums (Onkelos, Ps-Jonathan, Fragment Targum, and Neophyti) paraphrase Shiloh *(šîlōh)* as "King Messiah." LXX probably has the same tradition in mind in translating *yiqhat 'ammîm* ("the submission of the peoples") as *prosdokia ethnōn* ("the expectation of the peoples"), followed by the Vul-gate's *expectatio gentium* ("the expectation of the nations"). A fragmentary commentary on Genesis from Qumran Cave 4 likewise paraphrases Gen 49:10b as "until the Messiah of righteousness comes, the branch of Da-vid."[21] This paraphrase also brings into the intertextual complex the "Branch" *(ṣemaḥ)* of Jeremiah (Jer 23:5; 33:15) which, as was noted earlier, played such an important part in the role assigned to Zerubbabel. Also closely related to Gen 49:8-12, and no doubt known to the author of Zech 9:9-10, and certainly to the author of Mic 5:1-4a(Eng 2-5a), is the oracle of

---

20. Or "Until tribute comes to him" (NRSV), if one reads *šay lō* for MT *šîlōh* with E. A. Speiser, *Genesis* (AB 1; Garden City, 1964) 362, 366; or "Until he receives what is his due" (REB), reading *šĕlō*, "what is his." Other proposals in Claus Westermann, *Genesis 37–50*, trans. John J. Scullion (CC; Minneapolis: Augsburg, 1986) 231.

21. *'ad bô' māšîaḥ haṣṣedeq ṣemaḥ dāwîd*, 4 Q252 col. 5. The messianic interpretation is common in early Jewish and Christian paraphrase and commentary, e.g., *T. Jud.* 1:6; 22:3; Justin, *Apol.* 1:32; *Dial.* 53:1-2; 54:1-2; Irenaeus, *Haer.* 4.10.2.

Balaam in which the one to come is "a star (which) comes out of Jacob, a comet[22] which rises out of Israel" (Num 24:17). This messianic text is also represented at Qumran (1QM 11:4-9; CD 7:20), and here too the Targum identifies the star as King Messiah. The Deutero-Zecharian poem is therefore part of an interconnected web of messianic texts which focus on the person and descendants of David. In predicting that this astral figure will make war on, crush, and dispossess the Transjordanian kingdoms of Moab and Edom, together with two unidentified kingdoms,[23] the seer is replicating in some degree the review of David's conquests brought under the aegis of the God of Israel in Amos 1:3–2:3; 9:11-12.

The Good Shepherd

Both Zerubbabel and the shepherd-ruler in Zechariah 9–11 are presented, in the arcane symbolic language of prophecy, against the background of a critical international situation and an atmosphere of uncertainty and disorientation. With the earlier episode, set against the background of the violent pacification by Darius I of dynastic revolts in an emergent Persian Empire in mortal danger, we can at times follow the course of events to the month, even to the day. In Zechariah 9–11, on the contrary, dates are uncertain and the situation almost impenetrably obscure. The text gives little help towards establishing even an approximate date and only uncertain clues to the circumstances and events to which it refers. Among such clues may be listed the threat against Tyre (9:3-4), which makes best sense before that city's destruction by Alexander in 332 B.C.E., and the downfall of powerful nations, represented as cedars and oaks (11:1-3), which could stand for what happened on a massive scale during and for some time after the

---

22. The more common translation of *šēbeṭ* is "scepter" (as NRSV), but parallelism with *kôkāb* ("star") makes it preferable to follow REB and, before that, the proposal of Berend Gemser, "Der Stern aus Jacob (Num 24,17)," *ZAW* 43 (1925) 301-2, and others.

23. The "sons of Seth" are not mentioned elsewhere in biblical texts. The last named, *'îr*, was taken as a collective for "cities" by George Buchanan Gray, *A Critical and Exegetical Commentary on Numbers* (ICC; Edinburgh: T. & T. Clark, 1903) 372; and Martin Noth, *Numbers*, trans. James D. Martin (OTL; Philadelphia: Westminster, 1968) 170, but the context seems to call for a place name. The best guess seems to be Ar, an important town in Moab (Num 21:15, 28), as REB ("The last survivor from Ar will he destroy") and several recent commentators, including Philip J. Budd, *Numbers* (WBC 5; Waco: Word, 1984) 253; and Baruch A. Levine, *Numbers 21–36* (AB 4A; New York: Doubleday, 2000) 203-4.

conquests of Alexander. Egypt and Assyria, from which expatriated Judeans were to return (10:10-11), may be read as code for the Ptolemaic and Seleucid Empires, respectively, as in late passages in Isaiah where these two names occur together.[24] A final example: the end of any hope for the reunion of Ephraim and Judah, symbolized by the breaking of the staff called "Unity" (11:14), may have been occasioned by the revolt of Samaria, its destruction by either Alexander or Perdiccas, and its resettlement as a Macedonian colony, though clearly other options exist.[25]

The lack of a consistent line of thought or of imagery running through the section of Deutero-Zechariah between the messianic entry into Jerusalem (9:9-10) and the shepherd-ruler (11:4-14) is apt to leave the reader somewhat bewildered. An example with respect to imagery: In the messianic oracle in Zech 9:9-10 the war horse is to be banished, but then Judeans, represented as sheep, will be transformed into war horses (10:3), and in that capacity they will put to flight the enemy riding on horseback (10:5). The focus also moves back and forth between a future, eschatological perspective (9:11-17; 10:4-12) and the present, unsatisfactory situation (10:1-3; 11:1-3), which at least underlines the point about the political implications of eschatological and apocalyptic thinking. The familiar metaphor of shepherd and flock first appears in 9:16 and is further developed with reference to worthless shepherds in 10:2-3. The theme of the reunion of Judah and Ephraim, south and north, which will be represented by the shep-

24. Isa 10:24-27; 11:11; 19:23-25. See my *Isaiah 1–39* (AB 19; New York: Doubleday, 2000), 258.

25. The "City of Chaos," reduced to a heap of rubble, of Isaiah 24–27 has also been identified with Samaria, e.g. by Bernhard Duhm, *Das Buch Jesaia* (HKAT; 4th ed., Göttingen: Vandenhoeck & Ruprecht, 1922) 172, though he attributed the destruction in question to Hyrcanus between 113 and 105 B.C.E. Otto Plöger, *Theocracy and Eschatology*, trans. S. Rudman (Richmond: John Knox, 1968) 78-82, tentatively locates Zech 9:1-8 against the background of the attempts of Artaxerxes to bring Egypt back into the Persian fold, and he refers the breaking of the staffs to the Macedonian conquest and the Samaritan schism which he dates to about the same time. Plöger also provides a brief list of opinions on Deutero-Zechariah from Stade in the 1880s to Elliger and Eissfeldt in the 1960s. For other suggestions about the date(s) of Zech 9–11, see M. Delcor, "Les allusions à Alexandre le Grand dans Zech IX,1-8," *VT* 1 (1951) 110-24; Paul D. Hanson, "Zechariah 9 and the Recapitulation of an Ancient Ritual Pattern," *JBL* 92 (1973) 37-38; *The Dawn of Apocalyptic* (2nd ed., Philadelphia: Fortress, 1979) 287-92; Rudolph, *Haggai — Sacharja 1–8 — Sacharja 9–14 — Maleachi*, 159-61, 165-66; Carol L. Meyers and Eric M. Meyers, *Zechariah 9–14* (AB 25C; New York: Doubleday, 1993) 21, 356; Ralph L. Smith, *Micah — Malachi* (Dallas: Word, 1984) 242-49; Paul L. Redditt, "Nehemiah's First Mission and the Date of Zechariah 9–14," *CBQ* 56 (1994) 664-78.

herd's stick called *Ḥōbĕlîm* ("Union") in 11:7, is introduced in 10:6-12, as also the ingathering of exiled Judeans represented as sheep which have strayed from the fold, also in 11:4-17. The final intermediate verses (11:1-3) present a scene of disaster as the great cedars and cypresses of the Lebanon go up in flames, the mighty oaks of Bashan in northern Transjordan come crashing down, and the lions, deprived of their habitat in the Jordan thicket, are on the prowl. In the background we hear the wailing of the shepherds whose flocks have been destroyed.[26] The dependence of this passage on earlier prophecy, especially Jer 25:34-38, is evident, and the intertextual link is intended to prepare the reader for the autobiographical narrative which follows and which is acknowledged to be one of the most obscure passages in the entire biblical corpus (11:4-17). It reads as follows:

> [4]This is what Yahweh my God says: "Be shepherd to the flock destined for slaughter. [5]Those who buy them slaughter them and incur no guilt, while those who sell them say, 'Praised be God, I have become rich!' Their shepherds do not take pity on them. [[6]Surely, I will no longer take pity on the inhabitants of the earth" — oracle of Yahweh. "I am going to make each one fall into the hands of his neighbor, each into the hands of his king. They will wreak havoc on the earth, and I will deliver no one from their hands."][27] [7]So I became shepherd to the flock destined for slaughter by the dealers in sheep.[28] I took two sticks: the one I called Favor, the other Unity, and so I tended the sheep. [8]In one month I got rid of three shepherds.[29] However, I lost patience with the sheep, and they became sick and tired of me. [9]I said, "I will not be your

26. In 11:3 the shepherds are wailing because either "their glory" (NRSV) or "their rich pastures" (REB) are destroyed, translating MT *'addartām*. In view of the evident dependence of this passage on Jer 25:34-38, where *'addîrê haṣṣo'n* ("the strongest of the flock") occurs three times, it may be worth considering emending Zech 11:3 *'addartām* to *'addîrîm*.

27. I agree with Rudolph, *Haggai — Sacharja 1-8 — Sacharja 9-14 — Maleachi*, 205-6, that v. 6 has been inserted into the discourse, exploiting the catchword *lo' yaḥmôl* (v. 5). It contains no allusion to shepherding, but refers explicitly to kings, and *'ereṣ* must, in the context, be translated "earth," unlike 11:16 and 13:8, giving the verse a universalizing intent.

28. Reading *likĕna'ăniyyê* for MT *lākēn 'ăniyyê* prompted by LXX.

29. Rudolph, *Haggai — Sacharja 1-8 — Sacharja 9-14 — Maleachi*, 206-7, notes that this brief statement about the three shepherds (five words!) holds the record in the Old Testament for the number of interpretations it has elicited. He goes on to provide examples. For the Targum version *parnāsîn*, "community leaders," and the identification of the three shepherds with Moses, Aaron, and Miriam, see Kevin J. Cathcart and Robert P. Gordon, *The Targum of the Minor Prophets* (ArBib 14; Wilmington: Glazier, 1989) 213.

shepherd any longer. Those that are to die, let them die; those that are missing, let them stay missing; and as for the rest, let them devour each other's flesh." [10]So I took my stick called Favor and broke it, thereby annulling my covenant which I had made with all the peoples. [11]Since it was annulled on that day, the dealers in sheep who were observing my sign[30] recognized it as a message from Yahweh. [12]I then said to them, "If it please you, give me my wages; if not, let it be." They weighed out my wages, thirty silver pieces. [13]Yahweh said to me, "Throw it into the treasury,"[31] so I took the thirty silver pieces — the fine price at which I was valued by them! — and tossed them into the treasury of Yahweh's temple. [14]Then I broke my second stick called Unity, thereby annulling the kinship ties between Judah and Israel.

[15]Yahweh said to me, "Take once again the equipment of a shepherd, a worthless shepherd. [16]I am about to raise up in the land a shepherd who does not care for the sheep that are missing, or go after those that have strayed,[32] or heal the maimed, or nourish the healthy, but feeds on the flesh of the fat sheep, tearing off even their hooves."

[17]Woe to my worthless shepherd who abandons the flock!

May the sword strike his arm and his right eye!

May his arm shrivel up, his right eye be totally blind!

This piece of prophetic autobiography has been described in different ways and assigned to different genres including allegory, vision narrative, and prophetic sign-act or, rather, two sign-acts (11:4-14, 15-17), with the execution of the second unrecorded. It has one of the principal characteristics of allegory, in the many points of correspondence between the figurative and the mundane, but there seems to be too much action in rapid succession, event following event at a dizzying pace, for it to be easily recognized as such.[33] It may have a visionary origin, but is never

---

30. Reading *'ōtî* as substantive (*'ōt,* "sign," with pronominal suffix) which seems to fit the context somewhat better.

31. Reading *hā'ôṣār* for MT *hayyôṣēr,* the potter" or, if derived from *ṣwr* rather than *yṣr,* "the smelter" (e.g., Exod 32:4; 1 Kgs 7:15; 2 Kgs 12:11). The destination of the silver must in any case be a place, not a person.

32. Reading *hanne'deret > 'dr* for MT *hanna'ar.*

33. Rainer Albertz, *A History of Israelite Religion in the Old Testament Period.* Vol. 2: *From the Exile to the Maccabees,* trans. John Bowden (OTL; Louisville: Westminster/John Knox, 1994) 568-69, reads Zech 11:4-14 as allegoric with reference to either the Persian Empire or the succession of empires to which Israel had been subject to the time of composi-

described as a vision.[34] Prophetic sign-acts, some of them suggestive of a kind of street theater — for example, Jeremiah's public smashing of a ceramic pot (Jer 19:1-15) or wearing wooden and iron yoke-bars (27:1–28:17) — are meant to be seen and understood by the public the prophet is addressing. But there are sign-acts which could not have been performed very easily, if at all. Take, for example, the case of Ezekiel told to lie on his left side for three hundred and ninety days, then on his right side for forty more (Ezek 4:4-6). Deutero-Zechariah's simulation of the shepherd's role appears to be of this kind. It is difficult to see how he could have acted out this role, which entailed dismissing other shepherds over a period of a month, and then giving the whole thing up in disgust. The same for the second sign-act (11:15-16). We may ask how anyone could simulate or act out being guiltily inactive — not caring, not going after the strays, not healing, etc. or for that matter feeding on the fat sheep or tearing off their hooves.

The realistic performance of the sign-act comes only with the breaking of the sticks which, we are told, was observed by the sheep dealers and therefore worked as sign-act (11:11). But it is precisely at this point that the dependence on earlier prophetic texts, especially Ezekiel and Jeremiah, is most clearly in evidence and provides the best approach to getting at the meaning of the narrative. The breaking of the sticks reverses Ezekiel's sign-act in joining together two sticks named for Judah and Joseph-Ephraim, respectively, a symbolic anticipation of the eventual, much longed-for twelve-tribal reunion (Ezek 37:15-28). Ezekiel's symbolic action is explained at considerable length, which unfortunately is not the case with Zech 11:4-17. The description of the worthless shepherd in Zech 11:15-17 also draws, sometime practically verbatim, on denunciations of such shepherds (i.e., rulers) in Ezekiel (34:1-31) and Jeremiah (23:1-2; 25:34-38). These characteristics of the narrative, especially its description of actions which can be imagined but cannot practically be acted out, lead to the conclusion that Zech 11:4-17, to which we must add 13:7-9, is a purely literary phenomenon constructed on the basis of intertextual borrowing from earlier prophecy, especially Jeremiah and Ezekiel. At the same time, the amount of detail it contains — trading in sheep, the three shepherds, the wages and their disposal in the temple — suggests a veiled, symbolic ac-

---

tion. On that supposition, it would be interesting to know what to make of the two sticks, the three other shepherds, and the thirty silver pieces which ended up in the temple treasury.

34. Pace Rudolph, *Haggai — Sacharja 1–8 — Sacharja 9–14 — Maleachi,* 204.

count of a historical situation and events in real time rather than a purely eschatological scenario.[35]

With the help of Deutero-Zechariah's intertextual links we may therefore decode the narrative as follows. A community leader is inspired to achieve the goals represented by the two sticks, namely, good relations with neighboring peoples which will bring security ("Favor") and the eventual reunion of divided Israel ("Unity"). The prophet knows, however, that this task is doomed to failure. Other civic leaders, including the three dismissed, are indifferent to the needs of the people, many of whom are sold into slavery[36] and all of whom are subject to foreign domination. Eventually, the leader who has undertaken this impossible task meets with insuperable opposition from both colleagues and the people at large and resigns, his resignation symbolized by the breaking of the sticks. The low esteem in which he is held is shown by his wages, thirty silver pieces, equivalent to the value assessed for a slave (Exod 21:32). The contemptuous disposal of the shepherd's salary in the temple treasury, perhaps also the dismissal of the three shepherds, could suggest an allusion to one of several incidents of tension and outright hostility between the upper echelons of the temple clergy and the civic leaders during the late Persian and early Hellenistic period. This was, at any rate, a prominent feature of the social and political life in Judea at that time.[37]

It is characteristic of the kind of discourse represented by the account of the shepherd's brief and unsuccessful mission that the reader is left to speculate on the identity of the protagonist. There is no mention of

---

35. In disagreement with Rudolph, *Haggai — Sacharja 1-8 — Sacharja 9-14 — Maleachi*, 204-15, who excludes historical reference and identifies the good shepherd of Zech 11:4-14 and 13:7-9 with the Messiah *tout court* and, more surprisingly, the worthless shepherd of 11:15-16 (v. 17 is *eine spätere Zutat*) with the precursor of the antichrist, an embodiment of the forces of evil in the premessianic era.

36. The buying and selling is not just a metaphor for foreign domination. Trading in slaves was a common feature of the numerous wars waged during the early Hellenistic period, and of course later (e.g., Joel 4:3, 6-8[Eng 3:3, 6-8]; 1 Macc 3:41; 2 Macc 8:11). Indentured service for nonpayment of debt was also common (e.g., Neh 5:11-13). See Hengel, *CHJ*, 2:190-91.

37. Neh 12:44-47; 13:10-14, 22, 29; Mal 1:6-7; 2:8; Josephus, *Ant.* 11:297-301, 302-12. Josephus also has a report about Jerusalem priests claiming to be unjustly dismissed and taking refuge in Shechem (*Ant.* 11:346-47). On the subject of priest-prophet opposition during this period, I do not find that the dichotomizing and generalizing approach of Plöger and Hanson provides an adequate point of departure for the task of interpreting these key passages in Deutero-Zechariah. See Plöger, *Theocracy and Eschatology*, 78-96 (theocratic community/eschatological groups); Hanson, *The Dawn of Apocalyptic* (hierocratic priestly party/prophets and disenfranchised Levites).

David and no suggestion of monarchy or monocracy, but it can be argued that, in the prophet's mind, the disillusioned shepherd is a veiled allusion to a descendant of David whose name, if we only knew it, might be found in the Chronicler's Davidic genealogy (1 Chr 3:1-24). The identification of the shepherd as a community leader of Davidic descent is compatible with the high level of interest in David and the house of David sustained throughout Zechariah 9–14, indeed, throughout the entire book. The identification is also suggested by the principal intertextual links of Zech 11:4-17. The sequel to the condemnation of worthless shepherds (rulers) in Ezek 34:1-22 is the prospect of the Davidic good shepherd who will give security through a covenant of peace and will put an end to enslavement at the hands of foreigners (34:23-24). These essential goals are represented in Zech 11:4-14 by the stick called "Favor" which symbolizes a covenant "with all the (foreign) peoples" (v. 10). The uniting of the two sticks in Ezek 37:15-23 is followed by the promise of the Davidic shepherd-king and, again, the covenant of peace (37:24-28). Finally, Jeremiah's condemnation of worthless shepherds, i.e., contemporary Judean kings (23:1-4), is contrasted with the future reign of the house of David (23:5-6). What sequence of events lies behind Zech 11:4-14, whether the rise and fall of a descendant of David in the administration of the province or an incident similar to the prophetic enthusiasm for Zerubbabel, we have no means of knowing.

It remains to note the deliberate contrast in the second incomplete sign-act (Zech 11:15-17) between a good if unsuccessful and frustrated shepherd and a worthless one. That this is not a retrospective judgment on the failure of the shepherd in the preceding narrative should be obvious. It is clearly stated that that mission was doomed from the outset, there is no sign of divine reprobation of the shepherd whose mission failed, and the sheep are abandoned to their own devices but not abused. And even if his abandonment of the mission were to be judged the result of human weakness, it would hardly call for the extreme punishment threatened in the verses attached to the second sign-act (11:17).[38] The most natural sense of Yahweh's address to the prophet is that the worthless shepherd is to appear in the future,[39] perhaps as a successor to the first shepherd after his mis-

---

38. Rudolph, *Haggai — Sacharja 1-8 — Sacharja 9-14 — Maleachi*, 211, takes v. 17 to be a later addition to the vision which ends in the previous verse, but it is not clear why he does so. Zech 11:15-17 follows the common indictment-verdict pattern of prophetic discourse and is by no means the only instance of prose-verse alternation. It should not be attached to 13:7-9, which is not about a worthless shepherd.

39. The introductory *hinnēh-'ānokî mēqîm* ("See, I am about to raise up"), sometimes

sion came to a sudden end or after the latter's perhaps violent death. Like his predecessor, his identity remains in the shadows.

The Death of the Good Shepherd (Zechariah 13:7-9; 12:10-14)

The mission of the shepherd-ruler of Zech 11:4-14 who, as I have argued, was probably of the line of David, came to a sudden end, and we are not told what happened to him after he disposed of the derisory sum he received for his services. Since interest in David and the house of David is no less apparent in the third section of Zechariah (chs. 12–14) than in the first and second, it would make sense to look for clues to the shepherd's fate in these chapters. At the basic formal and redactional level, Trito-Zechariah consists in a series of about fourteen brief eschatological oracles introduced with the formula "On that day" *(bayyôm hahû').* This series has been bracketed at the beginning and end with a vivid description of a siege of Jerusalem and a life-and-death struggle with foreign powers in and around Jerusalem, combining realistic features (rape, looting, deportation) with traits characteristic of apocalyptic. This series of end-time scenarios has been interspersed at some point in the formation of the section with three longer pieces: the mourning for "the Pierced One" (12:10-14), the reprobation of contemporary prophets (13:2-6), and a poem about the death of a shepherd and the fate of his flock (13:7-9). All three deal in dark and obscure speech with violent death, the death of unnamed individuals. Our concern is with the first and third, and since the third, the only one in verse, connects in theme and language more directly with the shepherds of Zech 4:4-17, we will deal with it first. It may be translated as follows:

> Sword, awake against my shepherd,
> against the man who is my associate!
> Strike[40] the shepherd, that the sheep may be scattered,
> I will then turn my hand against the lambs.[41]

---

with slight variations, is used on numerous occasions to announce a future event or person. It would not be used to introduce the subject of the passage immediately preceding.

40. The variant represented by Matt 26:31 and Mark 14:27, "I shall strike the shepherd and the sheep will be scattered," also in some LXX manuscripts, presupposes *'akkeh* for MT *hak,* but MT is well supported and should stand.

41. Lit., "the young ones" or "the little ones" *(haṣṣōʿărîm).*

In all the land two-thirds will be struck down and perish,
the remaining one-third will be left in it.
I will bring that third to the fire,
refine them as one refines silver,
assay them as one assays gold.
I will then say, "These are my people,"
They will answer, "Yahweh is my God."

There is something close to a consensus that this poem is unrelated to its context and that its original location would have been with the shepherd passages in Zech 11:4-17.[42] The question then arises as to which of the two shepherds is the object of the threat of death by sword thrust. Those who read the poem as the continuation of the three lines of verse in 11:17 identify the victim of the sword as the worthless shepherd whose fate is described there. Less frequently, the reference is stated to be to the first shepherd who, however well-intentioned, is subject to punishment for failure to fulfil his mission.[43] But if the one threatened with the sword were the worthless shepherd, his death would not have the effects described in the poem; on the contrary, it would be to the benefit of the flock. We might also wonder why Yahweh would refer to this person as "my shepherd" and "my associate."[44] We may therefore conclude that the shepherd who is Yahweh's associate, and whose death is foreseen in the poem, is the one who first undertook the mission condemned to failure from the outset. Furthermore, the apostrophe to the sword does not imply that Yahweh will himself be the shepherd's executioner, or even that he wills his death. Here as elsewhere, the sword is an instrument of the permissive will of God in the hands of others. So, for example, in "the Song of the Sword" in Ezekiel 21, which may be the text the author of Zech 13:7-9 had in mind, it is

---

42. A distinguished commentator who, on this point, *cantat extra chorum* is Karl Elliger, *Das Buch der zwölf kleinen Propheten*, 2 (ATD 25; Göttingen: Vandenhoeck & Ruprecht, 1950) 165-67.

43. Theophane Chary, *Aggée, Zacharie, Malachie* (SB; Paris: Gabalda, 1969) 185, 194-95.

44. The incidence of the term *'āmît*, here translated "associate," occurs, apart from this instance, only in Leviticus and the Holiness Code (Lev 5:21 [6:2]; 18:20; 19:15; 24:19; 25:14-15) with the sense of either physical or biological proximity ("neighbor" or "relative"). Its occurrence here does not support the opinion that the worthless shepherd is the high priest, as proposed by Plöger, *Theocracy and Eschatology*, 88, or the leader of the hierocratic party (presumably also the high priest), or either the high priest or "the Davidic governor," as Hanson, *The Dawn of Apocalyptic*, 350.

Yahweh's sword that will be the instrument of death for many during the Babylonian conquest of Jerusalem.

The worst punishment is, however, reserved for the flock. Being the feckless creatures that they are, "sheep without a shepherd," that is, "sheep deprived of a shepherd,"[45] are sheep in big trouble. Worse is to follow. The reduction of the flock, that is, the people of Judea, by two-thirds, appears to have been suggested once again by Ezekiel (5:1-4), in this case by a sign-act more bizarre even than that of the reluctant shepherd of Zech 11:4-14. During the siege of Jerusalem, Ezekiel is told to take a razor and shave off his hair and beard. He then is to weigh it, burn one third, cut up another third as he walks around the city after the siege, and scatter the final third to the wind pursued by Yahweh with a drawn sword. Some of the few hairs left are to be kept in the fold of his robe, and of these some again are to be thrown into the fire and burned. Dividing, numbering, and weighing are symbolic of judgment, as we know from the mysterious writing on the wall during Belshazzar's banquet (Dan 5:24-28). What it says is that only a relatively small number of the people will survive, and this remnant must still undergo final purification by fire in order to emerge, and to be acknowledged by God, as God's own people (cf. Jer 31:33; Hos 2:25[Eng 23]; Zech 8:8)

We now turn to the first of the three intercalatory passages in Trito-Zechariah, which reads as follows (12:10-14):

> On that day . . . I shall pour out on the house of David and the inhabitants of Jerusalem a spirit of grace and supplication,[46] so that they will look to me concerning the one whom they pierced through;[47] they will lament over him like the lament over an only child, and will grieve bitterly over him like the bitter grieving for the firstborn son.

45. The prophet Micaiah has a vision of "sheep without a shepherd" in foreseeing the death of King Ahab (1 Kgs 22:17). It may not be coincidence that Jesus describes the crowd following him in the same way after hearing of the death of John the Baptist (Matt 26:31; Mark 14:27).

46. I take these terms, *ḥēn* and *taḥānûnîm,* as hendiadys, implying that the grace or favor bestowed on them will enable them to supplicate Yahweh for a change of heart which will express itself in mourning.

47. I retain MT *wěhibbîṭû 'ēlay* ("they will look to me") following LXX. One looks to God in prayer and in acknowledgement of sin (e.g., Isa 22:11; Ps 34:6[Eng 5]). Something may have fallen out or been elided at this point, perhaps a name, hence "concerning the one whom they pierced through" must be considered tentative. What is at least clear is that Yahweh cannot be the object of the piercing through.

> On that day, the lamenting in Jerusalem will be as great as the lamenting for Hadad-rimmon in the plain of Megiddon. The land will lament, each family for itself: the family of the house of David by itself and its women by themselves; the family of the house of Nathan by itself and its women by themselves; the family of the house of Levi by itself and its women by themselves; the family of Shimei by itself and its women by themselves. All the remaining families, family by family, by themselves and their women by themselves.

The mourning, and therefore the repentance, is for the future ("on that day") in which Jerusalem, currently under attack, will finally be free from foreign inroads. But the occasion for the mourning, the killing of a prominent person by the inhabitants of Jerusalem, was a recent and well-remembered event at the time of writing. The identity of the anonymous victim has been the subject of a vast amount of speculation. To document adequately even the interpretations in early Judaism and Christianity would call for a separate monograph.[48] A candidate whose name is often proposed is Josiah, but Josiah was put to death not by Jerusalemites but by Pharaoh Necho II, and therefore cannot be the victim referred to in Zech 12:10. However, the mourning at Megiddo could hardly have failed to bring Josiah to mind, given the place and circumstances of his death recorded in 2 Kgs 23:28-30; 2 Chr 35:20-25. Only here and in the Zechariah text is the location of Josiah's fateful encounter with the pharaoh referred to as "the plain of Megiddo(n)" *(biqʿat mĕgiddôn),* and the separation of male and female mourners in Zechariah brings to mind the male and female singers who, according to the Chronicler, perpetuated Josiah's memory in their

---

48. The identification of "the Pierced One" with Jesus in John 19:37 and Rev 1:7 is carried over by Jerome in his *editio vulgata* to Zech 12:10, *adspicient ad me quem confixerunt* ("They will look to me whom they have pierced through," close to *crucifixerunt*). Some rabbinic sources have in mind Messiah ben Joseph, precursor of the Davidic Messiah, slain by Gog at the entrance to Jerusalem (Rabbi Dosa in *b. Sukkah* 52a), an identification perhaps inspired by the failure of the Bar Kokhba revolt. On the Targum, which takes a quite different tack, see Cathcart and Gordon, *The Targum of the Minor Prophets,* 218-19. On older interpretations and identifications, see Hugo Gressmann, *Der Messias* (FRLANT 43; Göttingen: Vandenhoeck & Ruprecht, 1929) 329-36; Sigmund Mowinckel, *He That Cometh,* trans. G. W. Anderson (1959; repr. BRS; Grand Rapids: Eerdmans and Livonia: Dove, 2005) 290-91. For the more recent *Forschungsgeschichte,* see Joyce Baldwin, *Haggai, Zechariah, Malachi* (TOTC; Downers Grove: InterVarsity, 1972) 190-94; Samuel Amsler, André Lacocque, René Vuilleumier, *Aggée, Zacharie, Malachie* (CAT 11C; Neuchâtel: Delachaux & Niestlé, 1981) 190-93; Meyers and Meyers, *Zechariah 9-14,* 337-40.

threnodies (2 Chr 35:25). Most significant, however, is the participation in the mourning of the house of David and the house of Levi,[49] one of several indications of parallel features, thematic and ideological, between Zechariah and Chronicles, both of which show a strong interest in both temple and dynasty.[50]

The proposal, therefore, is that the victim of violence who will be mourned by the houses of David and Levi, and who was put to the sword in Jerusalem, perhaps during or after the siege alluded to at the beginning and end of Trito-Zechariah, was himself of the lineage of David. In the context of Zechariah 9–14 he is to be identified with the shepherd-ruler of Zech 11:4-14 and 13:7-9. The mourning, predicted for some time in the future, is probably a deliberate reprise of the mourning for Josiah which continued for long after his death and which, since Josiah was the last significant ruler in the line of David, was also a lament for the passing of the dynasty and all that it stood for.[51]

---

49. Nathan is David's son of that name (2 Sam 5:14; 1 Chr 3:5) and Shimei grandson of Levi (Num 3:18).

50. Klaus Seybold, "Spätprophetische Hoffnungen auf die Wiederkunft der davidischen Zeitalters in Sach 9–14," *Jud* 29 (1973) 99-111; Antti Laato, *Josiah and David Redivivus* (ConBOT 33; Stockholm: Almqvist & Wiksell, 1992) 260-332; Thomas Willi, "Das davidische Königtum in der Chronik," in *Ideales Königtum*, ed. Rüdiger Lux (Leipzig: Evangelische Verlagsanstalt, 2005) 71-87.

51. The death of Josiah and the mourning which followed are discussed more fully in my "Remembering Josiah," in *Bringing the Past to the Present in the Late Persian and Early Hellenistic Period: Images of Central Figures*, ed. Diana Vikander Edelman and Ehud Ben Zvi (Oxford: Oxford University Press, 2013) 331-61.

CHAPTER NINE

Resistance to Imperial Rome

When you see great empires at war with each other, look for the coming of Messiah.

Genesis Rabbah 4:7

The Jews and the Roman Empire

From beginning to end, attempts to restore the Davidic dynasty, or predictions of its future or its eschatological restoration, were without exception protests against imperial rule. By the time the empire of Republican Rome began to make its presence felt in the Hellenistic kingdoms towards the beginning of the second century B.C.E., Judea had accumulated a great deal of experience in living under imperial rule. In the collective memory of its inhabitants, Egypt was the paradigmatic imperial oppressor, and the death of Josiah at the hands of an Egyptian ruler had not been forgotten. With the conquest of the kingdom of Samaria and the subsequent deportation of many of its inhabitants Assyria had eliminated ten of the twelve tribes. Then, after barely surviving the wrath of Sennacherib in the last months of the eighth century, Judah finally succumbed to the Babylonians a little more than a century later, bringing the native dynasty to an end. Less than half a century after that, Babylon was conquered by the Persian Cyrus, and for the next two centuries Judah, its native dynasty extinguished, was a province of the Persian Empire. Then it was the turn of Alexander and his Macedonians, then the Ptolemies and Seleucids and, after a brief but ultimately unsuccessful experience of native rule with the Hasmoneans, finally the Romans. The situation of Judah/Judea as part of a land bridge or corridor between Egyptians to the south, Hittites and the Phoenician city-states to the north, Assyrians and Babylonians to the east and northeast, and Greeks, Macedonians, and, eventually, Romans to the west dictated its historical destiny. The accumulation of inscriptions of imperial conquerors — Egyptians, Assyrians, Babylonians, Macedonians, Romans, French, and British — at the mouth of the Nahr el-Kelb (Dog River) near the Lebanese-Israeli frontier, a key point on the north-south *Via Maris,* testifies to this fate.[1]

The experience of subjection to imperial rule is a primary theme in the prophetic books we have been interrogating, thus validating Max Weber's statement about the biblical prophets, to the effect that "their primary concern was with foreign politics, chiefly because it constituted the theater of their god's activity."[2] A critique of imperialism not of prophetic origin, couched in parabolic form, is the story about the City and Tower of Babel in Gen 11:1-9. The symbolism of this lively narrative points unmistakably to the city of Babylon, the center of the Babylonian Empire, a name of infamy for the Jewish people. The city built by the people from the east is emblematic of Babylonian political and military power, and the tower "with its top reaching to the heavens" is the seven-story Etemenanki ziggurat temple tower. Attached to the ziggurat was the Esagila sanctuary, residence of the imperial deity Marduk, ruler in heaven as the Babylonian king ruled on earth, who legitimated and sponsored the imperial ambitions of its rulers. Thus the story of Babel could be read as a denunciation not only of the wars of conquest, deportations, mass killings, and the sum of human misery inflicted in the pursuit of imperial power but also, in more satirical mode, the religious ideas and practices which served to undergird those ambitions. In that respect it can be compared with the anti-Babylonian diatribe and satire in Deutero-Isaiah.

For the author of this apparently artless little narrative the main point is ostensibly about the origin of linguistic differentiation. The people from the east start out having "one language with the same words" and end up all speaking different and mutually unintelligible languages. But the au-

---

1. See the comments on these inscriptions in Ethelbert Stauffer, *Jerusalem und Rom im Zeitalter Jesu Christi* (Bern: Francke, 1957) 11-12.

2. Max Weber, *Economy and Society,* ed. Guenther Roth and Claus Wittich (Berkeley: University of California Press, 1978) 1:443.

thor knew perfectly well that this is not how languages came into existence, and in fact the passage immediately preceding in Genesis, the Table of the Nations (10:1-32), presents the descendants of Shem, Ham, and Japhet settled in their own lands speaking their own languages (vv. 5, 20, 31). The author wishes us to understand that the loss of the one primordial language, the language of Eden shared even with the animals, is symbolic and symptomatic of a world of noncommunication, a damaged world. The point is made not only by means of the rather forced assonance of the name Babel with the verb *bālal,* meaning "confuse,"[3] but also, in a more subtle way, by presenting the builders talking among themselves in mutual reinforcement while Yahweh takes counsel with himself in interior monologue. For the first time in Genesis there is no communication between the human actors and the deity. Blinded by the delusion of permanence, self-sufficiency, and invulnerability to change, these pioneer imperialists mean to make a name for themselves to be achieved by unassailable political and military power backed by potent religious symbols. The critique of imperialism in Genesis 11 will be given a finer point in those rabbinic versions in which Nimrod, the first empire-builder (Gen 10:8-12), is the initiator and head of the building project (*b. Sanh.* 109a; *Pirqe R. El.* 24),[4] while the manifest satirical element in the story is taken further by those ancient authors who supplied their own ending in which the tower is blown down by a gust of wind.[5]

Readers of the book of Revelation will know that Babylon, emblematic of all evil empires, was also a symbol of Rome, the city itself, and the city as the center of the most powerful of all empires up to that time. In that book the fall of Rome is predicted in terms borrowed from Isa 21:9, "Fallen, fallen is Babylon!" (Rev 14:8; 18:2). Rome is the embodiment of the woman Babylon condemned to ruin (Isaiah 47), she will drink from the cup of God's fury (Rev 14:8; 16:19), and will be overthrown (Rev 18:10, 21-22).[6] The presence of Rome was brought forcibly to the attention of Levantine and Near Eastern countries after the defeat of Philip V of Macedon and, shortly afterwards, of Antiochus III at the decisive battle of

---

3. Cf. REB: "That is why it is called Babel, because there the Lord made a babble of the languages of the whole world."

4. The connection with Nimrod is also made by Josephus, *Ant.* 1:109-21.

5. *Jub.* 10:18-26; *Sib. Or.* 3:97-109. Other references in my *Creation — Un-Creation — Re-Creation* (London: T. & T. Clark, 2011) 164-70.

6. The downfall of Rome-Babylon is also predicted in 4 Ezra 15:44-45; 16:1-17. See further *Ps. Sol.* 2:25; 1 Pet 5:13; *Sib. Or.* 5:143.

Magnesia in Asia Minor in 190 B.C.E. The imposition of the heavy tribute of twelve thousand talents at the peace of Apamea two years later, payable by Antiochus and his successors, led to the looting of temples in territories ruled by the Seleucids, including the temple of Jerusalem. This in its turn led to armed resistance, the proscription of Jewish religious practices by Antiochus IV Epiphanes, the revolt of the Maccabee brothers, and a century of rule by the Hasmoneans. Judah Maccabee entered into a treaty of friendship with Rome which was renewed at intervals down to the time of Hyrcanus I (135-104).[7] However, friendship with Rome had the tendency to lead to the absorption of the "friend" into the Roman Empire. So with these overtures: within less than a century they led to the Roman takeover of the Hasmonean kingdom.

Enthusiasm for the Hasmoneans was, in any case, by no means universal and was tempered by the knowledge that they were not of Davidic lineage and therefore, to that extent, lacking legitimacy. The author of the *Psalms of Solomon* makes the same point about them: "With pomp they set up a monarchy because of their arrogance/They despoiled the throne of David with arrogant shouting" (*Pss. Sol.* 17:5-6). Mattathias, instigator of the revolt and great-grandson of Hashmonai ("Asamonaios" in Josephus, *Ant.* 12:265), after whom the family was named, was of priestly not royal descent (1 Macc 2:1). On his deathbed he urged his sons to follow the example not of David but of their zealous ancestor, the priest Phineas, son of Eleazar and grandson of Aaron (1 Macc 2:54). Independence was achieved by Simon while holding the office of the high priesthood (1 Macc 13:41-42), clearly the most important office for the Maccabees, though in this respect also legitimacy could be challenged since the Hasmoneans were not of the Zadokite line. None of them even claimed the royal title before Aristobulus I wore the crown, and that only for a year in 104 B.C.E. Opposition came from different quarters: the ranks of the devout *(ḥăsîdîm)* for whom the Maccabee rebellion represented no more than "a little help" (Dan 11:34), the dissident temple community of Leontopolis in Egypt founded by the banished Zadokite Onias IV, and probably also from sectarians who settled at Qumran in the mid-second century B.C.E. After Pompey was invited to resolve the struggle for succession between Aristobulus and Hyrcanus, sons of Queen Salome Alexandra, it was only a matter of time

---

7. Judah's treaty of friendship (1 Macc 8:1-32; *Ant.* 12:414-419) was renewed by Jonathan (1 Macc 12:1-23; *Ant.* 13:163), by Simon (1 Macc 14:16-24; 15:15-24), and by Hyrcanus I (*Ant.* 13:259-266).

before Judea was annexed and eventually incorporated into the Roman province of Syria. It was only from that point that the Davidic dynasty, never forgotten, came once more to the surface.

Spiritual Resistance to Rome and the Revival of the Dynastic Theme

Once the Hasmoneans began to occupy center stage in Jewish political and religious affairs the Davidic theme seems to have disappeared from view. However, we may be sure that the Davidic succession set out in 1 Chronicles 3 did not come to an end with the last named, the seven sons of Elioenai (1 Chr 3:24). One indication is that, long after this time, following on the First and Second Jewish Revolts, respectively, both Vespasian and Domitian gave orders to round up and kill any remaining descendants of the Davidic line.[8] Spiritual resistance to Rome was maintained by groups of the devout (*ḥăsîdîm*), and it remains to be determined to what extent their sentiments were shared in the population as a whole.

Since the dissemination of anti-Roman propaganda was a dangerous business, there is the additional problem of the coded and arcane language in which these views were expressed. This is the case with the *Psalms of Solomon,* composed within a few years of the occupation of Jerusalem by the Romans in 63 B.C.E. and representing the reaction of a conventicle of the devout to Pompey's desecration of the temple and cruel treatment of the population. For obvious reasons Pompey's name does not appear in the Psalms, but his siege of the temple area and entry into the holy of holies are referred to indirectly at 2:1-2 and his death in Egypt in 48 B.C.E. more overtly, and with evident *Schadenfreude,* at 2:26-30. The 17th psalm in this collection recalls the promise of a perpetual dynasty made to David, now however interrupted on account of sin, especially the sins of the Hasmoneans:

> Lord, you chose David to be king over Israel,
>> and swore to him about his descendants forever,
>> that his kingdom should not fail before you.

8. Eusebius, *Hist. eccl.* 3.12, 19-20. The information about Domitian in 3:20 includes a citation from Hegesippus about some grandsons of Judah, brother of Jesus, who admitted to being of Davidic descent, but explained that the kingdom proclaimed by Jesus the Messiah was not of this world. They were consequently dismissed as simple and harmless.

> But (because of) our sins, sinners rose up against us,
>> they set upon us and drove us out.
> Those to whom you did not (make the) promise,
> they took away (from us) by force;
> and they did not glorify your honorable name.
> With pomp they set up a monarchy because of their arrogance;
>> they despoiled the throne of David with arrogant shouting.
> But you, O God, overthrew them, and uprooted their descendants
>> from the earth.[9]

The implication is that the disappointed hopes placed in the Hasmoneans, a native dynasty but not of the one, authentic lineage, contributed to the revival, after long silence, of the Davidic theme. The psalmist goes on to pray for the raising up of one of David's lineage who will expel foreigners and aliens from the land, destroy those who invade it, purify Jerusalem, gather a holy people, and rule over foreign nations — in other words, fulfil the aspirations and predictions of the prophets of old (*Pss. Sol.* 17:21-32). In achieving these goals, the Lord Messiah,[10] their king, possessed by the spirit of God, will rely on God, not on military equipment, gold and silver, and great numbers of warriors, in keeping with the exhortation addressed to Zerubbabel, that he must rule "not by might, nor by power, but by my spirit" (Zech 4:6). Ps 18 in the collection, finally, gives voice to a longing for the reign of this Lord Messiah "in the days of mercy" still to come.[11]

The *Psalms of Solomon* demonstrate that the dynastic theme could still be a live issue in Judea of the early Roman period, but, to repeat, we do not know how widely these expectations were shared either in Judea or in the Diaspora. According to the third *Sibylline Oracle* originating in Egypt, probably in Alexandria, the savior figure who is to come and whose coming will bring fertility and well-being, put an end to warfare, impose peace

---

9. *Ps. Sol.* 17:4-7. The translation is that of Robert B. Wright in *OTP,* 2:665-66.

10. On the title "the Lord Messiah," sometimes emended to "the Lord's Messiah," see the note of Wright in *OTP,* 2:667.

11. On the *Psalms of Solomon,* see Nicholas R. M. de Lange, "Jewish Attitudes to the Roman Empire," in *Imperialism in the Ancient World,* ed. P. D. A. Garnsey and C. R. Whittaker (Cambridge: Cambridge University Press, 1978) 255-81; Emil Schürer, *The History of the Jewish People in the Age of Jesus Christ (175 B.C.–A.D. 135),* rev. and ed. by Geza Vermes, Fergus Millar, and Matthew Black (Edinburgh: T. & T. Clark, 1979) 2:503-5; Wright, in *OTP,* 2:639-70; George W. E. Nickelsburg, *Jewish Literature between the Bible and the Mishnah* (2nd ed., Fortress: Minneapolis, 2005) 238-47.

among the nations and even in the animal world will be "a king from the sunrise," a native ruler of the Ptolemaic dynasty, not one from the lineage of David.[12]

An earlier example of coded allusion to Rome is the use of the term *Kittim* (more properly *Kittiyyim*) attested in Daniel (Dan 11:29-30) and frequently in the Qumran archive. The term originally referred to Cyprus, and more specifically to Kition on the southeast coast of the island.[13] At Qumran, the allusion in the *Habakkuk Pesher* (commentary) to the Kittim sacrificing to their standards (1QpHab 6:1-8) has persuaded practically all Qumran scholars that "Kittim" stands for "Romans." As in Daniel 11, the fragmentary *Nahum Pesher* fits the Kittim into the history of the later Hasmoneans which ended with the Roman takeover in 63 B.C.E. In the *War Scroll* (1QM) the Kittim are the adversaries in the final, apocalyptic war, but we have the impression that, in this context, this term has a more general reference to the many oppressive forces experienced by the people of Israel throughout history of which the Romans were, for the author of this text, the last. The citation of Num 24:17-19, the oracle of Balaam about the star and the comet, in 1QM XI 5-7 names Moab and Seth, while Isa 31:8 cited in 1QM XI 11 recalls the Assyrians, a much greater and more oppressive power. A particularly interesting example occurs in the commentary on Habakkuk. In the pesher on Hab 1:6, "I am rousing the Chaldeans, that savage and impetuous nation," the commentator identifies the Chaldeans (Babylonians) with the Kittim (Romans) who take possession of many countries and do not believe in the precepts of God (1QpHab II 10-16). The Vulgate version of Num 24:24, which translates *kittîm* with *Italia*, seems to refer, Qumranlike, to the Roman defeat of the Seleucids and conquest of Judea, concluding with a prediction that they too will come to an end: "Ships will come from Italy; they will conquer the Assyrians and devastate the Hebrews, but they too will perish in the end." Rome is therefore the new Babylon.

The expectation of the future restoration of the *ṣemah dāwîd*, referring to the Davidic dynasty, is certainly represented at Qumran (4Q161; 4Q174; 4Q257; 4Q285), but the office and role of the king is not greatly emphasized and is overshadowed by the theocratic idea — the kingdom of God, God as universal ruler. In the *War Scroll* the king has virtually no

---

12. *Sib. Or.* 3:652-656; cf. 3:192-195, on which see John J. Collins, in *OTP*, 1:354-61, with further references in the same work, pp. 325-26.

13. Gen 10:4; 1 Chr 1:7; Num 24:24; Isa 23:1, 12; Jer 2:10; Ezek 27:6.

role. In the *Temple Scroll* the restrictions on the king laid out in Deut 17:14-20 are further extended. He is to take counsel with an advisory board of twelve priests and twelve Levites, and before waging war he must consult the deity by Urim and Thummim under the control of the high priest (11QT[a] LVI-LIX). As an eschatological figure, the Davidic messiah no longer stands alone. In 4QFlorilegium (4Q174:10-13), the sectarian version of the promise to David in 2 Sam 7:16, assurance is provided that the branch of David will arise in the latter days, but he will be accompanied by the Interpreter of the Law *(dôrēš hattôrâ),* certainly a priest. Along the same lines, the *Damascus Document* interprets the Star and the Comet (or Scepter) in the oracle of Balaam (Num 24:17) as referring, respectively, to the eschatological Interpreter of the Law and the Prince of all the Congregation, that is, to a priestly alongside a lay figure (CD VII 18-20). This duality corresponds to the frequent reference in the Scrolls to the messiah of Aaron alongside the messiah of Israel of the lineage of David.[14] One of the most explicitly apocalyptic of these texts, 4Q521, describes the messianic age in which the hungry will be fed, the blind will see, the deformed and sick will be healed, the dead will be raised to life, the good news will be proclaimed to the poor, and prisoners will be set free — a prediction in process of fulfillment in the reply of Jesus to the messengers sent by John the Baptist, himself at that time a prisoner (Matt 11:2-5; Luke 7:22; cf. Isa 61:1-4). The Qumran text begins by referring to God's Anointed One, the Messiah, but it is the Hasidim, the devout sectarians, not an individual messianic figure, who will occupy the throne of an eternal kingdom.[15]

This tilting of the emphasis away from a political messianic figure in the Qumran texts is understandable given the fundamentally priestly character of the sectarians responsible for the writings to which reference has been made. Looking beyond Qumran, it is also the outcome of the increas-

---

14. These are distinct figures. 1QS IX 11 enjoins fidelity to the early statutes of the community until the Prophet comes, and the messiahs of Aaron and Israel, three eschatological figures, therefore. The *Damascus Document* refers in one place to the messiah of Aaron alone (CD XII 23) and often to the messiahs of Aaron and Israel, two distinct figures (CD XII 23; XIV 19; XIX 10-11; XX 1), as also the *Community Rule* (1QS IX 2).

15. On messianism in the Dead Sea Scrolls, see John J. Collins, *The Scepter and the Star: Messianism in Light of the Dead Sea Scrolls* (2nd ed., BRS; Grand Rapids: Eerdmans, 2010) 56-89, 117-21; George J. Brooke, "The Kittim in the Qumran Pesharim," in *Images of Empire,* ed. Loveday Alexander (JSOTSup 122; Sheffield: JSOT, 1991) 135-39; "Kingship and Messianism in the Dead Sea Scrolls," in *King and Messiah in Israel and the Ancient Near East: Proceedings of the Oxford Old Testament Seminar,* ed. John Day (JSOTSup 270; Sheffield: Sheffield Academic, 1998) 434-55; Craig A. Evans, "Messiahs," in *EDSS,* 1:537-42.

ing role of the aristocratic priesthood in the governance of the province throughout the Second Temple period. We had occasion to consider some of the early indications of this development in the Deuteronomistic "law of the king" (Deut 17:14-20)[16] and the close cooperation between "the two sons of oil," Zerubbabel the governor and Jeshua the high priest. As we come to the end of an epoch with the advent of Roman rule, we hear how, according to Josephus (*Ant.* 14:41), Judeans complained to Pompey that Hyrcanus and Aristobuluus, though of priestly descent, were changing the form of government from rule by the priesthood to a state of slavery, meaning the absolute and often arbitrary monarchy that Hasmonean rule had become. The predominant priestly element is apparent in other writings in circulation during the Hasmonean period. It is evident throughout the book of *Jubilees* in which there is only a passing allusion to the future kingship from the progeny of Judah (*Jub* 32:18-20). In *Testaments of the Twelve Patriarchs* Judah predicts the permanence of the kingdom to be established by one of his descendants (*T. Jud.* 22:3), citing the messianic prophecy of Balaam (Num 24:17)[17] and the spirit-endowment of the eschatological ruler (Isa 11:1-2). At the same time, he bluntly admonishes his sons to remain subject to his brother Levi since "to me God has given the kingship and to him the priesthood; and God has subjected the kingship to the priesthood" (*T. Jud.* 21:1-2). It seems that it was only as the grim reality of Roman rule began to take hold, whether experienced directly or as administered through Herod and his successors, that the specifically political, and therefore specifically Davidic, aspect of eschatological thinking came once again into prominence.[18] Decades after the final catastrophe of 70 C.E. it will persist as one strand of a complex apocalyptic scenario in the

16. The "law of the king," which stipulates obedience to the law in the care of the levitical priests, may be alluded to in the pesher on the messianic text Isa 11:1-5, where the statement that "he will not judge by appearances, he will not decide by hearsay" is taken to mean that he will judge according to what one of the "priests of renown" teaches him (4Q161 III 22-25 = 4QpIsa^a).

17. In line with Num 24:17 LXX, *anthrōpos*, the author renders *šēbeṭ* as "a man."

18. The Similitudes of Enoch (*1 En.* 37–71) follows the book of Daniel in presenting the eschatological agent not identified, as in Daniel, with the community of "the saints of the Most High," but with an individual Son of Man, the Elect One, the Anointed One, who will lead in the eschatological war and will preside over the final judgment from his throne. The date, however, remains in doubt; compare George W. E. Nickelsburg and James C. VanderKam, *1 Enoch: A New Translation* (Minneapolis: Fortress, 2004) 6; and Nickelsburg, *Jewish Literature between the Bible and the Mishnah* (2nd ed., Minneapolis: Fortress, 2005) 254-56 (the turn of the era) with Ephraim Isaac, *OTP*, 1:6-7 (ca. 105-104 B.C.E.)

destruction of the Roman Eagle by the Messianic Lion of *4 Ezra* and the final triumph of "my Servant the Anointed One" of *2 Baruch*.[19]

Messianism and Active Resistance to Roman Rule

In his *Antiquities of the Jews* books 17 to 20, continued in the seven volumes of *The Jewish War*, Josephus tells the story of increasingly violent protest against Roman rule beginning with the last years of Herod's reign and moving to the deadly crescendo of open revolt, civil war, and the siege and capture of Jerusalem, a disaster of a magnitude even greater than the fall of the city to the Babylonians six and a half centuries earlier. The narrative is punctuated by acts of bravery and terror which included pulling down the golden eagle, symbol of imperial Rome, which Herod had placed on top of the temple (*Ant.* 17:149-67), storming the Roman armory at Sepphoris (*Ant.* 17:271-72; *B.J.* 2:118-19), and torching Herod's palace at Jericho (*Ant.* 17:273-77). Celebration of the festivals in Jerusalem, attended by thousands of pilgrims from every part of the country, provided the occasion for major displays of anti-Roman sentiment, riots, suppression, and bloodshed. This was the case on the occasion when Pilate (26-36 C.E.), as reported in Luke 13:1, mixed the blood of Galilean pilgrims with that of their sacrifices; or when, at a Passover during the administration of the procurator Cumanus (48-52 C.E.), a Roman soldier exposed himself to the crowd (*Ant.* 20:105-12; *B.J.* 2:224-27). The violence of this constant drumbeat of outrage and protest, compounded by the brutality or incompetence of several of the local Roman officials (*procuratores*), brought to the surface a sequence of leaders, some no doubt more opportunistic than idealistic as often happens in such situations, but all characterized by Josephus, whose prejudices are never hard to detect, as brigands and frauds.

While it is not always clear that these "disturbers of the peace" saw themselves playing a role in an eschatological drama, there are accounts suggesting the assumption of a prophetic role. This seems to have been the case with a certain Theudas, who led his followers to the Jordan proclaiming, in the guise of Joshua or perhaps Elijah, that the water would miraculously divide, providing them with passage, presumably from the east to the west bank (*Ant.* 20:97-98; Acts 5:36). Some time later, an Egyptian presented himself as a prophet and persuaded a large crowd to follow him to

---

19. *4 Ezra* 11–12; *2 Bar. (Syrian Apocalypse of Baruch)* 70.

the Mount of Olives, a numinous site, where, at his command, the walls of Jerusalem would collapse as those of Jericho under siege by Joshua (*Ant.* 20:169-72; *B.J.* 2:261-63).[20] Both were soon hunted down and dispatched.[21] Others claimed, directly or by implication, the title of king and the attributes of royalty. Prominent among these was Simon, a former slave or servant of Herod who, Josephus says, placed the diadem on his head and was proclaimed king (*Ant.* 17:273-77; *B.J.* 2:57-59).[22] Another was Athronges, a shepherd, who with his four brothers rebelled against Archelaus and the Romans (*Ant.* 17:278-84; *B.J.* 2:60-65). Their charisma may have been largely a matter of impressive physique, or so Josephus would give us to understand. He dismisses their claims with the remark that "anyone might make himself king at the head of a band of rebels" (*Ant.* 17:285).

By far the most significant of these leaders was Judas (Judah) son of Ezekias (Hezekiah), who commanded a band of irregulars which carried on guerilla activity and eventually open conflict against the occupying forces towards the end of the brief tenure of Archelaus (4 B.C.E.–6 C.E.). Josephus tells us that Judah aspired to royal status (*Ant.* 17:271-72; *B.J.* 2:56). In his report to the synedrium, Gamaliel refers to this same person, active at the time of the census, under the name Judas the Galilean (Acts 5:37). Josephus regarded him as a terrorist of the worst kind, but also admits that his anti-Roman activities were based on an explicit ideological and theological basis. His followers, he tells us, agree with Pharisee teachings but, in addition, "have an invincible passion for liberty and take God for their only leader and lord" (*Ant.* 18:23). In other words, their anti-imperialism was based on a literal understanding of the *Shema* and the absolute obligation of acting according to it even at the cost of one's life.[23]

20. This was the same Egyptian for whom Paul was mistaken by the Roman tribune (Acts 21:37-38). The tribune put him at the head of four thousand assassins, a more realistic number than the thirty thousand of Josephus.

21. On these and similar prophetic figures, including John the Baptist (*Ant.* 18:116-19), see Richard A. Horsley and John S. Hanson, *Bandits, Prophets and Messiahs: Popular Movements in the Time of Jesus* (San Francisco: Harper & Row, 1988) 135-89; Craig A. Evans, *Jesus and His Contemporaries: Comparative Studies* (AGJU 25; Leiden: Brill, 2001) 441-47.

22. He is also mentioned in passing by Tacitus, *Hist.* 5:9.

23. Josephus seems, at first reading, to be speaking of two individuals both named Judas: Judas son of Ezekias (*Ant.* 17:271-72; *B.J.* 2:56), in agreement with Acts 5:37, and Judas the Gaulanite from Gamala, founder of the fourth philosophy whose subversive activity came to fruition in the last years before the siege of Jerusalem (*Ant.* 18:4-10, 23-25). But the Judas active at the time of Archelaus is described as a *sophistēs*, a philosophical type, and founder of a sect (*B.J.* 118), and the Judas from Gamala (Gamla) in the Upper Transjordanian region lacks

From the undoubtedly incomplete information provided by Josephus we can reconstruct something like a Galilean dynasty committed to resistance to the death against Roman imperial domination. The first to be mentioned is Hezekiah father of Judah, described by Josephus as leader of a robber band *(archilēstēs)* and ravager of the countryside *(katatrechōn)*, but also as "a man of great power." He was hunted down and killed by Herod.[24] Judah the Galilean continued where his father left off after the appointment of Coponius, first of the Roman procurators (6-8 C.E.). Josephus's remark about his aspirations to monarchy (*Ant.* 17:272) may imply that, among his own people in Galilee, he was accepted and proclaimed as king. That he is also described as the founder of a sect and a *sophistēs* together with a certain priest called Zadok warns us against thinking of him as a simple "son of the people."[25] Two of his sons, James (Jacob) and Simon, were crucified by the procurator Tiberius Alexander (46-48 C.E.), no doubt for following their father's example (*Ant.* 20:102).[26] Another son, Menahem, occupied Masada after which, we are told, he returned to Jerusalem "like a true king" and entered the temple dressed in royal robes (*B.J.* 2:433-48). In the lead-up to the war he was murdered by the chief of a rival faction (*B.J.* 2:433-48; *Life* 21, 46-47). Finally, there is Eleazar ben Jair, also a *sophistēs* (*B.J.* 2:445), described as a close relative of Menahem (*B.J.* 2:449) and a descendant — perhaps grandson — of Judah the Galilean (*B.J.* 7:253). He was the leader of the final resistance on the rock of Masada, into whose mouth Josephus puts the speech advocating collective suicide rather than surrender (*B.J.* 7:32-336, 341-88).[27]

---

a patronymic which would distinguish him from his namesake. In addition, both were active about the same time. So it seems that Josephus is referring to one and the same person.

24. *Ant.* 14:159; 17:271-72; *B.J.* 1:204; 2:56.

25. *Ant.* 17:271-72; 18:9-10, 23; *B.J.* 2:56, 118-19; Acts 5:37.

26. By interesting coincidence, two disciples of Jesus with the same names, James son of Alphaeus and Simon the Zealot, are linked together in the list of the Twelve in Luke 6:13-16; Acts 1:13. In Matt 10:2-4; Mark 3:16-19 Simon the Zealot is paired with Judas Iscariot, by some thought to be involved in active resistance to Rome. According to *Ant.* 20:200, James the brother of Jesus was put to death by stoning in the year 62 C.E. at the insistence of the high priest Ananus.

27. On these "disturbers of the (imperial) peace," see Stauffer, *Jerusalem und Rom im Zeitalter Jesu Christi;* Horsley and Hanson, *Bandits, Prophets, and Messiahs;* Horsley, "Popular Prophetic Movements at the Time of Jesus," *JSNT* 26 (1986) 3-27; Martin Hengel, *The Zealots,* trans. David Smith (Edinburgh: T. & T. Clark, 1989); Rebecca Gray, *Prophetic Figures in Late Second Temple Jewish Palestine* (Oxford: Oxford University Press, 1993); Morton Smith, "The Troublemakers," in *CHJ.* Vol. 3: *The Early Roman Period,* ed. William Horbury, W. D. Davies, John Sturdy (1999) 501-68.

This cursory survey of events from the last years of Herod's reign as "king of the Jews,"[28] through the administration of the Herodians followed by successive procurators, to the siege and capture of Jerusalem reveals a surprising and unexpected feature, namely, the complete absence of any allusion to the Davidic dynasty and the hopes and expectations associated with it. It is possible that Josephus, for whom the priesthood was evidently more important than the monarchy, suppressed this aspect of the history, but it is more probable that, on account of their known antecedents, the aspirants to royalty who emerged at intervals during this period — Judah and his son Menahem in particular — were in no position to lay claim to Davidic lineage. In any case, since the narrative traditions about David never represent him as engaged in armed resistance to imperial control, he may not have been considered an appropriate model for Judah the Galilean and the others. It may nonetheless be significant that several who fought for freedom under Roman rule, and before that under Seleucid rule, bear the name of David's tribe. The first of the Maccabee brothers set the example followed by Judah the Galilean, Judah the Torah scribe whose disciples removed the Roman eagle from the roof of the temple and were involved in anti-Roman riots,[29] a Zealot Judah ben Ari (*B.J.* 6:92; 7:215), and several named Judah among the followers of Simon bar Giora, a prominent leader of the revolt. To these, some would add the Judah who betrayed Jesus.

Josephus attributes the anti-Roman uprisings leading to the final suppression of the revolt and fall of Jerusalem to an ambiguous oracle predicting world dominance for a ruler from Judea and the final eclipse of the Roman Empire:

> What more than all else incited them to the war was an ambiguous oracle, likewise found in their sacred scriptures, to the effect that, at that time, one from their country would become ruler of the world. (*B.J.* 6:312)

The identity of the "ambiguous oracle" has long been discussed. Among the leading candidates are Jacob's deathbed prediction about Shiloh to whom the nations will submit and offer tribute (Gen 49:10) and the oracle

---

28. The title conferred by the Roman senate (*Ant.* 1:282-85) and foretold by Menahem the Essene when Herod was still a child (*Ant.* 15:372-79).

29. *Ant.* 17:149-67, 213-18; *B.J.* 1:648-50, 655.

about the ruler to come whose dominion will be from sea to sea and from the River to the ends of the earth (Zech 9:9-10). For his own self-interested reasons, Josephus referred it to Vespasian, proclaimed emperor on Judean soil shortly before the fall of Jerusalem (*B.J.* 6:312), and the same identification is mentioned by Eusebius (*Hist. eccl.* 3.8.10-11), who, however, refers it to Jesus. The oracle also came to the attention of Tacitus as one element in a long-standing ideological war of words between east and west, Asia and Europe, the oriental provinces of the Roman Empire and Rome itself:

> The majority [in Judea] firmly believed that their ancient priestly writings contained the prophecy that this was the very time when the East should grow strong and that men starting from Judah should possess the world. This mysterious prophecy had in reality pointed to Vespasian and Titus, but the common people, as is the way of human ambition, interpreted these great destinies in their own favor, and could not be turned to the truth even by adversity.[30]

Since several of the leaders of the revolts against Rome were from the educated classes, it is quite possible that they were familiar with and motivated by the predictions of vast changes in international affairs in circulation at that time.

The leaders of the uprisings in Judea and the Diaspora under the emperors Trajan (98-117 C.E.) and Hadrian (117-38) likewise make no appeal to the memory of David. The Jewish revolt which broke out in 115 C.E. in Egypt and Cyrene was led by a rebel named Lukuas in Eusebius and Andreas in Cassius Dio. Eusebius reports that the rebels rallied round

---

30. *Hist.* 5:13; see also Suetonius, *Vesp.* 4. Dependence of Tacitus on Josephus is possible and is supported by his recording the prodigies preceding the fall of Jerusalem in the same paragraph of *Histories* (cf. Josephus, *B.J.* 6:288-309). See also Hegesippus in Eusebius, *Hist. eccl.* 3.8.1-11. The oracle is the Jewish contribution to an ideological and propagandistic war between east and west which can be traced back into the Achaemenid period (see Herodotus, *Hist.* 1:4), which then gathered strength in resistance to Hellenic influence, following on the conquests of Macedon, from Iranians, Parthians, Medes, Anatolians, and others as well as from Egypt (see *Sib. Or.* 4 and the Potter's Oracle), and was taken up with Rome as object after the Roman conquests in Asia. From the Near Eastern side, see Samuel K. Eddy, *The King Is Dead: Studies in the Near Eastern Resistance to Hellenism, 334-31 B.C.* (Lincoln: University of Nebraska Press, 1961). On the Roman side of this ideological warfare between East and West, in which Virgil's *Fourth Eclogue* also had a part to play, see Stauffer, *Jerusalem und Rom im Zeitalter Jesu Christi*, 20-39.

Lukuas "as their king," but nothing else is known about him.[31] The harsh proscription of Jewish practices, especially circumcision, and the plan to rebuild Jerusalem as Aelia Capitolina in the emperor's honor lit the fuse which had been smouldering during the intervening years. Much more is known about Shimʿon bar Koziba, leader of the revolt in Judea, than about Judah the Galilean. The information comes from the numerous artefacts and letters discovered in the Wadi Murabbaʿat and Naḥal Ḥever, coins minted by the rebels during the brief period of the revolt (132-35 C.E.), and commentary, both positive and negative, in early Jewish and Christian sources. The letters written by him, which deal with day-to-day affairs, complaints about orders disobeyed and the like, reveal no messianic consciousness. In these letters he refers to himself simply by name, but in other documents, mostly deeds and leases which have come to light, his title, *nāśî' yiśrā'ēl* ("prince" or "leader of Israel"), is added, but this too carries no evident royal-messianic implications.[32] The dating on documents and coins according to "the year of the redemption of Israel" has more messianic resonance, but can as readily be viewed as an early example of the practice of initiating a new calendar characteristic of revolutionary movements, for example, the *hejira* of Islam in 622 C.E. or Vendémiaire of the French revolutionaries in 1792. One rabbinic source states that Bar Kokhba claimed to be Messiah, but the claim is rejected in peremptory fashion, if for a decidedly odd reason.[33] It is also recorded of R. Akiva that,

---

31. Eusebius, *Hist. eccl.* 4.2.1-5; Cassius Dio, *Hist. rom.* 68:32; 69:12-13. On the disturbances in Egypt and Cyrene under Trajan (115-17), see Schürer, *The History of the Jewish People in the Age of Jesus Christ*, 1:529-34; Martin Hengel, "Messianische Hoffnung und politischer 'Radikalismus' in der jüdisch-hellenistischen Diaspora," in *Apocalypticism in the Mediterranean Hellenistic World and the Near East*, ed. David Hellholm (Tübingen: Mohr, 1983) 655-86. For documentation on the period 70-135 C.E., see Lester L. Grabbe, *Judaism from Cyrus to Hadrian*. Vol. 2: *The Roman Period* (Minneapolis: Fortress, 1992) 555-605.

32. In biblical texts *nāśî'* occurs in a Davidic-messianic context only twice, in Ezek 34:23-24; 37:24-25, though the Ezekielan authenticity of both is suspect. It should be noted that the same term is used throughout Ezekiel, especially in the Vision of the New Temple in chs. 40-48, precisely to avoid using the term *melek* ("king"). According to Eusebius (*Hist. Eccl.* 4.6.2), Bar Kokhba used his name ("Son of the Star") not in association with the Balaam messianic oracle in Num 24:17 but to persuade his gullible followers that he was a luminary come down from heaven. In the absence of supporting indications, the term *nāśî'* provides a rather insecure basis for assuming Bar Kokhba's messianic consciousness.

33. "Bar Kokhba reigned two and a half years, and then said to the rabbis, 'I am the Messiah.' They answered, 'Of Messiah it is written that he smells and judges: let us see whether he can do so.' When they saw that he was unable to judge by the scent they slew him" (*b. Sanh.* 93b).

on seeing Bar Kokhba, he exclaimed, "This is King Messiah," to which one of his disciples, R. Johanan ben Torta, replied, "Akiva, grass will grow through your jawbones and the Son of David will still not have come" (*y. Ta'an.* 68d).[34]

Jesus Son of David

Apart from Akiva's identification of Shim'on bar Koziba as King Messiah, the gospel record about Jesus is the only explicit attestation of royal, Davidic messianism throughout the entire period of Roman rule. According to rabbinic testimony (*y. Ta'an.* 68d), the messianic status of Bar Koziba was based on one of the fundamental messianic biblical texts, the oracle of Balaam about the star and the comet (Num 24:17):

> A star will come forth out of Jacob,
> a comet will arise from Israel;

hence the sobriquet "Son of the Star" (bar Kokhba in Aramaic) assigned to Shim'on bar Koziba by Akiva and later commentators on the revolt.[35] It remains uncertain whether in the course of the short-lived revolt Bar Kokhba succeeded in occupying Jerusalem; if he did, the occupation must have been short-lived. An event recorded in all four gospels is the entry of Jesus into Jerusalem presented as the climax of his public activity and the first in a chain of events leading to his death by crucifixion. All the versions reveal unmistakable messianic features. In Mark's account, the first indication occurs as Jesus and his disciples are leaving Jericho on their way to Jerusalem: a blind beggar, Bar Timaeus, petitions Jesus to restore his sight, and so it happens (Mark 10:46-52). In the Matthean version there are two unnamed blind beggars (Matt 20:29-34) and in Luke one only (Luke 18:35-43), but in all three versions they petition Jesus as Son of David. The

---

34. On the Bar Kokhba revolt: Schürer, *The History of the Jewish People in the Age of Jesus Christ*, 1:534-57; Benjamin Isaac and Aharon Oppenheimer, "The Revolt of Bar Kokhba: Ideology and Modern Scholarship," *JJS* 36 (1985) 33-60; "Bar Kokhba," *ABD*, 1:598-601; Peter Schäfer, *Der Bar Kokhba Aufstand: Studien zum zweiten jüdischen Krieg gegen Rom* (TSAJ 1; Tübingen: Mohr, 1981); Michael O. Wise, "Bar Kokhba Letters," *ABD*, 1:601-6; Collins, *The Scepter and the Star*, 201-4.

35. According to Eusebius or his source, probably Hegesippus (*Hist. eccl.* 4.6.2), the name is Barchōchebas, corresponding to the Aramaic bar Kokhba.

crowd accompanying Jesus also acclaims him as "the One who is to come" in anticipation of the restoration of the Davidic kingdom:

> Blessed is the kingdom of our father David which is coming! (Mark 11:10)
> Hosanna to the Son of David! (Matt 21:9)
> Blessed is the One who is to come in the name of the Lord! (Matt 21:9; Mark 11:9; Luke 19:38; John 12:13)

According to Luke, the joy of the disciples at the anticipation of the proximate restoration of the Davidic kingdom, which is to be a glorious and peaceful kingdom, breaks out as they descend the Mount of Olives, the place of revelation (Luke 19:37-40).[36] The restoration of sight to the blind on the way out of Jericho provides a first clue to what it means for Jesus to be addressed as "the One who is to come." It reinforces the reply of Jesus to John the Baptist, then in prison, who sought assurance that Jesus was "the One who is to come." Jesus invited John to observe that "the blind recover their sight, the lame walk, lepers are made clean, the deaf hear, the dead are raised to life, the poor have the good news brought to them" (Matt 11:2-6; Luke 7:18-23). The miraculous restoration of sight is, therefore, an anticipation of the vision of an eschatological kingdom more in accord with the Isaian predictions of a messianic age which will bring the removal of disabilities, the abolition of war, the triumph of justice and peace, and even the conquest of death itself.[37]

The presentation of the entry into Jerusalem as the fulfillment of prophecy is made explicit in the Matthean version (Matt 21:1-9) by citing an edited and abbreviated version of one of the key Davidic-messianic texts:

> Say to daughter Zion:
> See, your king is coming to you,
> humble, mounted on a donkey,
> on a colt, foal of a beast of burden.
>
> (Zech 9:9)[38]

36. See also Luke 21:37; Acts 1:12. Josephus reports the case of an Egyptian (pseudo)prophet who persuaded thirty thousand people to follow him to the Mount of Olives on his assurance that, once there, the walls of Jerusalem would fall down and he would enter the city in triumph (*Ant.* 20:169-71; *B.J.* 2:261-62).

37. Isa 29:18-19; 35:5-6; 42:6-7; 61:1-3.

38. Citing perhaps from memory, the gospel writer has substituted Isa 62:11 for the

The citation of Zech 9:9 opens up the event to a richer prophetic resonance by its association with the Judah oracle of Gen 49:8-12 in which Shiloh *(šîlōh)*, King Messiah, the One who is to come, "ties his colt to the vine, his donkey's foal to the red vine."[39] The untethering of the animal, an apparently trivial narrative detail present in all three Synoptic accounts, read against the background of Gen 49:8-12; Zech 9:9, confirms the true identity of the one to whom the animal belongs.

Beginning with the entry of Jesus into Jerusalem, the Davidic-messianic aspect of his mission is prominently and problematically in evidence in the Synoptic accounts of the events leading up to his death. It is also in evidence, with a different nuance, in the infancy narratives in the first and third gospels, preceded in the former and followed in the latter by a genealogy in which the antecedents of Jesus are traced back, respectively, to Abraham and Adam. Both, however, are essentially Davidic (Matt 1:1-17; Luke 3:23-38).[40] Both gospel writers state clearly the significance of bloodline in their accounts of the conception and birth of Jesus. Matthew's account of the birth and infancy (Matt 1:18–2:23) reads like a kind of midrash on interconnected biblical-messianic texts. These include the birth of Immanuel in Isa 7:14, the offering of tribute from the east in Isa 60:6, Balaam's oracle about the star and the comet in Num 24:17, and Micah's prophecy about Bethlehem, David's city, in Mic 5:1-4(Eng 2-5). The parallel in Luke's gospel, which also takes in the birth of John the Baptist, is more explicitly political, foreshadowing the eternal kingdom of David and the redemption of Israel, especially in the two canticles (Luke 1:5-80). The prophetically-warranted origin of the Messiah in Bethlehem seems to have been well known (John 7:41-42), and the Davidic descent of Jesus is mentioned occasionally outside of the infancy narratives[41] without seeming to carry much weight. In one disputed saying reported in three gospels which, exception-

---

first line of Zech 9:9 (cf. John 12:15, which cites Isa 40:9, "Do not be afraid, daughter Zion") and has been influenced by the LXX version of the Zechariah verse, *epibebēkōs epi hypozygion*, "mounted on a beast of burden." Significant omissions are "victorious over his foes" (v. 9) and the abolition of warfare and establishment of universal peace in v. 10.

39. On the interpretation of Gen 49:8-12 see above, pp. 147-49.

40. In Matthew, the arrangement in three groups of fourteen is meant to spell out the name David by gematria: the numerical value of *daleth — vav — daleth*, the consonants of David's name, is 4 + 6 + 4 = 14. In addition to the commentaries, see Marshall D. Johnson, *The Purpose of the Biblical Genealogies, with Special Reference to the Setting of the Genealogies of Jesus* (SNTSMS 8; 2nd ed., Cambridge: Cambridge University Press, 1988).

41. Rom 1:3; 2 Tim 2:8; Rev 5:5; 22:16.

ally, was initiated by Jesus, he deploys an exegetical argument based on Ps 110:1 ("The Lord says to my lord, sit at my right hand") which in fact appears to minimize rather than emphasize the significance of descent from David.[42]

This more explicitly political perspective on Davidic messianism probably originated in those early Christian circles which retained a distinctively Jewish identity while accepting Jesus as Messiah, the Anointed One of God. The most prominent figure among Jewish-Christians in the earliest period was James, brother of Jesus, who was put to death by the Sanhedrin at the instigation of the high priest Ananus in 62 C.E.[43] Eusebius remarks on the care with which the *desposynoi*, those claiming kinship with Jesus the Lord *(despotēs)*, preserved their genealogical records (*Hist. eccl.* 1.7, 14), among whom probably were some of those descendants of David whom Vespasian ordered hunted down and put to death after the fall of Jerusalem (*Hist. eccl.* 3.12).

Taking the gospel narrative as a whole, including the Fourth Gospel, the conclusion seems justified that the Davidic aspect of the profile of Jesus, understood as more explicitly political in nature, is marginal. Jesus is addressed as "Son of David" almost exclusively by people suffering from afflictions and disabilities — the blind, the dumb, the sick, the deaf, and the possessed — the alleviation of which disabilities by Jesus anticipates and prefigures the messianic age presented in the fullest and most compelling form in the book of Isaiah. As Jesus states in his reply to John the Baptist's query (Matt 11:2-6; Luke 7:18-23), these prodigious acts, including the raising of the dead to life, provided the clearest indication of the nature of his own messianic consciousness. Jesus never refers to himself as Messiah. In Mark's gospel Simon Peter proclaims him as such, to which the Jesus of Mark's gospel responds only by enjoining silence and then goes on at once to speak of himself as the Son of Man (Mark 8:27-33). Where Jesus speaks of himself in this gospel it is almost invariably as the Danielic Son of Man who will come in glory with the holy angels in the clouds of heaven at the end time,[44] but who must first be subject to suffering, contempt, and death, after the pattern of the Isaian Servant of the Lord.[45]

In the final phase of the gospel story the nature of the messianic sta-

---

42. Matt 22:41-46; Mark 12:35-37; Luke 20:41-44; cf. John 7:40-44.
43. *Ant.* 20:200; Eusebius, *Hist. eccl.* 2.23.11-25.
44. Dan 7:13-14; Mark 8:38; 13:26; 14:61-62.
45. Isa 52:13–53:12; Mark 8:31; 9:9, 12, 31; 10:33-34, 45; 14:21, 41.

tus claimed by Jesus himself, as opposed to the constructions and expectations placed on him by others, comes most explicitly to the fore. In the incident of the arrest, recorded in all four gospels, Jesus repudiates the violent intervention of one of his followers adding, in the Matthean version, that all who take up the sword perish by the sword (Matt 26:52). If he were a political messiah like the other "disturbers of the peace," would God his Father not send him twelve legions of angels, more than enough to deal with the three or four Roman legions stationed in the region at that time?[46] Placed on oath during his appearance before the high priest Caiaphas[47] to declare whether he is Messiah, Son of God, Jesus gives him an answer which is, in effect, a refusal to answer.[48] To the question "Are you king of the Jews?" put to him by Pilate,[49] Jesus gives a similar reply — "the words are yours," followed by silence.[50] Jesus met the same fate at the hands of the Romans as James and Simon, sons of Judah the Galilean. He would surely have sympathized with the suffering of the many who, by the time of his death, had died resisting imperial Rome, but he went his own way.

The suppression of the Bar Koziba revolt and the anti-Jewish measures of Hadrian marked the end of an epoch. The survivors among the religious leadership, the *Tannaim,* left Judea, devastated and depopulated after two centuries under Roman rule, and retreated to Galilee. Their goal was to lay the foundations for a way of life based on tradition, law, and the regular observance of Sabbath and the festivals, one which renounced apocalyptic

46. Matt 26:47-56; Mark 14:43-50; Luke 22:49-51; John 18:2-11.

47. According to Josephus, *Ant.* 18:35, 95, Joseph Caiaphas, son-in-law of Ananus (Annas), was appointed high priest in 18 C.E. and deposed by Vitellius in 36 C.E.

48. The brief reply *su legeis* is better translated with REB as "the words are yours" rather than "you have said so" (NRSV). The reply *ego eimi* of the Markan version (14:62) is equally ambiguous. When the Jesus of John's gospel replied in the same way during his arrest, those who confronted him, hearing the divine name *'ehyeh*, "I AM," revealed to Moses at Sinai, are said to have fallen to the ground (Jn 18:5).

49. Pilate, sent to Judea as procurator by Tiberius in 26 C.E. (*Ant.* 18:35, 177), a move perhaps made under the influence of the notoriously anti-Jewish Sejanus, was recalled ten years later after his ruthless suppression of disturbances in Samaria led to further trouble and a delegation to Rome to complain of his brutality (*Ant.* 18:85-89). He was also guilty of deliberate provocation by introducing medallions of the emperor attached to military standards into Jerusalem and expropriating funds from the temple treasury to finance the building of an aqueduct (*Ant.* 18:55-62; *B.J.* 2:169-77). While the gospel writers assign responsibility more to the Jewish authorities than to Pilate, a close reading of the accounts of the trial allow glimpses of the brutal official described by Josephus.

50. Matt 27:11-14; Mark 15:1-5; Luke 23:1-5.

visions and the political ambitions which so often accompanied them. David was not, however, forgotten. The sacred texts were still studied, the psalms recited, and his name repeated each time the fifteenth petition of the *Shemoneh Esreh* (the Eighteen Prayers) was recited:

> Speedily cause the branch of David, your servant, to flourish.
> Lift up his glory by your divine help, for we await your salvation
> all the day.
> Blessed are you, O Lord, you who cause the strength
> of salvation to flourish.

Bibliography

Ackroyd, Peter R. "Two Old Testament Historical Problems of the Early Persian Period." *JNES* 17 (1958) 13-27.

———. *Exile and Restoration.* OTL. Philadelphia: Westminster, 1968.

———. "The Temple Vessels — A Continuity Theme." In *Studies in the Religion of Ancient Israel.* VTS 23. Leiden: Brill, 1972, 166-81.

Albertz, Rainer. *A History of Israelite Religion in the Old Testament Period.* Vol. 2: *From the Exile to the Maccabees.* Trans. John Bowden. OTL. Louisville: Westminster John Knox, 1994.

Albright, William Foxwell. *The Biblical Period from Abraham to Ezra.* New York: Harper & Row, 1949.

Alcock, Leslie. *Arthur's Britain: History and Archaeology.* 2nd ed. London: Penguin, 1989.

Alt, Albrecht. "Die Rolle Samarias bei der Entstehung des Judentums." In *Kleine Schriften zur Geschichte des Volkes Israel.* Vol. 2. Munich: Beck, 1953, 316-37.

Alter, Robert. *The David Story.* New York: Norton, 1999.

Amit, Yairah. "The Saul Polemic in the Persian Period." In Lipschits and Oeming, *Judah and the Judeans in the Persian Period,* 647-61.

Amsler, Samuel, André Lacocque, and René Vuilleumier. *Aggée, Zacharie, Malachie.* CAT 11C. Neuchâtel: Delachaux & Nestlé, 1981.

Ashe, Geoffrey, ed. *The Quest for Arthur's Britain.* London: Pall Mall, 1968.

Avigad, Nachman. *Bullae and Seals from a Post-Exilic Judean Archive.* Qedem 4. Jerusalem: Hebrew University Institute of Archaeology, 1976.

———. *Discovering Jerusalem.* Nashville: Nelson, 1980.

———. *Hebrew Bullae from the Time of Jeremiah: Remnants of a Burnt Archive.* Jerusalem: Israel Exploration Society, 1986.

Bach, Robert. *Die Aufforderungen zur Flucht und zum Kampf im alttestamentlichen Prophetenspruch.* WMANT 9. Neukirchen: Neukirchener, 1962.

Badè, W. F. "The Seal of Jaazaniah." *ZAW* 51 (1933) 150-56.

Balcer, Jack Martin. "The Athenian Episcopos and the Achaemenid King's Eye." *AJP* 98 (1977) 252-63.

————. *Sparda by the Bitter Sea.* BJS 52. Chico: Scholars, 1984.

Baldwin, Joyce. *Haggai, Zechariah, Malachi.* TOTC. Downers Grove: IVP, 1972.

Baltzer, Klaus. *Deutero-Isaiah.* Trans. Margaret Kohl. Hermeneia. Minneapolis: Fortress, 2001.

Barkay, Gabriel. "A Bulla of Ishmael, the King's Son." *BASOR* 290/91 (1993) 112-13.

Bartal, Aryeh. "Again, Who Was Sheshbazzar?" *BM* 24 (1979) 357-69. (Hebrew)

Barth, Hermann. *Die Jesaja Worte in der Josiazeit: Israel und Asshur als Thema einer produktiven Neuinterpretation der Josiaüberlieferung.* WMANT 48. Neukirchen: Neukirchener, 1977.

Barton, John. *Amos' Oracles against the Nations: A Study of Amos 1.3–2.5.* SOTSMS 6. Cambridge: Cambridge University Press, 1980.

Batten, Loren W. *A Critical and Exegetical Commentary on the Books of Ezra and Nehemiah.* ICC. Edinburgh: T. & T. Clark, 1913.

Beaulieu, Paul-Alain. *The Reign of Nabonidus, King of Babylon, 556-539 B.C.* New Haven: Yale University Press, 1989.

Becking, Bob. "Baalis King of the Ammonites: An Epigraphical Note on Jeremiah 40:14." *JSS* 38 (1993) 15-24.

————. "Inscribed Seals as Evidence for Biblical Israel? Jeremiah 40.7–41.15 *par exemple*." In *Can a 'History of Israel' Be Written?* ed. Lester L. Grabbe. JSOTSup 245. Sheffield: Sheffield Academic, 1997, 80-82.

————. *From Babylon to Eternity: The Exile Remembered and Constructed in Text and Tradition.* London: Equinox, 2009.

Begg, Christopher T. "The Interpretation of the Gedaliah Episode (2 Kgs 25:22-26) in Context." *Anton* 62 (1987) 3-11.

Begrich, Joachim. "Sōpher und Mazkīr: Ein Beitrag zur inneren Geschichte der davidisch-salomonischen Grossreiches und des Königreiches Juda." *ZAW* 58 (1940-41) 1-29.

Bentzen, Aage. *King and Messiah.* London: Lutterworth, 1955.

Ben-Yashar, Menahem. "On the Problem of Sheshbazzar and Zerubbabel." *BM* 27 (1981) 46-56. (Hebrew)

Berger, P. -R. "Zu den Namen *ššbssr* und *šn'sr*." *ZAW* 83 (1971) 98-100.

Berges, Ulrich. *Das Buch Jesaja: Komposition und Endgestalt.* Freiburg: Herder, 1998.

Betlyon, John W. "The Provincial Government of Persian Judah: Judah and the Yehud Coins." *JBL* 105 (1986) 633-42.

Beuken, Willem A. M. *Haggai-Sacharja 1–8: Studien zur Überlieferungsgeschichte der frühnachexilischen Prophetie.* SSN 10. Assen: Van Gorcum, 1967.

———. "Isa 55.3-5: The Restoration of David." *Bijdr* 35 (1974) 49-64.

———. *Jesaja 1–12*. HTKAT. Freiburg: Herder, 2003.

Bickerman, Elias. "La seconde année de Darius." *RB* 88 (1981) 23-28.

Blenkinsopp, Joseph. "The Quest of the Historical Saul." In *No Famine in the Land: Studies in Honor of John L. McKenzie,* ed. James W. Flanagan and Anita Weisbrod Robinson. Missoula: Scholars, 1975, 75-99.

———. *Prophecy and Canon: A Contribution to the Study of Jewish Origins.* Notre Dame: University of Notre Dame Press, 1977.

———. "The Mission of Udjahorresnet and Those of Ezra and Nehemiah." *JBL* 106 (1987) 409-21.

———. *Ezra-Nehemiah.* OTL. Philadelphia: Westminster, 1988.

———. *A History of Prophecy in Israel.* 2nd ed. Louisville: Westminster/John Knox, 1996.

———. "The Judaean Priesthood during the Neo-Babylonian and Achaemenid Periods." *CBQ* 60 (1998) 25-43.

———. "Judah's Covenant with Death (Isaiah xviii 14-22)." *VT* 40 (2000) 472-83.

———. *Isaiah 1–39.* AB 19. New York: Doubleday, 2000.

———. *Isaiah 40–55.* AB 19A. New York: Doubleday, 2002.

———. *Isaiah 56–66.* AB 19B. New York: Doubleday, 2003.

———. "Bethel in the Neo-Babylonian Period." In Lipschits and Blenkinsopp, *Judah and the Judeans in the Neo-Babylonian Period,* 93-107.

———. "Hezekiah and the Babylonian Delegation." In *Essays on Ancient Israel in Its Near-Eastern Context: A Tribute to Nadab Na'aman,* ed. Yairah Amit et al. Winona Lake: Eisenbrauns, 2006, 107-22.

———. "Benjamin Traditions Read in the Early Persian Period." In Lipschits and Oeming, *Judah and the Judeans in the Persian Period,* 630-33.

———. *Judaism, the First Phase.* Grand Rapids: Eerdmans, 2009.

———. "The Cosmological and Protological Language of Deutero-Isaiah." *CBQ* 73 (2011) 493-510.

———. "Remembering Josiah." In *Bringing the Past to the Present in the Late Persian and Early Hellenistic Period: Images of Central Figures,* ed. Diana Vikander Edelman and Ehud Ben Zvi. Oxford: Oxford University Press, 2013, 331-61.

Boling, Robert G. *Judges.* AB 6A. Garden City: Doubleday, 1975.

Bordreuil, Pierre. "Les 'grâces de David' et I Maccabee ii 57." *VT* 31 (1981) 73-76.

Bresciani, Edda. "Egypt, Persian Satrapy." In *CHJ,* 1: *Introduction; The Persian Period,* 1984, 358-72.

Briant, Pierre. *Histoire de l'Empire perse de Cyrus à Alexandre.* Vol. 1. Paris: Fayard, 1996. Eng. *From Cyrus to Alexander: A History of the Persian Empire.* Trans. Peter T. Daniels. Winona Lake: Eisenbrauns, 2002.

Bright, John. *A History of Israel.* 3rd ed. Philadelphia: Westminster, 1981.

Brooke, George. "The Kittim in the Qumran Pesharim." In *Images of Empire,* ed. Loveday Alexander. JSOTSup 122. Sheffield: JSOT, 1991, 135-39.

———. "Kingship and Messianism in the Dead Sea Scrolls." In *King and Messiah in Israel and the Ancient Near East: Proceedings of the Oxford Old Testament Seminar,* ed. John Day. JSOTSup 270. Sheffield: Sheffield Academic, 1998, 434-55.

Budd, Philip J. *Numbers.* WBC 5. Waco: Word, 1984.

Cameron, George G. "Darius, Egypt, and 'the Lands beyond the Sea.'" *JNES* 2 (1943) 307-13.

Caquot, André. "Les 'grâces de David': À propos d'Isaïe 55,3b." *Sem* 15 (1965) 45-59.

Carter, Charles E. "Ideology and Archaeology in the Neo-Babylonian Period: Excavating Text and Tell." In Lipschits and Blenkinsopp, *Judah and the Judeans in the Neo-Babylonian Period,* 301-22.

Cathcart, Kevin J., and Robert P. Gordon. *The Targum of the Minor Prophets.* ArBib 14. Wilmington: Glazier, 1989.

Charlesworth, James H. *The Old Testament Pseudepigrapha.* 2 vols. Garden City: Doubleday, 1983-85.

Chary, Theophane. *Aggée, Zacharie, Malachi.* SB. Paris: Gabalda, 1969.

Childs, Brevard S. *Isaiah.* OTL. Louisville: Westminster John Knox, 2001.

Clements, Ronald E. "The Ezekiel Tradition: Prophecy in a Time of Crisis." In *Israel's Prophetic Tradition: Essays in Honour of Peter Ackroyd,* ed. Richard Coggins, Anthony Phillips, and Michael Knibb. Cambridge: Cambridge University Press, 1982, 119-36.

Cogan, Mordechai, and Hayim Tadmor. *II Kings.* AB 11. Garden City: Doubleday, 1988.

Collins, Adela Yarbro, and John J. Collins. *King and Messiah as Son of God: Divine, Human, and Angelic Messianic Figures in Biblical and Related Literature.* Grand Rapids: Eerdmans, 2008.

Collins, John J. *Daniel.* Hermeneia. Minneapolis: Fortress, 1993.

———. *The Scepter and the Star: The Messiahs of the Dead Sea Scrolls and Other Ancient Literature.* 1995; 2nd ed. BRS. Grand Rapids: Eerdmans, 2010.

Cook, J. M. *The Persian Empire.* New York: Schocken, 1983.

Cooke, G. A. *The Book of Judges.* Camb. B. Cambridge: Cambridge University Press, 1913.

———. *A Critical and Exegetical Commentary on the Book of Ezekiel.* ICC. Edinburgh: T. & T. Clark, 1936.

Coote, Robert B. *Amos among the Prophets: Composition and Theology.* Philadelphia: Fortress, 1981.

Cowley, Arthur E. *Aramaic Papyri of the Fifth Century b.c.* 1923; repr. Osnabrück: Zeller, 1967.

Cross, Frank Moore, Jr. "Aspects of Samaritan and Jewish History in Late Persian and Hellenistic Times." *HTR* 59 (1966) 201-11.

————. *Canaanite Myth and Hebrew Epic.* Cambridge, MA: Harvard University Press, 1973.

————. "Samaria and Jerusalem in the Era of the Restoration." In *From Epic to Canon: History and Literature in Ancient Israel.* Baltimore: Johns Hopkins University Press, 1998, 173-202.

Dahood, Mitchell. "Zechariah 9:1, 'En 'Adam," *CBQ* 25 (1963) 123-24.

Dandamaev, M. A. *Persien unter den ersten Achämeniden (6. Jh. v. Chr.).* Wiesbaden: Reichert, 1976.

————. *A Political History of the Achaemenid Empire.* Trans. W. J. Vogelsang. Leiden: Brill, 1989.

Davies, Philip R. *The Origins of Biblical Israel.* LHB/OTS 485. New York: T. & T. Clark, 2007.

Davies, W. D., and Louis Finkelstein, eds. *The Cambridge History of Judaism.* Vol. 2: *The Hellenistic Period.* Cambridge: Cambridge University Press, 1989.

Delcor, M. "Les allusions à Alexandre le Grand dans Zech IX, 1-8." *VT* 1 (1951) 110-24.

Dietrich, Walter. *Prophetie und Geschichte: Eine redaktionsgeschichtliche Untersuchung zum deuteronomistichen Geschichtswerk.* FRLANT 108. Göttingen: Vandenhoeck & Ruprecht, 1972.

Dion, Paul. "ששבצר and ססנור." *ZAW* 95 (1983) 111-12.

Duhm, Bernhard. *Das Buch Jesaja.* 4th ed. HKAT 3/1. Göttingen: Vandenhoeck & Ruprecht, 1922.

Eddy, Samuel K. *The King Is Dead: Studies in the Near Eastern Resistance to Hellenism, 334-31 B.C.* Lincoln: University of Nebraska Press, 1961.

Edelman, Diana V. "Did Saulite-Davidic Rivalry Resurface in Early Persian Yehud?" In *The Land That I Will Show You: Essays on the History and Archaeology of the Ancient Near East in Honour of J. Maxwell Miller,* ed. J. Andrew Dearman and M. Patrick Graham. JSOTSup 343. Sheffield: Sheffield Academic, 2001, 77-80.

Eissfeldt, Otto. "The Promises of Grace to David in Isaiah 55:1-5." In *Israel's Prophetic Heritage,* ed. Bernhard W. Anderson and Walter Harrelson. New York: Harper & Row, 1962, 196-207.

————. *The Old Testament: An Introduction.* New York: Harper & Row, 1966.

Elliger, Karl. *Das Buch der zwölf kleinen Propheten.* Vol. 2. ATD 25. Göttingen: Vandenhoeck & Ruprecht, 1950.

————. *Deuterojesaja 40,1–45,7.* BKAT 11/1. Neukirchen-Vluyn: Neukirchener, 1978.

Ellis, Richard S. *Foundation Deposits in Ancient Mesopotamia.* New Haven: Yale University Press, 1968.

Evans, Craig A. "Messiahs." *EDSS* 1:537-42.

————. *Jesus and His Contemporaries: Comparative Studies.* AGJU 25. Leiden: Brill, 2001.

Finkelstein, Israel, and Amihai Mazar. *The Quest for the Historical Israel*. Ed. Brian B. Schmidt. Atlanta: Society of Biblical Literature, 2007.

Finkelstein, Israel, and Neil Asher Silberman. *David and Solomon: In Search of the Bible's Sacred Kings and the Roots of the Western Tradition*. New York: Free Press, 2006.

Finley, T. J. "The Apple of His Eye *(bābat 'ênô)* in Zechariah ii 12." *VT* 38 (1988) 337-38.

Flusser, David. "The Four Empires in the Fourth Sybil and in the Book of Daniel." *IOS* 2 (1972) 148-75.

Friedman, Richard E. *The Exile and Biblical Narrative: The Formation of the Deuteronomistic and Priestly Codes*. HSM 22. Chico: Scholars, 1981.

Fritz, Volkmar. "Die Deutungen des Königtums Sauls in den Überlieferungen von seiner Entstehung, 1 Sam 9–11." *ZAW* 88 (1976) 246-62.

Galling, Kurt. "Die Ausrufung des Namens als Rechtsakt in Israel." *TLZ* 81 (1956) 65-70.

———. *Studien zur Geschichte Israels im Persischen Zeitalter*. Tübingen: Mohr, 1964.

Gelston, Anthony. "The Foundations of the Second Temple." *VT* 16 (1966) 232-35.

Gemser, Berend. "Der Stern aus Jacob (Num 24,17)." *ZAW* 43 (1925) 301-2.

Gese, Helmut. "Zur Geschichte der Kultsänger am Zweiten Tempel." *Abraham unser Vater: Juden und Christen im Gespräch über die Bibel*, ed. Otto Betz, Martin Hengel, and Peter Schmidt. AGSU 5. Leiden: Brill, 1963, 222-34.

Gibson, J. C. L. *Textbook of Syrian Semitic Inscriptions*. Vol. 1: *Hebrew and Moabite Inscriptions*. Oxford: Clarendon, 1971.

Ginzburg, Carlo. *The Judge and the Historian*. Trans. Antony Shugaar. London: Verso, 1999.

Goldingay, John, and David Payne. *Isaiah 40–55*. Vol. 2. ICC. London: T. & T. Clark, 2006.

Gould, G. P. *Virgil, Eclogues, Georgics, Aeneid 1-6*. Rev. ed. LCL 63. Cambridge, MA: Harvard University Press, 1996.

Grabbe, Lester L. *Judaism from Cyrus to Hadrian*. Vol. 2: *The Roman Period*. Minneapolis: Fortress, 1992.

Gray, George Buchanan. *A Critical and Exegetical Commentary on Numbers*. ICC. Edinburgh: T. & T. Clark, 1903.

Gray, John. *Joshua, Judges and Ruth*. NCBC. Grand Rapids: Eerdmans, 1967.

Gray, Rebecca. *Prophetic Figures in Late Second Temple Jewish Palestine*. Oxford: Oxford University Press, 1993.

Gressmann, Hugo. *Der Messias*. FRLANT 43. Göttingen: Vandenhoeck & Ruprecht, 1929.

Gunkel, Hermann. *Schöpfung und Chaos in Urzeit und Endzeit: Eine religionsgeschichtliche Untersuching über Gen. 1 und Ap. Jon 12*. Göttingen: Vandenhoeck & Ruprecht, 1895. Eng. *Creation and Chaos in the Primeval Era and the Eschaton*. Trans. K. William Whitney Jr. BRS. Grand Rapids: Eerdmans, 2006.

Gunneweg, Antonius H. J. "'AM HA'ARES — A Semantic Revolution." *ZAW* 95 (1983) 437-40.

Hagedorn, Anselm C. "Edom in the Book of Amos and Beyond." In *Aspects of Amos: Exegesis and Imagination*, ed. Hagedorn and Andrew Mein. LHB/OTS 536. London: T. & T. Clark, 2011, 41-57.

Halpern, Baruch. *David's Secret Demons: Messiah, Murderer, Traitor, King*. BIW. Grand Rapids: Eerdmans, 2001.

Hanson, Paul D. "Zechariah 9 and the Recapitulation of an Ancient Ritual Pattern." *JBL* 92 (1973) 37-48.

―――. *The Dawn of Apocalyptic*. 2nd ed. Philadelphia: Fortress, 1979.

Healey, John P. "Am Ha'arez." *ABD* 1:168-69.

Hengel, Martin. *Judaism and Hellenism: Studies in Their Encounter in Palestine during the Early Hellenistic Period*. Trans. John Bowden. Vol. 1. Philadelphia: Fortress, 1974.

―――. "Messianische Hoffnung und politische 'Radikalismus' in der jüdisch-hellenistischen Diaspora." In *Apocalypticism in the Mediterranean Hellenistic World and the Near East*, ed. David Hellholm. Tübingen: Mohr, 1983, 655-86.

―――. *The Zealots*. Trans. David Smith. Edinburgh: T. & T. Clark, 1989.

Hentschel, Georg. "Die Hinrichtung der Nachkommen Sauls (2 Sam 21,1-14)." In *Nachdenken über Israel, Bibel und Theologie: Festschrift für Klaus-Dietrich Schunck zu seinem 65. Geburtstag*, ed. H. Michael Niemann, Matthias Augustin, and Werner H. Schmidt. BEATAJ 37. Frankfurt am Main: Lang, 1994, 93-116.

Hermisson, Hans-Jürgen. "Einheit und Komplexität Deuterojesajas: Probleme der Redaktionsgeschichte von Jes 40–55." In Vermeylen, *The Book of Isaiah/Le Livre d'Isaïe*, 286-312.

Herr, Larry G. "The Servant of Baalis." *BA* 48 (1985) 169-72.

Hiers, Richard H. "Day of the Lord." *ABD* 2:82-83.

Hillers, Delbert R. *Micah*. Hermeneia. Philadelphia: Fortress, 1984.

Hooke, Samuel H. "A Scarab and Sealing from Tell Duweir." *PEQ* 67 (1935) 171-97.

Horsley, Richard A. "Popular Prophetic Movements at the Time of Jesus." *JSNT* 26 (1986) 3-27.

Horsley, Richard A., and John S. Hanson. *Bandits, Prophets, and Messiahs: Popular Movements in the Time of Jesus*. San Francisco: Harper & Row, 1985.

Houtman, Cornelis. "Queen of Heaven." *DDD* 678-80.

Hübner, Ulrich. *Die Ammoniter: Untersuchungen zur Geschichte, Kultur und Religion in eines transjordanischen Volkes im 1. Jahrtausend v. Chr*. Wiesbaden: Harrassowitz, 1992.

Humphreys, W. Lee. "The Rise and Fall of King Saul: A Study of an Ancient Narrative Stratum in 1 Samuel." *JSOT* 18 (1980) 74-90.

———. "From Tragic Hero to Villain: A Study of the Figure of Saul and the Development of 1 Samuel." *JSOT* 22 (1982) 95-117.

Isaac, Benjamin, and Aharon Oppenheimer. "The Revolt of Bar Kokhba: Ideology and Modern Scholarship." *JJS* 36 (1985) 33-60.

Jankulak, Karen. *Geoffrey of Monmouth.* Cardiff: University of Wales Press, 2010.

Japhet, Sara. "Sheshbazzar and Zerubbabel — Against the Background of the History and Religious Tendencies of Ezra-Nehemiah." *ZAW* 94 (1982) 66-98.

———. *I & II Chronicles.* OTL. Louisville: Westminster/John Knox, 1993.

Jeremias, Christian. *Die Nachtgesichte des Sacharja.* FRLANT 117. Göttingen: Vandenhoeck & Ruprecht, 1977.

Johnson, Aubrey R. *The Cultic Prophet in Ancient Israel.* 2nd ed. Cardiff: University of Wales Press, 1962.

———. *The Cultic Prophet and Israel's Psalmody.* Cardiff: University of Wales Press, 1979.

Johnson, Marshall D. *The Purpose of the Biblical Genealogies.* 2nd ed. SNTSMS 8. Cambridge: Cambridge University Press, 1988.

Jolles, André. *Einfache Formen: Legende, Sage, Mythe, Rätsel, Spruch, Kasus, Memorabile, Witz.* Darmstadt: Wissenschaftliche Buchgesellschaft, 1958.

Joyce, Paul M. *Ezekiel.* LJB/OTS 482. New York: T. & T. Clark, 2007.

Kaiser, Walter C. "The Unfailing Kindnesses Promised to David: Isaiah 55:3." *JSOT* 45 (1989) 41-98.

Kapelrud, Arvid. "Temple Building, a Task for Gods and Kings." *Or* 32 (1963) 56-62.

Karageorghis, Vassos. *Cyprus, from the Stone Age to the Romans.* London: Thames & Hudson, 1982.

Keel, Othmar. *Jahwe-Visionen und Siegelkunst: Eine neue Deutung der Majestätsschilderungen in Jes. 6, Ez. 1 und 10 und Sach. 4.* Stuttgart: Katholisches Bibelwerk, 1977.

Keel, Othmar, and Christoph Uelinger. *Gods, Goddesses, and Images of God in Ancient Israel.* Trans. Thomas H. Trapp. Minneapolis: Fortress, 1998.

Kellermann, Ulrich. *Nehemia: Quellen, Überlieferung und Geschichte.* BZAW 102. Berlin: Töpelmann, 1967.

Kirsch, Jonathan. *King David: The Real Life of the Man Who Ruled Israel.* New York: Ballantine, 2000.

Kittel, Rudolph. "Cyrus und Deuterojesaja." *ZAW* 18 (1898) 149-62.

Koch, Klaus. *The Prophets.* Vol. 1: *The Assyrian Period.* Philadelphia: Fortress, 1983. German ed. 1978.

Kratz, Reinhard. *Kyros in Deuterojesaja-Buch: Redaktionsgeschichtliche Untersuchungen zu Entstehung und Theologie von Jes 40-55.* FAT 1. Tübingen: Mohr Siebeck, 1991.

————. *Die Propheten Israels.* Munich: Beck, 2003.

————. *Prophetenstudien.* FAT 74. Tübingen: Mohr Siebeck, 2011.

Kuhrt, Amélie. "The Cyrus Cylinder and Achaemenid Imperial Policy." *JSOT* 25 (1983) 83-97.

————. *The Ancient Near East c. 3000–330 B.C.* Vol. 2. London: Routledge, 1995.

Laato, Antti. *Josiah and David Redivivus.* ConBOT 33. Stockholm: Almqvist & Wiksell, 1992.

————. "Zechariah 4:6b-10a and the Akkadian Royal Building Inscriptions." *ZAW* 106 (1994) 53-69.

Lange, Nicholas R. M. de. "Jewish Attitudes to the Roman Empire." In *Imperialism in the Ancient World,* ed. P. D. A. Garnsey and C. R. Whittaker. Cambridge: Cambridge University Press, 1978.

Lemche, Niels P. "David's Rise." *JSOT* 10 (1978) 2-25.

Lescow, Theodor. "Das Geburtsmotiv in den messianischen Weissagungen bei Jesaja und Micha." *ZAW* 79 (1967) 172-207.

Levin, Christoph. "Das Amosbuch der Anawim." *ZTK* 94 (1997) 407-36 = *Fortschreibungen: Gesammelte Studien zum Alten Testament.* BZAW 316. Berlin: de Gruyter, 2003, 265-90.

Levine, Baruch A. *Numbers 21–36.* AB 4A. New York: Doubleday, 2000.

Lipiński, Edouard. "Recherches sur le livre de Zacharie." *VT* 20 (1970) 25-55.

————. "Royal and State Scribes in Ancient Israel." In *Congress Volume, Jerusalem, 1986,* ed. J. A. Emerton. VTS 40. Leiden: Brill, 1988, 157-64.

————. "The People of the Land of Judah." *TDOT* 11 (2001) 174-75.

Lipschits, Oded. "The History of the Benjamin Region under Babylonian Rule." *TA* 26 (1999) 155-90.

————. *The Fall and Rise of Jerusalem.* Winona Lake: Eisenbrauns, 2005.

Lipschits, Oded, and Joseph Blenkinsopp, eds. *Judah and the Judeans in the Neo-Babylonian Period.* Winona Lake: Eisenbrauns, 2003.

Lipschits, Oded, Gary N. Knoppers, and Rainer Albertz, eds. *Judah and the Judeans in the Fourth Century B.C.E.* Winona Lake: Eisenbrauns, 2007.

Lipschits, Oded, and Manfred Oeming, eds. *Judah and the Judeans in the Persian Period.* Winona Lake: Eisenbrauns, 2006.

Macchi, Jean-Daniel. "Le Thème du 'jour de YHWH' dans les XII petits prophètes." In *Les Prophètes de la Bible et le fin des temps,* ed. Jacques Vermeylen. LD 240. Paris: Cerf, 2010, 141-81.

Machinist, Peter. "Palestine, Administration of." *ABD* 5:69-81.

Macintosh, A. A. *A Critical and Exegetical Commentary on Hosea.* ICC. Edinburgh: T. & T. Clark, 1997.

Malamat, Abraham. "The Historical Setting of Two Biblical Prophecies on the Nations." *IEJ* 1 (1950/51) 149-59.

Malul, Meir. "Was David Involved in the Death of Saul on the Gilboa Mountain?" *RB* 103 (1996) 517-45.

Mays, James Luther. *Hosea.* OTL. Philadelphia: Westminster, 1969.

McCarter, P. Kyle. "The Apology of David." *JBL* 99 (1980) 489-504.

———. *II Samuel.* AB 9. Garden City: Doubleday, 1984.

McEvenue, Sean E. "The Political Structure in Judah from Cyrus to Nehemiah." *CBQ* 43 (1981) 353-64.

McKenzie, Steven L. *King David: A Biography.* Oxford: Oxford University Press, 2000.

———. "Saul in the Deuteronomistic History." In *Saul in Story and Tradition,* ed. Carl S. Ehrlich and Marsha C. White. Tübingen: Mohr Siebeck, 2006, 59-70.

Mettinger, T. N. D. *Solomonic State Officials: A Study of the Civil Government Officials of the Israelite Monarchy.* ConBOT 5. Lund: Gleerup, 1971.

Meyers, Carol L., and Eric M. Meyers. *Haggai, Zechariah 1–8.* AB 25B. Garden City: Doubleday, 1987.

———. *Zechariah 9–14.* AB 25C. New York: Doubleday, 1993.

———. "The Future Fortunes of the House of David: The Evidence of Second Zechariah." In *Fortunate the Eyes That See: Essays in Honor of David Noel Freedman in Celebration of His Seventieth Birthday,* ed. Astrid B. Beck et al. Grand Rapids: Eerdmans, 1995, 207-22.

Miller, J. Maxwell, and John H. Hayes. *A History of Ancient Israel and Judah.* 1986; 2nd ed. Louisville: Westminster John Knox, 2006.

Miller, John Wolf. *Das Verhältnis Jeremias und Hesekiels sprachlich und theologisch untersucht.* Assen: Van Gorcum, 1955.

Mitchell, Hinckley G., J. M. Powis Smith, and Julius A. Bewer. *A Critical and Exegetical Commentary on Haggai, Zechariah, Malachi, and Jonah.* ICC. New York: Scribner, 1912.

Moore, George Foot. *A Critical and Exegetical Commentary on Judges.* ICC. New York: Scribner's, 1895.

Mowinckel, Sigmund. *He That Cometh.* Trans. G. W. Anderson. 1959; repr. BRS. Grand Rapids: Eerdmans and Livonia: Dove, 2005.

———. *The Psalms in Israel's Worship.* Trans. D. R. Ap-Thomas. 1967; repr. BRS. Grand Rapids: Eerdmans and Livonia: Dove, 2004.

Na'aman, Nadab. "The Kingdom of Judah under Josiah." *TA* 18 (1991) 3-71.

———. "The Pre-Deuteronomistic Story of King Saul and Its Historical Significance." *CBQ* 54 (1992) 638-58.

Naumann, Thomas. *Hoseas Erben: Strukturen der Nachinterpretation im Buch Hosea.* BWANT 7/11. Stuttgart: Kohlhammer, 1981.

Nelson, Richard D. *The Double Redaction of the Deuteronomistic History.* JSOTSup 18. Sheffield: JSOT, 1981.

Nicholson, Ernest W. "The Meaning of the Expression 'am ha'arez in the Old Testament." *JSS* 10 (1965) 59-66.

Nickelsburg, George W. E. *Jewish Literature between the Bible and the Mishnah.* 2nd ed. Minneapolis: Fortress, 2005.

Nickelsburg, G. W. E., and James C. VanderKam. *1 Enoch: A New Translation*. Minneapolis: Fortress, 2005.

Nissinen, Martti. *Prophetie, Redaktion und Fortschreibung im Hoseabuch*. AOAT 231. Kevalaer: Butzon & Bercker and Neukirchen: Neukirchener, 1991.

Nogalski, James. *Literary Precursors to the Book of the Twelve*. BZAW 217. Berlin: de Gruyter, 1993.

Noth, Martin. *Numbers*. Trans. James D. Martin. OTL. Philadelphia: Westminster, 1968.

Oakley, Francis. *Kingship: The Politics of Enchantment*. Oxford: Blackwell, 2006.

Oates, Joan. "The Fall of Assyria (635-609 B.C.)." In *CAH*, 2nd ed., 3/2, ed. John Boardman et al. (1991) 162-88.

O'Brien, Mark A. *The Deuteronomistic History Hypothesis: A Reassessment*. OBO 92. Freiburg: Universitätsverlag and Göttingen: Vandenhoeck & Ruprecht, 1989.

Olmstead, Albert T. *History of the Persian Empire: Achaemenid Period*. Chicago: University of Chicago Press, 1948.

Oppenheim, A. Leo. "The Eyes of the Lord." *JAOS* 88 (1968) 173-80.

Orr, Avigdor. "The Seventy Years of Babylon." *VT* 6 (1956) 304-6.

Otzen, Benedict. *Studien über Deuterosacharja*. ATDan 6. Copenhagen: Munksgaard, 1964.

Parker, Richard A. "Darius and His Egyptian Campaign." *AJSL* 58 (1941) 373-77.

Parker, Richard A., and Waldo H. Dubberstein. *Babylonian Chronology 626 B.C. to A.D. 45*. Brown University Studies 19. Providence: Brown University Press, 1956.

Paul, Shalom. *Amos*. Hermeneia. Minneapolis: Fortress, 1991.

Petersen, David L. "Zerubbabel and Jerusalem Temple Construction." *CBQ* 36 (1974) 366-72.

―――. *Late Israelite Prophecy*. SBLMS 23. Missoula: Scholars, 1977.

―――. *Haggai and Zechariah 1-8*. OTL. Philadelphia: Westminster, 1984.

Petitjean, Albert. *Les Oracles du Proto-Zacharie*. EBib. Paris: Gabalda, 1969.

Pinsky, Robert. *The Life of David*. New York: Schocken, 2005.

Plöger, Otto. *Theocracy and Eschatology*. Trans. S. Rudman. Richmond: John Knox, 1968.

Plumb, John Harold. *The Death of the Past*. Boston: Houghton Mifflin, 1970.

Pohlmann, Karl-Friedrich. *Ezechiel: Der Stand der theologischen Forschung*. Darmstadt: Wissenschaftliche Buchgesellschaft, 2008.

Polley, Max E. *Amos and the Davidic Empire: A Socio-Historical Approach*. New York: Oxford University Press, 1989.

Pomykala, Kenneth E. "Jerusalem as the Fallen Booth of David, Amos 9:11." In *God's Word for Our World*. Vol. 1: *Theological and Cultural Studies in Honor of Simon John de Vries*, ed. J. Harold Ellens et al. JSOTSup 388. London: T. & T. Clark, 2004, 275-93.

Porton, Bezalel, and Ada Yardeni. *Textbook of Aramaic Documents from Ancient Egypt.* Vol. 1: *Letters.* Jerusalem: Hebrew University, 1986.

Pury, Albert de, Thomas Römer, and Jean-Daniel Macchi. *Israël construit son histoire: L'historiographie deutéronomiste à la lumière des recherches récentes.* MdB 34. Geneva: Labor et Fides, 1996.

Redditt, Paul L. "Nehemiah's First Mission and the Date of Zechariah 9–14." *CBQ* 56 (1994) 664-78.

Redditt, Paul L., and Aaron Schart, eds. *Thematic Threads in the Book of the Twelve.* BZAW 325. Berlin: de Gruyter, 2003.

Redford, Donald B. *Egypt, Canaan, and Israel in Ancient Times.* Princeton: Princeton University Press, 1992.

Reventlow, Henning Graf, Yair Hoffman, and Benjamin Uffenheimer, eds. *Politics and Theopolitics in the Bible and Post-Biblical Literature.* JSOTSup 171. Sheffield: Sheffield Academic, 1994.

Robertson, Edward. "The Apple of the Eye in the Masoretic Text." *JTS* 38 (1937) 56-59.

Römer, Thomas C. *La première histoire d'Israël, l'école deutéronomiste à l'oeuvre.* Geneva: Labor et Fides. 2007.

———. *The So-Called Deuteronomistic History.* London: T. & T. Clark, 2007.

Römer, Thomas C., ed. *The Future of the Deuteronomistic History.* BETL 147. Leuven: Leuven University Press and Peeters, 2000.

Rudolph, Wilhelm. *Esra und Nehemia samt 3. Esra.* HAT 20. Tübingen: Mohr, 1949.

———. *Haggai — Sacharja 1–8 — Sacharja 9–14 — Maleachai.* KAT 13/4. Gütersloh: Mohn, 1976.

Ruzicka, Stephen. *Politics of a Persian Dynasty: The Hecatomnids in the Fourth Century B.C.* Norman: University of Oklahoma Press, 1992.

Sack, Ronald H. "Nebuchadnezzar II and the Old Testament: History versus Ideology." In Lipschits and Blenkinsopp, *Judah and the Judeans in the Neo-Babylonian Period,* 221-33.

Salway, Peter. *Roman Britain.* New York: Oxford University Press, 1981.

Sanders, James A. *The Psalms Scroll of Qumrân Cave 11 (11QPs^a).* DJD 4. Oxford: Oxford University Press, 1965.

Sarna, Nahum M. "Psalm 89: A Study in Inner-Biblical Exegesis." In *Biblical and Other Studies,* ed. Alexander Altmann. Cambridge, MA: Harvard University Press, 1963, 29-46.

Schäfer, Peter. *Der Bar Kokhba Aufstand: Studien zum zweiten jüdischen Krieg gegen Rom.* TSAJ 1. Tübingen: Mohr, 1981.

Scholem, Gershom. *The Messianic Idea in Judaism.* New York: Schocken, 1971.

Schürer, Emil. *The History of the Jewish People in the Age of Jesus Christ (175 B.C.–A.D. 135).* Vol. 2. Rev. and ed. Geza Vermes, Fergus Millar, and Matthew Black. Edinburgh: T. & T. Clark, 1979.

Scott, Robert B. Y. "Secondary Meanings of Ahar." *JTS* 50 (1949) 178-79.

Sellin, Ernst, *Das Zwölfprophetenbuch überstezt und erklärt.* KAT 12. 3rd ed. Leipzig: Scholl, 1930.

Seybold, Klaus. "Spätprophetische Hoffnungen auf die Wiederkunft der davidischen Zeitalters in Sach 9–14." *Jud* 29 (1973) 99-111.

Smart, James D. *History and Theology in Second Isaiah.* Philadelphia: Westminster, 1965.

Smith, Morton. "II Isaiah and the Persians." *JAOS* 83 (1963) 415-21.

———. "The Troublemakers." In *CHJ.* Vol. 3: *The Early Roman Period,* ed. William Horbury, W. D. Davies, and John Sturdy, 1999, 501-68.

Smith, Ralph L. *Micah — Malachi.* Waco: Word, 1984.

Smith, Sydney. *Isaiah, Chapters XL–LV.* Oxford: Oxford University Press, 1944.

Soggin, J. Alberto. *Judges.* Trans. John Bowden. OTL. Philadelphia: Westminster, 1981.

Speiser, E. A. *Genesis.* AB 1. Garden City: Doubleday, 1964.

Spek, R. J. van der. "Did Cyrus the Great Introduce a New Policy towards Subdued Nations?" *Persica* 10 (1982) 278-83.

Starbuck, Scott R. A. "Theological Anthropology at a Fulcrum: Isaiah 55:1-5, Psalm 89, and Second Stage Traditio in the Royal Psalms." In *David and Zion: Biblical Studies in Honor of J. J. M. Roberts,* ed. Bernard F. Batto and Kathryn L. Roberts. Winona Lake: Eisenbrauns, 2004, 247-65.

Starkey, J. L. "Excavations at Tell el-Duweir 1934-1935." *PEQ* 67 (1935) 198-208.

Stauffer, Ethelbert. *Jerusalem und Rom im Zeitalter Jesu Christi.* Berne: Francke, 1957.

Steck, Odil Hannes. *Gottesknecht und Zion: Gesammelte Aufsätze zu Deuterojesaja.* FAT 4. Tübingen: Mohr (Siebeck), 1992.

Sweeney, Marvin A. *King Josiah of Judah: The Lost Messiah of Israel.* Oxford: Oxford University Press, 2001.

Tcherikover, Victor. *Hellenistic Civilization and the Jews.* Trans. S. Applebaum. New York: Atheneum, 1975.

Thomas, D. Winton. "A Note on *mhlswt* in Zechariah 3:4." *JTS* 33 (1931-1932) 279-80.

Thorpe, Lewis, trans. *Geoffrey of Monmouth, the History of the Kings of Britain.* London: Penguin, 1966.

Toorn, Karel van der, and Cees Houtman. "David and the Ark." *JBL* 113 (1994) 209-31.

Tuell, Steven. *Ezekiel.* NIBCOT. Peabody: Hendrickson, 2009.

Tufnell, Olga. *Lachish III: The Iron Age.* Oxford: Oxford University Press, 1953.

Vaggione, Richard P. "Over All Asia? The Extent of the Scythian Domination in Herodotus." *JBL* 92 (1973) 523-30.

Vanderhooft, David Stephen. *The Neo-Babylonian Empire and Babylon in the Latter Prophets.* HSM 59. Atlanta: Scholars, 1999.

VanderKam, James C. *From Joshua to Caiaphas: High Priests after the Exile.* Minneapolis: Fortress, 2004.

Van Seters, John. *The Biblical Saga of King David.* Winona Lake: Eisenbrauns, 2009.

Vaux, Roland de. *Ancient Israel: Its Life and Institutions.* 1961; repr. BRS. Grand Rapids: Eerdmans and Livonia: Dove, 1997

Vermeylen, Jacques. *Du Prophète Isaïe à l'Apocalyptique: Isaïe I–XXXV.* EB. Paris: Gabalda, 1977.

———. *The Book of Isaiah/Le Livre d'Isaïe: Les oracles et leur relecture.* BETL 81. Leuven: University Press and Peeters, 1989.

———. "La maison de Saül et la maison de David: Un écrit de propagande théologico-politique de 1 Sm 11 à 2 Sm 7." In *Figures de David à travers la Bible.*, ed. Louis Doreusseaux and Vermeylen. LD 177. Paris: Cerf, 1999, 35-74.

Vincent, J. M. *Studien zur literarische Eigenart und zur geistigen Heimat von Jesaja, Kap. 40-55.* BBET 5. Frankfurt am Main: Lang, 1977.

Weber, Max. *Ancient Judaism.* Trans. and ed. Hans H. Gerth and Don Martindale. Glencoe: Free Press, 1952.

———. *Economy and Society.* Ed. Guenther Roth and Claus Wittich. Berkeley: University of California Press, 1978.

Weidner, E. F. "Joachin, König von Juda in babylonischen Keilschrifttexten." In *Mélanges syriens offert à Monsieur René Dussaud II.* Paris: Geuthner, 1939.

Weimar, Peter. "Der Schluss des Amos-Buches: Ein Beitrag zur Redaktionsgeschichte des Amos-Buches." *BN* 16 (1981) 60-100.

Wellhausen, Julius. *Die Composition des Hexateuchs und der historischen Bücher des Alten Testaments.* 4th ed. Berlin: de Gruyter, 1963.

Westermann, Claus. *Isaiah 40–66.* OTL. Philadelphia: Westminster, 1969.

———. *Genesis 17–50.* Trans. John J. Scullion. CC. Minneapolis: Augsburg, 1986.

Whitley, Charles. "The Term Seventy Years Captivity." *VT* 4 (1954) 60-72.

———. *Genesis 1–11.* Neukirchen: Neukirchener, 1979.

Whybray, Norman. *Isaiah 40–66.* NCBC. Grand Rapids: Eerdmans, 1975.

Willi, Thomas. "Das davidische Königtum in der Chronik." In *Ideales Königtum,* ed. Rüdiger Lux. Leipzig: Evangelische Verlagsanstalt, 2005.

Williamson, H. G. M. "'The Sure Mercies of David': Subjective or Objective Genitive?" *JSS* 23 (1978) 31-49.

———. *1 and 2 Chronicles.* NCBC. Grand Rapids: Eerdmans, 1982.

———. "The Composition of Ezra i–vi." *JTS* 33 (1983) 1-30.

———. *Ezra, Nehemiah.* WBC 16. Waco: Word, 1985.

———. "The Governors of Judah under the Persians." *TynBul* 39 (1988) 59-82.

Wilson, Robert R. "The Old Testament Genealogies in Recent Research." *JBL* 94 (1975) 169-89.

———. *Genealogy and History in the Biblical World.* Yale Near Eastern Researches 7. New Haven: Yale University Press, 1977.

————. "Genealogy, Genealogies." *ABD* 2:929-32.

Wise, Michael O. "Bar Kokhba Letters." *ABD* 1:601-6.

Wiseman, Donald J. *Chronicles of the Chaldaean Kings (626-556 B.C.) in the British Museum.* London: Trustees of the British Museum, 1961.

Wöhrle, Jacob. *Die frühen Sammlungen des Zwölfprophetenbuch: Entstehung und Komposition.* BZAW 360. Berlin: de Gruyter, 2006.

Würthwein, Ernst. *Der 'amm ha'aretz im Alten Testament.* BWANT 17. Stuttgart: Kohlhammer, 1936.

Zimmerli, Walther. *Ezekiel 2.* Trans. James D. Martin. Hermeneia. Philadelphia: Fortress, 1983.

Index of Modern Authors

Index of Subjects

Index of Biblical and Other Ancient Texts